The Medical Review Officer's Manual ■

The Medical Review Officer's Manual

Medical Review Officer Certification Council

Robert Swotinsky, MD, MPH
Fallon Clinic
Worcester, MA

Donna Smith, PhD
Substance Abuse Management, Inc.
Boca Raton, FL

OEM Press
Beverly Farms, MA

ISBN 1-883595-24-X

Printed in the United States of America

Library of Congress Cataloging-in-Publication Data
Swotinsky, Robert B.
        The medical review officer's manual / Robert Swotinsky, Donna
Smith, — 1st ed.
                    p.   cm.
        Includes bibliographical references and index.
        ISBN 1-883595-24-X
        1. Employees—Drug testing. 2. Drug testing—Law and legislation-
-United States. I. Smith, Donna, Ph. D. II. Title.
        [DNLM: 1. Automatic Data Processing—methods. 2. Laboratory
Techniques and Procedures. 3. Specimen Handling—methods.
4. Substance Abuse Detection—methods. 5. Urinalysis.
6. Workplace.   HV 5823 H976m 1999]
HF5549.5.D7   IN PROCESS
658.3'822—dc21
DNLM/DLC
for Library of Congress   99-12452
                                                            CIP

Published by OEM Press
8 West Street
Beverly Farms, MA 01915

To my parents, Anita and Jack Swotinsky
RS

To my mother, Harriett Riggs Runkle, in memoriam
DS

Contents

4 ■ Laboratory Analysis and Performance Testing   29

5 ■ Receiving and Reviewing Drug Test Results   45

List of Figures and Tables

Preface

The Medical Review Officer's Manual is a reference for physicians and other providers or workplace drug and alcohol testing services. The manual reviews workplace drug and alcohol testing procedures, interpretation of drug test results, and other topics important to medical review officers. We have based the procedures in this book on those used in programs regulated by the federal government, for example. the U.S. Department of Health and Human Services and the U.S. Department of Transportation. We have also addressed practices and issues specific to nonregulated testing—that is, tests not subject to the federal workplace drug testing rules.

Chapter 1 describes the medical review officer's role in workplace drug testing. The history of workplace drug and alcohol testing regulations is summarized in Chapter 2. Chapters 3 and 4 review the procedures for collecting and analyzing urine drug test specimens. Chapters 4 through 9 describe the MRO's interpretation and handling of drug test results; Chapter 10 reviews alternative technologies for drug and alcohol testing; and Chapter 11 discusses workplace alcohol testing. An overview of the substance abuse professional's role in workplace substance abuse testing is the subject of the last chapter (Chapter 12). Appendices A through F offer reference material and copies of the regulations, current through January 1, 1999.

We wrote this manual after a decade of practice under federal regulations. While the field of substance abuse testing continues to evolve in response to new technologies, regulations and case laws, we trust that this manual will provide helpful guidelines for years to come.

We are grateful to the Medical Review Officer Certification Council (MROCC) for supporting this project. Our particular thanks to MROCC's chairman, Elias Shaptini, and executive director, Brian Compney, for their support and patience. We also thank Kent Peterson for his inspiration and dedication to MRO training. Excellent and thorough comments on drafts of this book were provided by John Ambre, Benjamin Gerson, Jay Hammett, Joseph Johnson, Alan B. Jones, Donald Ian Macdonald, Kent Peterson, and Scott Phillips.

RBS
DS

About the Authors

Robert B. Swotinsky, MD, MPH, is an occupational physician and medical review office with Fallon Clinic and MetroWest Medical Center in central Massachusetts. He was Editor of *The Medical Review Officer's Guide to Drug Testing* (1992, Van Nostrand Reinhold), is Founding Editor of the *MRO Update* newsletter, is on the Medical Review Officer Certification Council Examination Development Committee, and has taught in MRO training courses. Dr. Swotinsky lives in Sudbury, MA with his wife, Michelle, and three children, Eric, Jenna, and Alex.

Donna R. Smith, PhD, is Senior Vice President at Substance Abuse Management, Inc. (SAMI), one of the largest MRO and third-party administrator companies in the United States. Prior to joining SAMI, Dr. Smith served as Director, Drug Enforcement and Program Compliance, U.S. Department of Transportation (DOT), where she was a principal author of the DOT drug and alcohol testing rules. Dr. Smith is a widely acclaimed speaker, educator, and author and serves on the Examination Development Committee of the Medical Review Officer Certification Council. She also serves on the anti–doping task force of the International Olympic Committee. Dr. Smith lives with her husband in Boca Raton, FL, and has two grown children, Matthew and Stephen.

Acronyms

AAMRO	American Association of Medical Review Officers
ACOEM	American College of Occupational and Environmental Medicine
ADA	Americans with Disabilities Act
ASAM	American Society of Addiction Medicine
BAC	blood alcohol concentration
BAT	breath alcohol technician
CPA	College of American Pathologists
CCF	custody and control form
CDL	commercial driver's license
CEAP	Certified Employee Assistance Professional
CME	continuing medical education
CLIA	Clinical Laboratories Improvement Act
CMV	commercial motor vehicle
CPL	Conforming Products List
COC	chain of custody (see also CCF)
DEA	Drug Enforcement Administration
DOL	Department of Labor
DOT	Department of Transportation
DWI	driving while intoxicated
EAP	employee assistance program
EBT	evidential breath test
EMIT	enzyme multiplied immunosassay test
FAA	Federal Aviation Administration
FHWA	Federal Highway Administration
FPIA	fluorescence-polarization immunoassay
FRA	Federal Railroad Administration
FTA	Federal Transit Administration

DHHS   Dept of Health & Human Services

GC/MS	gas chromatography/mass spectrometry
GPO	Government Printing Office
HHS	Department of Health and Human Services
IV	intravenous
KIMS	kinetic interaction of microparticles
MFR	Memorandum for Record
MIS	management information system
MRO	medical review officer
MROCC	Medical Review Officer Certification Council
NHTSA	National Highway Traffic Safety Administration
NIDA	National Institute on Drug Abuse
NLCP	National Laboratory Certification Program
NRC	Nuclear Regulatory Commission
RIA	radioimmunoassay
RSPA	Research and Special Programs Administration
SAMHSA	Substance Abuse and Mental Health Services Administration
SAP	Substance Abuse Professional
SAPAA	Substance Abuse Program Administrators Association
STT	screening test technician
TAC	tetracaine, adrenaline, cocaine
TPA	third-party administrator
USCG	United States Coast Guard

The Medical Review Officer's Manual ■

The Medical Review Officer ■

Medical review officers (MROs) function as "gatekeepers," receiving laboratory drug test results and determining if positive results can be explained by legitimate medical uses of controlled substances or if they indicate illicit drug use. For each positive test result, the MRO allows the donor an opportunity to discuss the result and present explanations, such as use of prescription medications. If there is an alternative medical explanation, the MRO declares the result negative and reports it to the employer. If the donor has no alternative medical explanation, the MRO verifies the result as positive and reports it to the employer.

Workplace drug testing is a three-step process:

1. *The collection process,* which documents the link between the specimen and its donor through use of a custody and control form (CCF).
2. *The specimen analysis,* which consists of a screening test and, if the screening result is positive, a confirmation test.
3. *Medical review of the test result* conducted, by the MRO. The MRO's review is a required element in tests conducted under federal and certain state laws.

Qualifications ■

FEDERAL REQUIREMENTS

Federal rules define the MRO as "a licensed physician (medical doctor or doctor of osteopathy) . . . who has knowledge of substance abuse disorders and has appropriate medical training to interpret and evaluate an individual's positive test result together with his or her medical history and any other relevant biomedical information." Federal regulations require that MROs be medical doctors or doctors of osteopathy because of their training, responsibility, and credibility.

STATE REQUIREMENTS

As of 1998, five states—Hawaii, Iowa, Louisiana, Montana, and Oklahoma—require use of MROs in drug testing programs. In Connecticut, Oregon and some other states, laboratory tests, including workplace drug tests, can be ordered only by physicians and other health care professionals. An increasing number of states—including Alaska, Florida, Ohio, Tennessee, and Washington—require use of MROs for employers who wish to receive insurance discounts or protection from liability. Most of these state laws refer to physician MROs. Oklahoma is an exception, defining the "review officer" as a licensed physician or someone who has earned a doctoral degree in clinical chemistry, forensic toxicology, or a similar biomedical science [§310:638-1-9]. Iowa is another exception, defining the MRO as ". . . a licensed physician, osteopathic physician, chiropractor, nurse practitioner, or physician assistant" [§730.5].

Several states have rules that address qualifications for MROs in more detail:

- *Florida [Chapter 59A-24.008(1)(c)].* Florida's Drug-Free Workplace Program standards, which affect employers who participate in the workers' compensation discount program, require that MROs attend a training course provided by the American Association of Medical Review Officers (AAMRO), American College of Occupational and Environmental Medicine (ACOEM), or American Society of Addiction Medicine (ASAM).
- *Hawaii [Title 11,Chapter 113, Hawaii Administrative Rules].* A Hawaiian MRO license is required to review positive drug test specimens collected in Hawaii. The license application can be obtained from:

  State of Hawaii Department of Health
  State Laboratories Division
  Attn: Substance Abuse Testing
  2725 Waimano Home Road
  Pearl City, HI 96782-1496
  (808)453-6658

  The applicant submits a four-page form with a picture, documentation of training and experience, a photocopy of his or her MD diploma, and verification of medical licensure in Hawaii or another state. The license must be renewed every 24 months. The Hawaii Department of Health can revoke the license if the MRO is addicted to drugs or alcohol, reviews results while impaired by drugs or alcohol, is grossly negligent in functioning as an MRO, or is convicted of a crime directly related to functioning as an MRO.
- *Oklahoma [Workplace Drug and Alcohol Testing Act, Chapter 638, Section 310, Oklahoma Administrative Code, 1995].* The review officer must have a medical license or hold a doctoral degree in clinical chemistry, forensic toxicology, or a similar biomedical science. The review officer must also have completed at least 12 hours of MRO training.
- *New York [State Public Health Law, Title V, S 571, and Title 10, 58-1.8].* Laboratories must report clinical test results, including workplace drug tests, directly to physicians. New York's law does not address physician interpretation of the results nor does it use the term *medical review officer.*

LICENSURE

Federal rules require that MROs be licensed physicians. States regulate licensure and medical practice, and most physicians maintain active licenses for only the state in which they practice. There is some controversy as to whether the MRO function is a medical practice (see "The Practice of Medicine" later in this chapter). This has important implications for licensure because it is common practice for MROs to review results from collections performed out-of-state and to interview donors by phone across state lines. No legal authority specifically states whether MROs must obtain a state medical license before calling into that state to conduct a telephone interview; however, violation of state licensure laws may have serious consequences. Thus, MROs who practice in just a few states may find that peace of mind outweighs the cost of several state licenses. MROs in the largest, national firms do not maintain licenses in all states; this would be impractical.

TRAINING

MROs should be knowledgeable in the following areas:

- Medical uses of prescription drugs.
- Pharmacology and toxicology of illicit drugs.
- Drug testing procedures, especially the review and handling of test results.

Several professional organizations offer MRO training courses (see Appendix A). The courses last from one to three days and cost between $350 and $600. There is no federal requirement that a licensed physician attend one of these courses before serving as an MRO.

CERTIFICATION

The federal government's definition of an MRO is sufficiently broad that it may include almost all physicians. As with other medical specialties, credentialing of MROs has been developed to promote quality. In 1992, two groups—the American Association of Medical Review Officers (AAMRO) and the Medical Review Officer Certification Council (MROCC)—started certifying the competency of MROs, based on completion of a training course (usually two days) and passing the group's written examination. However, neither group authorizes use of the term *board certified* to describe MRO competency certification. This term is commonly reserved for broader medical disciplines (e.g., internal medicine, dermatology, rheumatology), particularly those recognized by the American Board of Medical Specialties (ABMS). Neither MROCC nor AAMRO are recognized by the ABMS as specialty boards.

To be a certified MRO, one must demonstrate the specific competencies necessary to review and properly report the results of drug tests, as well as perform related administrative and program-management duties.

Several thousand MROs have been certified by AAMRO, MROCC, or both organizations. Both AAMRO and MROCC certifications expire after five years. MROCC requires that the MRO take six hours of relevant continuing medical education (CME) and pass the examination again to remain certified. AAMRO does not require CME for recertification and offers the certified MRO the opportunity of remaining in "good standing" by taking an in-home (by mail) test.

Federal rules do not require MRO certification. Some employers and labor unions prefer that their MROs be certified. Certification might help distinguish the MRO in marketing his or her services and validate the MRO's competency in case of a legal or other challenge.

Responsibilities ■

The MRO is responsible for protecting the specimen donor from false accusations of illicit drug use when the result is positive because of an alternative medical explanation. There is no need for the MRO to interview the donor if the laboratory result is negative. If the result is positive, the MRO verifies the forensic integrity of the record and offers the donor an opportunity to present an alternative medical explanation for the positive result.

The MRO's role can extend to several additional responsibilities:

■ If the MRO learns medical information about the donor that suggests the individual may pose a safety risk at work, the MRO can notify the employer (see Chapter 6).
■ MROs can participate in the treatment recommendations and fitness-for-duty assessments of donors who have tested positive (see Chapter 12).
■ Some MROs help employers with drug testing policies, particularly the procedural and technical aspects of these policies.
■ In contrast to drug testing, MROs have no required role in federally mandated alcohol testing programs.

The Practice of Medicine ■

When an MRO contacts a donor to ask about alternative medical explanations for a positive test result, no doctor-patient relationship is created. A doctor-patient relationship exists when an individual seeks the assistance of the physician for the purpose of obtaining a diagnosis or treatment. This is not the case with verifying drug test results, wherein the employer has initiated the MRO engagement and the MRO's primary duty is to the employer. Under the Americans with Disabilities Act (ADA), workplace drug tests are not considered medical tests and are exempt from the same restrictions that the ADA places on medical tests. (Workplace alcohol tests are, however, considered medical tests under the ADA.) The inclusion or exclusion of MRO functions from medical practice may have important implications for professional medical liability insurance, licensure, and record keeping. While drug test records may not be medical records per se, they are of an equally sensitive nature and demand confidential treatment.

In-House versus Off-Site MROs ■

Most companies use MROs based elsewhere—at clinics or third-party administrators. Some companies with in-house physicians also use off-site MROs because of concern that their physicians might be placed in an adversarial role against employees or because off-site MROs offer attractive and reason-

Table 1-1. In-House and Off-Site MROs ■

In-House MROs	Off-Site MROs
Can more easily locate and contact employees when reviewing positive results	Have economies of scale by handling a high total volume of tests
Often, better understand company policies and procedures	Have broad experience through working with many employers
Can better integrate drug testing with other health and safety programs	Offer broad range of service options, e.g., collections, random selections, summary reports

ably priced service packages as well as expertise. It is nevertheless common for physicians who perform company-sponsored examinations to serve as MROs for the same companies, and this has worked successfully. Good MROs position themselves as neutral and nonadversarial. There are certain advantages to using in-house MROs and other advantages to using off-site, contract MROs, as listed in Table 1-1.

MROs and Collection Sites ■

Collection of specimens for drug testing by MROs or their staff offers several advantages: If the collection was performed at his or her location, the MRO can easily get copy 4 (the MRO copy) of the CCF, can more easily get corrective statements (see Chapter 2), and can more readily perform shy bladder evaluations and examinations for clinical signs of opiate abuse, when needed. On the other hand, MROs who are independent of the collection site may offer more objectivity in their review of CCFs and collection-site performance. The same issue applies to laboratories and collection sites: While some laboratories offer collection services, laboratories that are independent of the collection site may offer more objectivity in their review of the CCFs. Federal rules do not prohibit MROs or laboratories from collecting drug test specimens.

MROs and Laboratories ■

In federally regulated testing, laboratories cannot require their clients to use particular MROs, nor can an MRO be employed by, be a contractor for, or have a financial interest in the laboratory that analyzes tests that the MRO reviews. This helps to ensure the MRO's objectivity if concerns arise about laboratory performance. Laboratories can, however, *refer* their clients to particular MROs, and the MROs can bill for laboratory services, often bundled into packages they offer to employer clients. An MRO's services can be billed through the laboratory as a convenience to the employer, provided they are itemized separately on the invoices, to help preserve the distinction between the laboratory and the MRO and their individual charges.

MROs and Third-Party Administrators ■

Third-party administrators (TPAs) provide testing-management services through subcontractors, for example, collection sites, laboratories, and/or MROs. The federal rules use the term *consortia* to refer to TPAs, including those formed by employee groups or associations. The largest TPAs employ one or more full-time MROs. Smaller administrators usually contract with off-site MROs to review positive results. The off-site MROs report both negative and verified positive determinations to the administrators, who serve as the gatekeepers for reporting all results to the employers. In 1995, DOT stated: "DOT never intended, nor can it condone, a practice which allows MROs to appoint outside 'agents' to perform [the administrative] review [of negative results]. The MRO should have a direct supervisory relationship with the reviewer and not simply have access to the 'process' of the administrative review"[1]. Thus, while some TPAs receive results and send only positives to off-site MROs, this is not what DOT intended.

The Substance Abuse Program Administrators Association (SAPAA) is a national organization of drug and alcohol testing TPAs. SAPAA offers training courses, a certification examination, and periodic national and regional conferences. (See Appendix A for SAPAA's address.)

Other Roles of the Medical Review Officer ■

Under the Federal Aviation Administration (FAA) and United States Coast Guard (USCG) rules, the MRO's role includes return-to-duty determinations on employees who have had a positive drug test and have completed the recommended program of assistance (see Chapter 12).

While the MRO role, as defined by federal rules, is otherwise limited to review and interpretation of positive drug test results, employers often rely on MROs for related services. These include litigation support, performance testing programs, assistance with development of policies and procedures, and clinical medical services, such as commercial driver's license (CDL) medical examinations.

LITIGATION SUPPORT AND EXPERT TESTIMONY

The employer may ask the MRO to provide expert testimony and/or factual depositions in administrative or legal proceedings initiated by an employee who challenges a drug test result or an employment action taken as a result of a positive test. In this situation, the MRO will be asked to identify the specific actions and decision-making process he or she took in reviewing and interpreting a drug test result. The MRO usually provides testimony on behalf of the employer to explain the test verification process upon which an employment action (e.g., termination, withdrawal of offer to hire) has been made. Service agreements or contracts between the MRO and the employer should identify the MRO's fees for litigation support and expert testimony.

POLICY AND PROCEDURES DEVELOPMENT

Employers may ask their MROs for help in developing and implementing their drug-free workplace programs. This help may involve assisting with policy and procedures, establishing employee assistance programs (EAPs), coordinating employee and supervisory education and training, and monitoring compliance with federal or state requirements. These consultation roles require a broad knowledge base beyond the core elements of reviewing, interpreting, and reporting drug test results.

Each employer who conducts drug testing should have a formal written substance abuse policy. Model policies are available from several federal agencies (Department of Health and Human Services, Department of Labor, Department of Transportation) and community and service agencies (e.g., Chamber of Commerce, safety councils). Each employer should have its policy reviewed by a competent attorney familiar with labor and case law related to drug testing. At a minimum, each employer's drug testing policy should include provisions for an employee assistance program, employee awareness education, and supervisory training. The policy should clearly identify prohibited alcohol- and drug-related conduct, the sanctions or consequences for engaging in prohibited conduct, the rights and responsibilities of employees in substance abuse testing programs, and the procedures for testing, referral to the EAP, and disciplinary actions. MROs should avoid rendering any legal opinion about the employer's policy or the company's compliance with federal or state laws.

The MRO in the Drug Testing Marketplace ■

Workplace drug and alcohol testing is a mature market. Most large companies that would conduct testing already have their programs in place. Much of the recent growth in drug and alcohol testing is attributable to new programs established by smaller companies. In general, large third-party administrators (TPAs) serve large companies' programs, and small local providers serve small companies' programs. The prices presented below reflect observations made in the mid-1990s. Actual prices vary by region, volume, and provider and have generally decreased over time.

Only a handful of physicians serve as full-time MROs. Most of these work for large TPAs that offer packages of services such as collection-site networks, laboratory analyses, off-hours testing, and/or SAP services. There is not great demand for "MRO only" services. Efforts to market MRO services should focus on laboratories, since they often refer employers to MROs, particularly those who bring high volumes of tests to the laboratory. MROs who handle both negative and positive test results charge approximately $5 to $15 per test, depending on volume. Some MROs handle only positive results and let TPAs handle negative results. MROs who handle only positive results charge approximately $25 to $50 per test.

Thousands of occupational health clinics perform drug and alcohol testing. For many, this is a small part of their services and may be limited to collecting urine specimens and performing breath alcohol tests. TPAs, through aggressive marketing, networks of affiliated clinics and low prices, effectively compete with occupational health clinics. Many employers view drug tests as a commodity, that is, a product undifferentiated by quality and purchased based on price alone.

Clinics charge approximately $35 to $70 per test for collection, analysis, review, reporting, and record keeping. Most clinics offer a default laboratory for those clients who have not already selected a laboratory. Clinics pay laboratories approximately $13 to $20 for the analysis of a drug test specimen, and as little as $9 to $10 when annual volume exceeds several thousand. These are bundled prices—that is, they include any necessary confirmation testing. When ordered separately, confirmation testing costs approximately $100. Through volume discounts and experience in negotiating laboratory fees, clinics can usually obtain lower laboratory prices than employers. Clinics generally mark up laboratory fees to cover indirect costs and to make some profit. Some clinics also provide their clients with random selections, summary reporting, and other expanded services. Several software packages are available to help with these services (see Chapter 9).

If a local provider cannot compete against national providers on price, it should instead identify and promote features that distinguish and add value to its services. All other things being equal, local employers prefer using one provider for drug testing, preplacement examinations, injury care, and other occupational health services. Local clinics offer the ability to perform evaluations for clinical signs of opiate abuse and to evaluate donors who do not provide enough urine or breath for testing purposes. Some companies value the personalized services (e.g., face-to-face interviews with donors) that only local MROs can offer. The personal relationships that clinics have with local employers help attract and retain business. Nevertheless, the role of the local clinic is often reduced to collecting specimens on behalf of TPAs. Urine collections take 20 to 30 minutes each, and, at market fees of $10 to $20, generate little revenue unless they are performed efficiently and at high volume.

Clinics are well positioned to provide alcohol testing services because the tests lend themselves to a decentralized approach. The breath specimens are analyzed on-site and the results can be reported immediately and directly from the test site to the employer. Like collections, breath alcohol tests take 20 to 30 minutes each and, at market rates of $25 to $30 per screening or confirmation test, are not highly profitable.

OFF-HOURS SERVICES

Employers may ask their local providers to make arrangements for off-hours testing. The use of this service is often less than anticipated; nevertheless, providers feel obliged to respond to their clients and make the arrangements. Some options include:

- *Hospitals.* Emergency room waiting times, procedural errors, and staff turnover can be problematic. In some cases, other 24-hour/day hospital departments, such as security and respiratory therapy, have been enlisted to perform off-hours urine collections and breath alcohol tests.
- *Independent technicians.* Some medical technicians and other medically trained persons offer services in which they come to the accident scene or other designated locations to perform the test.

- *On-call staff.* Some freestanding clinics require their nurses and medical assistants to share responsibility and be on-call for off-hours testing. Some clinics affiliated with other nearby clinics share the responsibility for off-hours testing.
- *Third-party administrators.* Several regional and national TPAs manage off-hours testing services. The TPA refers its clients to local providers who perform the collections or breath tests. As a practical matter, it is easier to allow the TPA to use its own laboratory account rather than try to impose each employer's specific laboratory account and forms on the off-hours collector(s).

Establishing and ensuring reliable systems for off-hours testing requires significant administrative effort and cost, which should be recouped through setup fees or high per-test fees. Fees of $150 to $300 per collection are not unreasonable.

Risk Management ∎

To date, drug testing litigation has focused more on employers and laboratories than MROs, possibly because the MRO role is new and less visible to plaintiffs and attorneys. Also, lawsuits usually broadly challenge drug testing programs instead of focusing on procedural details. Typical drug testing lawsuits have alleged wrongful discharge, civil rights and disability discrimination, and other traditional tort causes of action. Fewer lawsuits have attacked the persons doing the tests and the procedures used.

Federal regulations impose detailed requirements that have become a standard of practice. Adherence to the procedures has been presented as a defense in litigation, and deviation from them has been cited as improper. As MROs become involved in areas beyond those covered under the federal regulations—for example, in policy development, litigation support, and assessments and referrals for assistance—they can no longer cite the rules to justify their actions if they are challenged. Physician involvement beyond the mere review of positive drug test results can help ensure the quality and success of testing programs. However, physicians must recognize that they acquire additional responsibility and liability when they take on these other roles.

An employee who loses his or her job due to a positive drug test may file an action against the MRO. He or she may sue the MRO for defamation, claiming false reporting of a drug test as positive or charging that the MRO inadequately considered his or her medical history, did not allow presentation of alternative explanations, denied the individual the right to a reanalysis, or released information to unauthorized persons without permission. Or the employee may make other allegations. The employee, employer, or a third party may sue an MRO who recommended that someone return to work if that person subsequently causes an injury while under the influence of drugs. In this case, the suit would allege negligence on the part of the MRO for not making a decision that a reasonable MRO would have made in the same circumstance.

LIMITING RISKS

Workplace drug testing is paper intensive. Service providers should be meticulous in their record keeping. Each record's documentation should enable an outsider to readily understand the process and the reasoning employed in reaching the outcome. Each record is a potential courtroom exhibit. Furthermore, good records can persuade a plaintiff's attorney that no case exists.

Adherence to standard operating procedures helps ensure consistency and makes potential courtroom testimony based on these procedures more credible. These procedures should treat applicants and current employees with an equally high degree of diligence and confidentiality.

A lapse in confidentiality may give rise to a claim, based on a breach of contract or invasion of privacy. All information obtained in the course of testing is sensitive and must be protected as confidential information. As a technique for reducing risk, each donor should be asked to sign a release prior to testing. The release should allow all those in the chain of drug testing—collector, laboratory personnel, MRO, and employer—access to all relevant information. This information must not be shared with anyone else without the prior written consent of the donor unless required or permitted by law.

As with any clinical specialty, to ensure that current practice guidelines are followed, an MRO must keep abreast of new information and regulations. The technology is evolving quickly, federal regulations continue to be issued, and an increasing body of case law and state legislation has developed. The typical MRO needs help to keep abreast of new information. One of the best ways to keep current is to participate in continuing education specifically oriented toward MROs. Various training programs and certification examinations offered by professional organizations serve an important role in providing continuing education programs (see Chapter 1). A number of newsletters and journals also feature information relevant to workplace substance abuse testing (see Appendix A).

INSURANCE COVERAGE

MROs who have medical liability insurance may want to ask their insurance carrier to state, in writing, if their policy covers MRO activities. Some medical professional liability insurers do not cover MRO activities because of uncertainty about the risk, unfamiliarity with the activities, or because the activities do not involve a physician-patient relationship. If the MRO's current insurance carrier does not include MRO activities, the MRO may need to change carriers or consider supplemental MRO insurance. MRO-specific insurance coverage is offered by several insurance carriers, for example:

Davis, Jones, Lamb Insurance Agency, Inc.
4080 First Avenue, NE, #101
Cedar Rapids, IA 52402-9867
(319)364-5193

MGIS Companies
1849 West North Temple, Bldg. #D
Salt Lake City, UT 84116
(800)969-6447

MRO insurance costs less than traditional forms of medical professional liability insurance. Standard business insurance (errors and omissions) may also be sufficient for nonmedical claims that occur as a result of MRO activities.

CONTRACTS

Written contracts that define responsibilities can help manage the MRO's risk. Figure 1-1 presents a sample scope-of-services document for a clinic-based MRO. Any contract or service agreement between the MRO and the employer should include a statement of work, outlining the responsibilities of each party. MROs and employers are often reluctant to get involved with contracts. Many MROs provide services without contracts, even though contracts can help limit the MRO's liability for errors or poor judgments made by the collector, laboratory, or employer.

Figure 1-1. Sample Scope-of-MRO-Services Document ■

Section 1. Statement of Work: Clinic Will Provide Services as Follows:

A. Receipt, review, and reporting of drug test results conducted through the COMPANY's program.

   1. The CLINIC will receive results from the laboratory that analyzes drug test specimens on behalf of the COMPANY. The CLINIC will report as "canceled" to the COMPANY those tests that have significant procedural or technical errors.

   2. The CLINIC will provide review and interpretation of each laboratory-positive test. Each review will be conducted by a physician trained to serve as a Medical Review Officer (MRO). The MRO will determine if there is an alternative medical explanation for positive results. In carrying out this responsibility, the MRO will make a reasonable effort to contact the individual, conduct an interview, and review his/her medical history and other relevant factors. The MRO will review all medical records made available by the individual when a positive test could have resulted from legally prescribed medication. The MRO may also arrange for a medical evaluation to determine if the individual has clinical signs of drug abuse that correlate with opiate abuse. Only those laboratory-positive results that have no alternative medical explanation will be reported to the employer as positive. The MRO will be available to the COMPANY for consultation regarding the use of prescribed medications.

   3. The CLINIC will furnish the COMPANY with a written report of the results of each test.

   4. When the COMPANY has specified drug testing regulations to which it is subject, the CLINIC will perform in conformance with those regulations.

B. Record keeping

   The CLINIC will maintain drug test records on behalf of the COMPANY. The records will include the laboratory reports, custody and control forms, and documentation of the MRO's evaluation for laboratory-positive results. The CLINIC will maintain these records for at least five years for verified positive results and at least one year for other test results. If requested in writing, the MRO will maintain these records for longer periods.

Figure 1-1. Sample Scope-of-MRO-Services Document (continued) ■

C. Return-to-work determinations

If requested, the CLINIC's MRO will recommend to the COMPANY when a worker may return to his/her position after failing or refusing to take a drug test. If reinstatement is recommended, the MRO will establish a schedule for follow-up testing of that worker.

D. Consultation and expert testimony

The CLINIC's MRO will be available for telephone consultation concerning drug testing procedures and will provide expert testimony in drug test-related cases on an as-needed basis.

Section 2. Employer Responsibilities: The COMPANY Will:

A. Provide the CLINIC with a copy of the COMPANY's current drug abuse/drug testing policy and procedures; the name and phone number of a representative to assist with contacting individuals; and the name, phone number, and address of the person in the COMPANY to whom results should be reported.

B. Before performance begins, inform the CLINIC of applicable drug testing regulations, if any, and furnish the MRO with a copy of the MRO's responsibilities with regard to the COMPANY's Employee Assistance Program.

C. Assure that the means of receiving results from the MRO (e.g., fax transmissions) are secure and confidential and that individual drug test results will be kept confidential and will be disclosed only to individuals with a business need for the information or otherwise in accordance with law.

D. Assume responsibility for the performance of the collection site(s) and/or laboratory, if the COMPANY has contracted directly with these providers for services.

E. Be responsible for laboratory costs of reanalyses and additional tests performed on specimens.

F. Have sole responsibility for decisions about the employment, termination, retention, or disciplining of any employee, former employee, or applicant for employment.

Reference ■

1. Guidance on the role of consortia and third-party administrators in DOT drug and alcohol testing programs. *Federal Register* 1995;60(July 25):38,204–5.

Drug and Alcohol Testing Laws ∎

Federal Laws ∎

On September 15, 1986, President Ronald Reagan signed Executive Order (E.O.) 12564, requiring each executive-branch federal agency to establish a comprehensive drug-free workplace program, including drug testing of federal employees in safety-sensitive positions. Under E.O. 12564, each program included these elements:

1. Formal written policy.
2. Employee assistance program.
3. Supervisory training.
4. Employee education.
5. Methods for detecting illicit drug users, for example drug testing.

Executive Order 12564 also directed the Department of Health and Human Services (DHHS) to develop scientific and technical guidelines for all aspects of drug testing—that is, collection of specimens, chain of custody, laboratory accreditation, and medical review of results. In 1988, DHHS issued its *Mandatory Guidelines for Federal Workplace Drug Testing Programs*[1]. The Department of Transportation (DOT) issued more elaborate procedures in 1989 for testing private-sector transportation workers under its jurisdiction [2]. Six DOT "modal" offices—the Federal Aviation Administration (FAA), Federal Highway Administration (FHWA), Federal Railroad Administration (FRA), Federal Transit Administration (FTA), Research and Special Programs Administration (RSPA, which regulates pipelines), and United States Coast Guard (USCG, which regulates maritime commerce)—issued implementation rules that defined who would be tested, how often they would be tested, the consequences of a positive result, and so forth. DOT-mandated testing programs began in 1990, except for testing in the mass transit industry. The FTA did not implement a DOT drug testing program in 1989 because of an adverse court decision on its regulation.

In 1991, a fatal crash of a New York City subway was attributed to alcohol abuse by the driver. Shortly thereafter, Congress passed the Omnibus Transportation Employee Testing Act [3], which required DOT to add alcohol testing to its existing drug testing rules and to add split-specimen procedures and certain other modifications to the drug testing rules for FAA, FHWA, FRA, and FTA. (The Omnibus Act did not cover RSPA or USCG.) The FTA was also authorized to reissue its drug testing regulations. DOT implemented these changes in February 1994.

In 1989, the Nuclear Regulatory Commission (NRC) issued drug and alcohol testing procedures covering the nuclear power industry [4]. NRC's rules are similar but more stringent than those of DHHS. The NRC rules are focused on "fitness-for-duty" issues and extend beyond the general deterrence objectives of drug-free workplace programs. The federal rules continue to undergo refinement through amendments, interpretations, and guidance documents, many of which are published in the *Federal Register*. The federal rules are "codified" as official documents in the *Code of Federal Regulations (CFR)*, published annually by the Government Printing Office.

Tests conducted under federal authority are called *regulated* tests. Regulated testing follows applicable federal rules and procedures, for example, FHWA implementation rules and DOT procedures. Nonregulated testing usually follows similar procedures but has greater flexibility. Several state drug testing laws require employers to use DHHS or DOT procedures. Many employers make certain exceptions, for instance, by conducting on-site tests, testing for additional drugs, or using different laboratory cutoff levels.

The federal drug testing rules authorize testing only for marijuana, cocaine, amphetamines (amphetamine and methamphetamine), opiates (codeine, morphine, and 6-acetylmorphine 6-AM), and phencyclidine. They define six kinds of testing:

1. *Preemployment or preplacement.* A preemployment test is given before an offer of employment has been made. A preplacement test is given after an offer of employment has been made. Either of these tests can be given to an individual who is being considered for a position covered by federal rules. Each of the DOT agencies defines who is "covered" under their rules. For example, under FHWA rules, covered positions are those for which the worker must have a commercial driver's license (CDL). Nearly all employers who conduct drug testing require preemployment or preplacement tests.
2. *Reasonable suspicion (also known as "reasonable cause," "for cause").* A reasonable suspicion test is given to an employee who performs in a covered position and is suspected of using a prohibited drug. In DOT-regulated programs, "reasonable suspicion" occurs when a trained supervisor—some DOT modes require two supervisors—has observed behavior (i.e., performance issues), conduct (i.e., demeanor), or appearance indicative of drug use. In non-DOT programs, the basis for reasonable suspicion may be defined by state law, company policy and, in a unionized setting, collective bargaining agreements.
3. *Post-accident (also known as "post-incident").* A test is given to a surviving employee after occurrence of an accident in which the employee's performance may have caused or contributed to the accident. Each DOT mode sets forth criteria that define which accidents warrant post-accident testing. For example, FHWA requires post-accident testing after fatal accidents involving commercial motor vehicles (CMVs) and after nonfatal accidents in which the covered drivers are cited for moving violations and the vehicles must be towed, or in which there are personal injuries requiring medical treatment.

4. *Random.* A random test is one given to a covered employee selected by chance on an unannounced basis. DOT's drug and alcohol testing rules started with annual random drug and alcohol testing rates of 50 percent and 25 percent of covered employees, respectively. Thus, if an employer had 100 covered employees, the rules required at least 50 random drug tests each year. The DOT rules allow test rates to be adjusted as often as every year, based on industry-wide positive rates during the preceding two years.

5. *Return-to-duty.* This is a test given to a covered employee before he or she returns to duty following a positive test or refusal to submit to testing, the individual having met any additional conditions required to return to work.

6. *Follow-up.* Follow-up testing performed on a frequent, unannounced basis after a covered employee has passed a return-to-duty test and resumed safety-sensitive functions is also federally authorized. Most DOT rules require a minimum of six follow-up tests in the first 12 months after return to safety-sensitive duties, and allow follow-up testing for up to 60 months (five years).

Some employers perform *periodic testing,* that is, tests performed on a scheduled basis such as annually. Periodic tests were required under the original DOT rules but have been largely phased out with the implementation of random testing. Under DOT rules, only the FAA and USCG authorize periodic testing of certain employees when renewing a federal license or certificate.

State Laws ■

Many states and some localities have also passed laws on drug and alcohol testing. Some of these laws serve to protect individuals from invasions of privacy or denial of due process, and others offer employers discounts in their workers' compensation insurance premiums if they have qualifying drug-free workplace programs. In some states, a positive drug test or an alcohol level above a certain cutoff is considered presumptive evidence of intoxication that can be used to deny workers' compensation benefits and/or unemployment benefits. The array of different rules can result in nonuniform treatment of employees working for multistate companies. For example, an employer may be able to conduct nonregulated random testing in one state but not in another. DOT rules, where applicable, preempt conflicting state and local laws, so multistate companies can have uniform policies and procedures.

References ■

1. Department of Health and Human Services. Mandatory guidelines for federal workplace drug testing programs. *Federal Register* 1988;53(April 11):11,970–89.
2. U.S. Department of Transportation. Procedures for transportation workplace drug testing programs. *Federal Register* 1989;54(Dec 1):49,854–84.
3. Omnibus Transportation Employee Testing Act of 1991. Public Law 102-143, 102nd Congress, October 28, 1991.
4. Nuclear Regulatory Commission. Fitness-for-duty programs. *Federal Register* 1989;54(June 7):24,468–508.

Urine Collection Procedures ■

Specimen collections involve some of the most sensitive and difficult aspects of workplace drug testing. It is here that the specimen donor's needs for privacy and confidentiality most conflict with forensic demands for specimen integrity and proper identification. The procedures for collecting specimens offer a balance between forensic standards and individual privacy rights. For the test results of a urine specimen to meet forensic standards, all of the following must be documented:

- The urine specimen was properly identified with its donor.
- No adulteration or tampering took place.
- No unauthorized access to the specimen was possible.
- Secure transfer of the specimen was made to each person handling it.

Chain of custody is the term used to describe the process of documenting the transfer of a specimen from the donor to the collector, from the collector to the courier, from the courier to the laboratory, and from one person or department to another within the laboratory. Urine specimen collection for workplace drug testing is a detailed procedure that consists of many steps. The following sections address specific aspects of the procedure. For further guidance about federal agency programs, consult the Substance Abuse and Mental Health Services Administration's (SAMHSA) *Urine Specimen Collection Handbook for Federal Workplace Drug Testing Programs* [1] and DOT's *Urine Specimen Collection Procedures Guidelines* [2].

Custody and Control Forms ■

Each collection procedure is documented on a custody and control form (CCF), also known as a *chain-of-custody form* (COC). Regulated programs use the seven-copy federal CCF (OMB No. 9999-0023), which is also called the *DOT form*, or *NIDA form* (see Appendix E). Laboratories preprint CCFs with their logos and program-specific account information, including the name and address of the medical review officer (MRO) who is expected to review and interpret the results. An MRO or other program administrator may use a single account and the same preprinted information for multiple employers; in this instance, the collector would write each "employer's name and address" in Step 1 of the form. Laboratories provide preprinted CCFs at no direct cost to their clients. The forms are also sold by Government Printing Offices (GPOs), which are listed in the government listings of local phone directories. Each copy of the CCF is different from the others. For example, the laboratory result appears only on copies 1, 2, and 3, and the donor's name appears only on copies 4, 5, 6, and 7. The flow chart in Figure 3-1 shows where each copy is sent.

Use of the Federal Drug Testing Custody and Control Form, with its title and references to federal regulations, implies that the test is authorized by federal rules. To avoid misrepresentation, this form should be used *only* for regulated testing. Forms that do not reference the federal regulations—sometimes called *non-DOT (non-NIDA) forms*—should be used for nonregulated testing. These forms may have seven copies and look like DOT forms, or they may be quite different, often simpler. Every form has a chain-of-custody block that is used to record the person-to-person transfer of the specimen. Figure 3-2 presents an example of a non-DOT form.

Person-to-person transfers of the specimen should be kept to a minimum until the specimen is sealed in its shipping package. Once it is sealed in its shipping package with the appropriate copies of the CCF, no entries are made in the chain-of-custody block. Transport personnel do not sign the form, nor must they maintain a separate chain of custody to track handling of the pack-

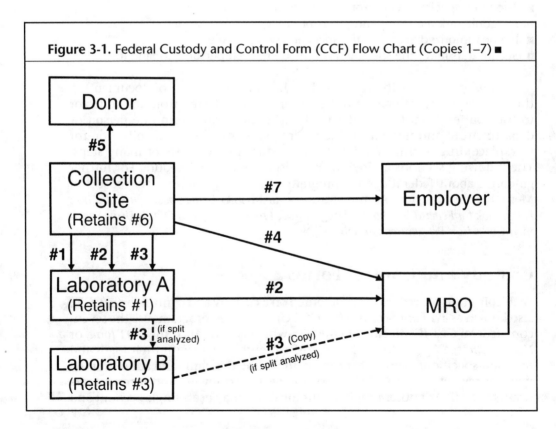

Figure 3-1. Federal Custody and Control Form (CCF) Flow Chart (Copies 1–7) ■

Figure 3-2. Non-DOT Substance Abuse Chain-of-Custody (COC) Form ■

Substance Abuse Chain-of-Custody Form C (NON-NIDA)

COLLECTOR

LabOne

8915 Lenexa Drive • Overland Park, KS 66214
(800) 728-4064 for Client Services

06548601

CLIENT
ACCOUNT #:   0022
SALES DEPARTMENT SAMPLE ACCT
ABC COMPANY
12345 E. 1 STREET
ANYTOWN   XX   10101

COLLECTION SITE NAME/NUMBER

COLLECTION SITE ADDRESS

COLLECTION SITE PHONE

TESTS TO BE PERFORMED:

REFERRING PHYSICIAN/MRO
DR. JOHN SMITH
XYZ MRO COMPANY
123 ANY STREET
ANYTOWN   XX   12345

Donor I.D. Verified ◯ Photo I.D.
                    ◯ Employee Representative I.D.

SPECIMEN TEMPERATURE:
Has been read within 4 minutes? ◯ Yes ◯ No
Within range of 90°-100°F/32°-38°C? ◯ Yes ◯ No***
***If NO, record actual temp.: _____ °F

REASON FOR TEST: (Check one)
◯ Pre-employment   ◯ Random   ◯ Return to duty   ◯ Reasonable suspicion/cause
◯ Post-accident   ◯ Periodic   ◯ Other_____

DONOR

DONOR INSTRUCTIONS

1. PROVIDE SPECIMEN(S); GIVE TO COLLECTOR.
2. OBSERVE COLLECTOR AFFIX NUMBERED SEAL ACROSS LID OF SPECIMEN CONTAINER(S).
3. VERIFY BY INITIALING THE SPECIMEN SEAL(S).
4. FILL IN DONOR INFORMATION. **PLEASE PRINT LEGIBLY.**
5. SIGN AND DATE DONOR AFFIDAVIT BELOW.

DONOR AFFIDAVIT

DONOR NAME _____

DONOR PHONE NUMBER _____

DATE OF BIRTH _____ SEX _____
I CERTIFY THAT THE SPECIMEN(S) SEALED WITH THE ABOVE SPECIMEN ID NUMBER
WAS PROVIDED BY ME ON THIS DATE AND THE SPECIMEN(S) HAS NOT BEEN ALTERED.

SIGNATURE _____ DATE _____

DONOR INFORMATION

SOC. SEC. NO. _____/_____/_____

OTHER I.D. _____

CONTACT NAME _____

EMPLOYER _____

MEDICATIONS (OPTIONAL)_____

CHAIN OF CUSTODY

COLLECTOR INSTRUCTIONS

1. VERIFY DONOR'S I.D. WITH VALID DRIVER'S LICENSE OR PICTURE I.D. AND FILL OUT FORM.
2. RECORD TEMPERATURE
3. SEAL EACH SPECIMEN WITH TAMPER EVIDENT SEAL.
4. CONFIRM PRESENCE OF DONOR'S SIGNATURE AND DATE IN DONOR AREA ABOVE.
5. INDICATE SPECIMEN(S) SUBMITTED ___ URINE AND/OR ___ BLOOD. INDICATE NUMBER AND TYPE OF SPECIMEN(S) SUBMITTED: ___ urine ___ blood
6. SIGN AND DATE COLLECTOR AFFIDAVIT BELOW.

COLLECTOR AFFIDAVIT - MUST BE COMPLETED

I CERTIFY THAT THE SPECIMEN(S) WAS/WERE PROVIDED BY THE ABOVE DONOR ON THIS DATE IN ACCORDANCE WITH SPECIFIED COLLECTION
PROCEDURES. I FURTHER CERTIFY THE PROPERLY IDENTIFIED SPECIMEN(S) HAS BEEN PREPARED FOR TRANSPORT TO THE LABORATORY.

SIGNATURE X _____ DATE __/__/__ TIME ____ AM PM

FORM#11 4/98

COPY 1 - ORIGINAL - SEND TO LABORATORY WITH SPECIMEN

age [3]. The laboratory will initiate a chain-of-custody document to track the transfer of the specimen during the laboratory testing process.

Most CCFs include the bottle label and shipping container seal, attached on a perforated flap. Each CCF has a preprinted unique specimen identification number, both on the form and the bottle label, and usually printed as both a number and a bar code. It is essential that the specimen identification number on the bottle(s) match the specimen identification number on the CCF copies.

Specimen Collection Kits ■

The supplies necessary to process a urine specimen are usually provided by the laboratory. These specimen collection kits generally contain:

- *One or two specimen bottles:* plastic containers with sealable caps that can hold at least 60 mL of urine. For split specimen collections, in which the sample is divided, the kit has two bottles.
- *Collection container:* wide-mouth single-use container into which the donor urinates.
- *Heat-sensitive temperature strip:* affixed to either the specimen bottle or the collection container.
- *Plastic bag:* specimen bottle(s) placed in the bag with a desiccant material in case there is leakage during shipment.
- *Shipping container:* hard-sided box or cylinder for shipping the specimen bottle(s) and CCF copies to the laboratory.

The specimen kits should be wrapped or sealed when presented to the specimen donor to ensure that they have not been tampered with or previously used. The donor should take only the collection container into the bathroom when providing the specimen. The bottle(s), wrapped or otherwise sealed, should remain with the collector and should be opened in view of the donor when the specimen is transferred from the collection container into the specimen bottle(s).

Release and Consent Forms, Medication Lists ■

Although the donor's consent for testing and release of test results is implied by his or her signature on the CCF, many collection sites ask the donor to sign a release and consent statement on a separate form. Many health professionals consider use of release and consent forms good medical practice. Each should indicate that results are being released to both the MRO and the employer. The sample release and consent form in Figure 3-3 includes a mechanism for documenting the start and stop time, in case the donor is unable to provide a sufficient urine specimen within the allowed time period. If the donor refuses to sign the release and consent form, the collector should note this and proceed with the collection. If the release and consent form is incomplete or omitted by mistake, the test should not be canceled unless the employer's policy requires cancellation.

Federal rules neither require nor prohibit the use of release and consent forms. Some employers use these or other forms to ask the donor for indemnification or for a list of medications taken before the test, and DOT explicitly prohibits this. Furthermore, asking about medications is considered a medical inquiry and, as such, is prohibited in a pre-offer setting under the ADA. The federal drug testing rules include an option for the donor to list medications

Figure 3-3. Release and Consent Form for Substance Abuse Testing ■

_____   _____
NAME   EMPLOYER

_____   _____
SOCIAL SECURITY NO.

_____   _____
HOME TELEPHONE NO.   HOME ADDRESS

In accordance with and subject to the terms and safeguards of the above-referenced employer's substance abuse prevention policy, I hereby consent to give breath, urine, and/or blood specimen(s) to the employer's agents, including any medical facility or laboratory, for testing for the presence of alcohol and/or prohibited drugs. I further consent and agree that the laboratory will provide the results of any tests performed on such specimens to the employer's designated medical review officer, to the employer's substance abuse prevention program manager, and, where required by regulations, to the appropriate federal (e.g., DOT) and state agencies. I also authorize the release of this information to any physician who needs it to determine my physical qualification in accordance with applicable federal regulations. This authorization will remain valid for 12 months from the signature date.

I understand that the employer's agents will hold the test results confidential and not release them except in accordance with the employer's substance abuse prevention policy.

_____   _____
DONOR'S SIGNATURE   WITNESS' SIGNATURE

                                                              ❑ AM
_____, _____ ❑ PM
                     DATE

Collector's note:
If a urine volume of < 30mL for a single specimen, or < 45mL for a split specimen, is obtained, offer the donor up to 40 ounces of fluid to drink and try collection again. If no suitable specimen is obtained within three hours, enter the stop time: _____ ❑ AM / ❑ PM
reason for stopping (❑ time limit, ❑ patient left/refusal to submit, ❑ other: _____)
and fax this form to the employer representative.

```
To: _____
Secure Fax #: _____
Initials:_____ Date: _____
```

on the back of copy 5, the donor copy, of the CCF. This list is intended to serve as a memory jogger, to refresh the donor's memory if he or she is later contacted by the MRO. If medications are entered on other copies of the CCF by mistake, the test should not be canceled unless the employer's policy requires cancellation.

A "mature minor," typically at least age 15, can consent to medical tests that are not high risk [4]. Workplace drug tests are not medical care, and parental consent when testing a minor, especially one 15 years or older, is optional. Signature verification can be problematic, because parents usually sign consent forms at home, not at collection sites or company premises. If the parent is asked to provide consent, the parent should also be asked to waive access to the results. Workplace drug tests are for employment purposes, not family disputes. (See also Chapter 9, "Releasing Records to a Third Party.")

Regulated and Nonregulated Collections at the Same Visit ■

Employers with regulated testing programs may also have nonregulated programs to test for additional drugs and/or test employees not covered by the federal rules. If the regulated and nonregulated collections occur at the same visit, the regulated specimen takes priority and should be collected first. One person can perform both collections but should collect the specimens using separate forms and bottles and separate acts of urination.

Use of the Urine Sample for Nondrug Tests ■

Under DOT guidance, after urine has been set aside for the DOT drug test, any remaining portion of the sample may be used for nondrug testing, but only if such testing is required by the FHWA, such as a dipstick test for glucose and protein as part of a CDL physical [5]. The DOT does not permit "adulteration" or specimen integrity checks (pH, specific gravity, creatinine) to be conducted at the collection site to determine the specimen's suitability for drug testing.

Measuring the Temperature Range of the Specimen ■

The recommended procedure for determining the specimen temperature is through the use of a heat-sensitive strip affixed to the collection container or specimen bottle. The temperature measuring device must be able to indicate if the temperature is outside the acceptable range. The DOT and DHHS rules set the acceptable temperature range at 32–38°C (90–100°F). The Nuclear Regulatory Commission (NRC) and certain nonregulated employers—for example, the U.S. Postal Service—use narrower ranges, for example, starting at 94°F or 96°F. The urine's temperature is measured within four minutes of voiding to determine if its temperature is consistent with a freshly voided specimen. The collector notes the temperature on the CCF as within range or as a specific value. The urine temperature decreases from body temperature by about 2°F as it equilibrates with the relatively cooler container. Thus, the temperature of a freshly voided urine specimen in a container is approximately 97° F. Specimens held against the groin or axillary region are less than 93°–96° F [6,7].

Directly Observed Collections ∎

In regulated testing, the donor provides his or her specimen in privacy unless one or more of the events in Table 3-1 has taken place, thereby raising suspicion of substitution or adulteration. The collector does not decide whether to conduct a direct observation but instead, if adulteration is suspected, asks a higher level supervisor or the employer representative for authorization to conduct a second collection under direct observation. The collector submits

Table 3-1. Events That Trigger Directly Observed Collections ∎

Triggering Events	Comments
Suspected adulteration at the collection site	
1. A specimen *outside the temperature range* and not within 1° C/1.8° F—in either direction—of the donor's body temperature.	The collector, with concurrence from his/her supervisor or from the employer, *must* collect a second specimen under direct observation. Specimens from both collections, observed and nonobserved, go to the laboratory with separate CCFs and are analyzed and reported separately.
2. *Observation of the donor attempting to submit a substituted or adulterated specimen,* e.g., the donor provides a urine specimen that is blue, presumably because of blue water from the toilet.	
Last specimen dilute or drug-positive	
3. A *dilute* specimen (specific gravity < 1.003 and creatinine < 0.20 g/L) unless the "substituted" specimen criteria are met.	The employer *may* require a directly observed collection if the donor's previous specimen was diluted or verified positive. In regulated testing, the occurrence of a dilute specimen is not "reasonable cause" for requiring a second specimen collection. Some employers require automatic retests anyway, but this is not authorized by the federal regulations.
4. *Return-to-duty and follow-up tests,* i.e., tests performed after the donor has tested positive.	
Last specimen was unsuitable	If the laboratory cannot analyze the specimen because of its condition and cannot identify an adulterant, and the donor denies adulteration of the specimen and has not taken a medication known to interfere with immunoassays, the MRO reports to the employer that the test is canceled, the reason for cancellation, and that a second collection must take place immediately under direct observation.
5. *"Specimen unsuitable: cannot obtain valid drug test result"*	

specimens from both collection procedures, nonobserved and observed, to the laboratory. The donor is subject to disciplinary action if either specimen is verified positive.

The observer must be in the bathroom while the donor urinates and sees the urine pass from the body to the collection container. The person who directly observes, or *witnesses,* the urination must be of the same gender as the donor. If someone other than the collector observes the urination, that person's name is entered on the CCF in the "Comments" section or chain-of-custody block.

State laws in Connecticut, Maine, Oklahoma, and Rhode Island and a city ordinance in Boulder, Colorado, prohibit direct observation of urine drug test specimen collections. DOT's provisions for direct observation supersede state laws in DOT-mandated testing.

Shy Bladders ■

The urine specimen—30 mL for a single specimen or 45 mL for split specimens—must come from one voiding of the bladder. In regulated testing, one cannot combine specimens from separate voids to reach 30 or 45 mL because this would undermine sample security and identification. In DOT-regulated testing, if the donor provides insufficient volume from a single void, the collector should:

1. Discard the specimen and its container(s).
2. Ask the donor to stay at the collection site and drink up to 40 ounces of fluids.
3. Wait and try again for up to three hours.

Three hours starts when the donor returns from the restroom with insufficient urine. The donor is allowed up to three hours, even if the collector must stay late. If the donor has been allowed up to three hours and has not provided a sufficient specimen, the collector records what has occurred—for example, the start and end times of the three-hour period—and notifies the employer. In regulated testing, if the donor is already employed at the company, the employer must then offer a shy bladder evaluation. If the donor is an applicant, the employer has the alternative option of rescheduling the test. Employees have always been entitled to shy bladder evaluations. In 1998, the DOT stated that applicants are also entitled to shy bladder evaluations [8].

Each shy bladder evaluation should be conducted promptly after the attempted collection. A shy bladder evaluation is a medical assessment that determines if the donor has a physiologic, anatomic, or psychological reason for the insufficient urine volume. Unsupported claims of situational anxiety and dehydration are not acceptable explanations for a shy bladder. A preexisting psychological disorder—that is, one designated in the *Diagnostic and Statistical Manual of Mental Disorders (DSM IV)*—that can cause insufficient urine volume may be considered an acceptable explanation. The protocol of the evaluation is at the examiner's discretion, based on the circumstances. A medical history usually suffices; ancillary testing is rarely necessary.

The physician who performs the shy bladder evaluation submits his or her written report to the MRO. The MRO then reports to the employer, in writing, whether the shy bladder situation represents a medical condition that justifies cancellation of the test or whether it represents a refusal to provide a specimen. If the donor has a permanent or long-term medical inability to provide sufficient fresh urine (for example, has an indwelling catheter or is on dialysis), and it is established that the applicant has no clinical evidence of illicit drug use, the MRO should report the result as negative (see Figure 3-4)

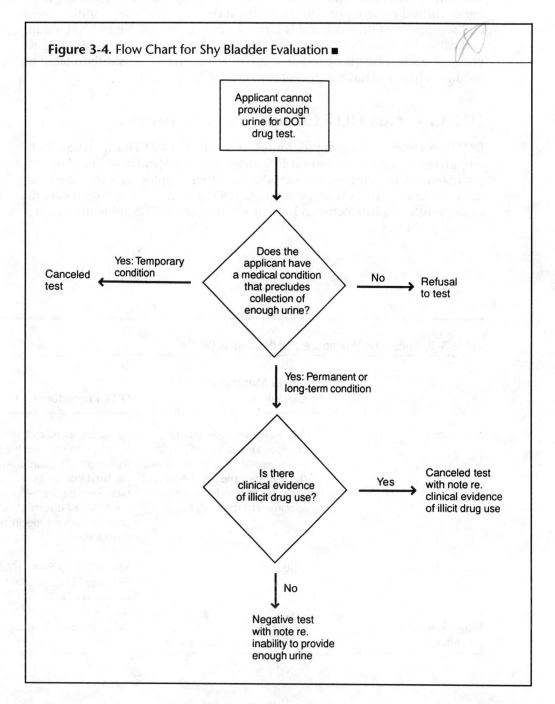

Figure 3-4. Flow Chart for Shy Bladder Evaluation ■

[8], thereby facilitating hiring of the worker. The MRO can perform the evaluation for clinical evidence of illicit drug use or can arrange for another qualified physician to perform the evaluation. The evaluation protocol may include a physical examination, blood test, information from the donor's personal physician, and information from the physician who conducted the shy bladder evaluation. If this evaluation reveals signs and symptoms of drug use, the MRO reports the result to the employer as canceled and reports the finding of clinical evidence of illicit drug use. If the applicant does not have signs and symptoms of drug use and is hired, he or she remains subject to random and other kinds of DOT drug tests. The employer, through the MRO, must verify at each subsequent test that an anuric donor is physically unable to produce urine and has no clinical evidence of drug abuse.

DHHS versus DOT Collection Procedures ■

DOT's specimen collection procedures, as detailed in 49 CFR Part 40, apply to employers in the transportation industries. DHHS's *Mandatory Guidelines* apply to federal agencies (other than NRC) and their employees, including civilian personnel in Department of Defense (DOD) agencies. The collection procedures differ slightly between DOT procedures and DHHS guidelines, as presented in Table 3-2.

Table 3-2. Collection Procedures: DHHS versus DOT ■

	DHHS Mandatory Guidelines	DOT Procedures
Minimum	30 mL. If a split specimen collection is attempted but the donor produces only 30–44 mL, the split specimen is waived and the collector sends the single specimen to the laboratory.	45 mL for splits, and 30 mL for single specimens. If a split specimen collection is attempted but the donor produces less than 45 mL, the collector discards the urine and a new specimen is collected.
Split specimens	Optional	Mandatory for FAA, FHWA, FRA, and FTA. Optional for RSPA and USCG.
Insufficient volume procedures	Drink 8 fl oz every 30 min, up to 24 oz; wait up to 2 hr.	Drink up to 40 fl oz; wait up to 3 hr.

References ■

1. Substance Abuse and Mental Health Services Administration. *Urine Specimen Collection Handbook for Federal Workplace Drug Testing Programs.* DHHS Publication No. (SMA)96-3114, 1996.
2. U.S. Department of Transportation. *Urine Specimen Collection Procedures Guidelines.* Washington, DC, December 1994.
3. U.S. Department of Transportation. Procedures for transportation workplace drug and alcohol testing programs. *Federal Register* 1994;59(Aug 19):42,996–43,019.
4. English A, Matthews M, Extavour K, et al. *State Minor Consent Statutes: A Summary.* San Francisco, CA: National Center for Youth Law for Continuing Education in Adolescent Health, April 1995.
5. Bennett D. *Letter to S Russ.* Washington, DC: U.S. Department of Transportation, Jan. 4, 1994.
6. Peron NB, Ehrenkranz JRL. Fake urine samples for drug analysis: hot but not hot enough. *JAMA* 1988;259:841.
7. Judson BA, Himmelberger DU, Goldstein A. Measurement of urine temperature as an alternative to observed urination in a narcotic treatment program. *Am J Drug Alcohol Abuse* 1979;6:197.
8. Office of Drug and Alcohol Policy. *Policy Statement.* Washington, DC: U.S. Department of Transportation, June 26, 1998.

Laboratory Analysis and Performance Testing ■

4

A forensic urine drug-testing laboratory must reliably, and in a legally defensible manner, discriminate between those specimens that contain drugs and/or drug metabolites at or above the specified cutoff levels and those that do not. Testing is designed to be 100-percent accurate for positive results. While claims of 100-percent accuracy may meet with skepticism, forensic urine drug testing, when properly performed, appears to have no false positives. This accuracy is achieved primarily by use of a definitive analytic technique—gas chromatography/mass spectrometry (GC/MS)—for confirmatory testing.

In regulated testing, each sample is analyzed at least twice (screen and confirmation) before it is reported as positive. If collected, the "split" portion of the specimen may be analyzed at a second laboratory to corroborate the first positive result. This method, together with chain-of-custody procedures and medical review of laboratory-positive results, virtually eliminates the possibility of false-positive results (detecting drugs when they are not present) or misidentification (detecting the presence of drugs but identifying the wrong drugs).

Certification of Laboratories ■

Federally regulated drug tests must be analyzed at laboratories certified by the Department of Health and Human Services (DHHS) National Laboratory Certification Program (NLCP). The Department of Transportation (DOT) allows tests of Mexican commercial motor vehicle drivers to be performed at laboratories certified by DHHS or by laboratories that are deemed equivalent to U.S. standards by DOT [1]. The National Institute on Drug Abuse (NIDA) originally administered the NLCP, and this gave rise to the expression *NIDA certified laboratory*. The NLCP is now administered by the Substance Abuse and Mental Health Services Administration (SAMHSA), a division of DHHS, thus giving rise to the current expressions, *SAMHSA certified* or *DHHS certified*.

A laboratory becomes and remains DHHS certified by passing on-site inspections and periodic proficiency testing. The DHHS standards for certification and the proficiency testing requirements constitute the most stringent laboratory accreditation program available in forensic urine drug testing. The

DHHS certification program assures that laboratories follow certain principles and similar procedures and that they perform satisfactorily in proficiency testing programs. As of 1998, approximately 70 laboratories were DHHS certified. A list of DHHS certified laboratories appears in the *Federal Register* during the first week of each month. The list is also available from SAMHSA (see Appendix A). Many laboratory companies operate separate noncertified laboratories at the same locations; these noncertified facilities provide nonregulated forensic urine drug testing services.

DHHS's certification authority is limited to laboratories in the United States, to Drug Enforcement Administration (DEA) Schedule I and II drugs, and to testing performed under federal regulations. The College of American Pathologists Forensic Urine Drug Testing (CAP-FUDT) program certifies performance for the five drugs (and drug classes) in the federal panel; it also certifies performance for other drugs, and at other cutoff values, upon request. Most DHHS certified laboratories are also CAP-FUDT certified.

Laboratories that are DHHS certified under the NLCP are exempt from the requirements set forth under the Clinical Laboratory Improvement Amendments of 1988. This exemption is limited to the certified laboratories' immunoassay and GC/MS confirmatory testing processes for the five drug classes for which DHHS certifies.

Cutoff Values ■

A cutoff value is established for each assay and is used to determine if a given specimen is negative or positive. If the specimen's drug concentration is at or above the cutoff, the result is positive. Conversely, if the specimen's drug concentration is below the cutoff, the result is negative. Thus, in forensic urine drug testing, *negative* does not mean "no drug present" or "undetected," but rather that the apparent concentration of analyte was less than the cutoff concentration for that assay.

DHHS certified laboratories are certified only for the drugs, and at the cutoffs, listed in Table 4-1. Most laboratories offer a variety of drug testing panels, combinations of drugs, and cutoff values. The employer should consult the laboratory when selecting nonstandard panels and cutoff values to make sure the lab can reliably test for those drugs and at those cutoff values.

The cutoff levels established for federal drug testing serve an administrative function in the final interpretation of test results. The confirmation cutoff values are set to prevent positive results due to "incidental" or "external" exposure to drugs, that is, passive or second-hand smoke inhalation or absorption from handling items with drug residues. Drug concentrations above the confirmatory cutoff levels are consistent with direct use of drug(s).

Accessioning ■

The flow chart in Figure 4-1 illustrates laboratory handling of urine specimens. At accessioning, the laboratory receives the specimen and checks the Custody and Control Form (CCF) for completeness and accuracy before specimen analysis. The specimen is then examined for evidence of tampering. If

Table 4-1. Federal Drug Testing Cutoff Concentrations ■

Drugs	Initial Test Cutoff Levels (ng/mL)	Confirmatory Test Cutoff Levels (ng/mL)
Marijuana metabolites	50	15[a]
Cocaine metabolites	300	150[b]
Opiate metabolites	2,000	
Morphine		2,000
Codeine		2,000
6-Acetylmorphine[c]		10
Phencyclidine	25	25
Amphetamines	1,000	
Amphetamine		500
Methamphetamine[d]		500

[a.] Assayed as 11-nor-delta-9-THC-9-carboxylic acid (a THC metabolite).

[b.] Assayed as benzoylecognine (a cocaine metabolite).

[c.] Test for 6-AM when the morphine concentration exceeds 2,000 ng/mL.

[d.] Specimen must also contain amphetamine at a concentration greater than or equal to 200 ng/mL.

the specimen appears adequate for testing—that is, the packaging is intact and the specimen does not appear adulterated—the laboratory transfers an aliquot into a labeled vial and starts an internal chain-of-custody form for recording handling of the specimens for the screening tests.

Screening and Confirmation Tests ■

Most laboratories process specimens as batches (groups) of aliquots. The number of aliquots in each batch varies, depending on the laboratory's size and workload. Each batch includes an appropriate number of performance test samples to monitor the accuracy of test results. The batches are submitted for screening tests, typically performed by a sophisticated, automated device that draws off a small sample as each aliquot is individually conveyed to a sampler. The sampling device draws in water between real samples, thereby rinsing it and avoiding contamination between real samples.

Screening serves to eliminate most specimens from further testing and to identify presumptive positive specimens that need confirmatory testing.

Figure 4-1. Flow Chart for Laboratory Handling of Urine Specimens ■

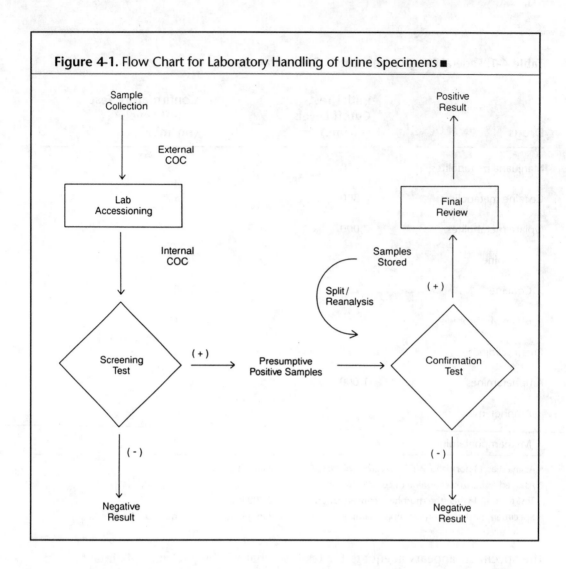

In regulated testing, each screening test must be performed using an FDA-approved immunoassay. Immunoassays are semiquantitative: They distinguish between ranges of concentrations but generally do not measure specific concentrations. Each immunoassay is based on competitive binding of a drug for a limited number of antibody binding sites. The antibodies may also bind to other, similar chemicals; thus, the tests are nonspecific. In testing for drugs that belong to large classes of similar drugs, such as benzodiazepines and barbiturates, the antibodies often react with many drugs in that class. Most manufacturers optimize the performance of their assays for one or more of the most common members of a given class of drug. Table 4-2 lists the common commercially available immunoassays.

If the screening result is below the cutoff, the laboratory reports the result as negative and discards the specimen without further testing. If the screen-

Table 4-2. Common Immunoassays ■

Immunoassay	Brand Name(s)	Manufacturer	Comments
Enzyme (EIA)	EMIT, CEDIA	Syva, Boehringer Mannheim/Microgenics	Widely used. Inexpensive. Equipment is available for automated, high-volume rapid screening by EIA. Sensitive to some adulterants.
Fluorescence polarization (FPIA)	ADx, TDx	Abbott Diagnostics	Resistant to a number of adulterants. Gives reasonably good quantitative estimates of concentrations. Slower and more expensive than EIA and KIMS.
Kinetic interaction of microparticles	OnTrak, TesTcup OnLine	Roche Diagnostics	Equipment is available for automated, high-volume rapid screening by KIMS. Used by some large laboratories.
Colloidal metal (CMI)	Triage	Biosite Diagnostics	Used in on-site testing.
Radioimmunoassay (RIA)	Abuscreen	Roche Diagnostics	Labor-intensive. Resistant to a number of adulterants. Not widely used.

ing result is at or above the cutoff for one or more drug classes, the laboratory takes a new aliquot from the specimen for each identified drug class, starts a new internal chain-of-custody form for that aliquot, and performs confirmatory testing.

In regulated testing, confirmatory testing is performed by a combination of two analytical techniques: gas chromatography and mass spectrometry (GC/MS). Gas chromatography physically separates the various substances that have been extracted from the specimen. Mass spectrometry identifies specific substances that the gas chromatograph separated. GC/MS is used to identify the specific molecule that corresponds with the drug or drug metabolite. The technique is highly sensitive and can detect most drugs in low ng/mL concentrations. However, it is also expensive (for example, more than $100) and time-consuming, and for this reason, specimens are screened by faster, less expensive immunoassays to identify specimens that should undergo GC/MS.

An aliquot from the specimen is prepared for GC/MS by extracting the drug or drug metabolite and, in most cases, chemically combining it with another compound to form a derivative. The drug (or derivative) is then separated by the gas chromatograph and detected by the mass spectrometer. The magnitude of the response to GC/MS testing is proportional to the concentration of analyte in the specimen.

Certified laboratories are authorized to conduct certain additional analyses to provide definitive evidence of specific drug metabolites or isomer forms of drugs. The most commonly performed additional analyses are for the *d*- and *l*-isomer forms of amphetamine and methamphetamine. Special analyses are usually performed at the request of the medical review officer (MRO); however, some laboratories routinely perform *d*- and *l*-isomer analyses on amphetamine-positive results if the concentrations are high or if they meet other predefined criteria. This can be based on a preestablished contract between the employer and the laboratory. Laboratories are also authorized to conduct analyses for detection of dilution, substitution, and adulteration, as described later in this chapter.

Review and Determination ■

Based on the drug/metabolite assay(s), the laboratory makes one of three determinations, as outlined in Table 4-3. If the result is negative, the signature of the laboratory's certifying scientist—the actual signature or a stamped signature—is entered in Step 7, which appears on copies 1, 2, and 3 of the CCF (see Appendix E). If the result is positive, the report must indicate which drug or drug metabolite(s) was detected, and the certifying scientist must review the record and write his or her signature in Step 7. In regulated testing, if the determination is "Test not performed," the laboratory includes an appropriate statement on the "Remarks" line in Step 7 of the CCF. If the additional comments cannot be fully described on the "Remarks" line, the laboratory may attach a separate sheet describing the problem, and reference the attachment on the "Remarks" line.

Dilute, Substituted, and Adulterated Specimens ■

A donor may try to avoid a positive drug test result by adding something to, or substituting another fluid for, his or her own urine. Federal guidelines require that the laboratory perform procedures to screen for adulteration. Federal guidance authorizes, but does not require, testing for nitrite concentration, creatinine concentration, specific gravity, and pH. This panel of tests is designed to identify common adulterants. A laboratory may also test for

Table 4-3. Laboratory Determinations ■

Determination	Interpretation
Negative	No drug/drug metabolite was detected at or above the cutoff concentration either in the screening or confirmatory assays.
Positive	The drug/drug metabolite was detected at or above the cutoff concentration on both the screening and confirmatory assays.
Test Not Performed	
Fatal flaw, <flaw stated> or Uncorrected flaw, <flaw stated>	The specimen was not tested because of a fatal flaw (e.g., broken seal; specimen ID numbers do not match) or uncorrected flaw (e.g., a collector's signature was omitted and no signed statement is received to correct the error).
Specimen unsuitable: cannot obtain valid drug test result	The laboratory could not complete the screening or confirmation analyses and the specimen has not been determined to be adulterated or substituted.
Specimen adulterated:	
Nitrite is too high	Nitrite concentration $\geq$ 500 µg/dL.
pH is too high (or too low)	pH $\geq$ 11 (or $\leq$ 3).
Presence of _____ (specify) detected	A foreign substance was detected.
Specimen substituted: not consistent with normal human urine	Specific gravity $\leq$ 1.001 or $\geq$ 1.020 and creatinine concentration $\leq$ 5 mg/dL.

one or more specific adulterants—for example, glutaraldehyde—if the presence of the adulterant(s) is suspected because of the urine's color, smell, consistency, or other properties. Table 4-4 lists examples of specific adulterants. Glutaraldehyde, bleach, nitrites, surfactants, and certain other adulterants can be identified using GC/MS, colorimetry, and other procedures. When a DHHS certified laboratory suspects adulteration and is unable to identify the adulterant, the laboratory may, upon authorization by the MRO, send an aliquot from the specimen to another DHHS-certified laboratory that can perform the appropriate test(s). According to DHHS, a specimen is defined to be [2]:

Table 4-4. Examples of Urine Adulterants ■

Adulterant	Test(s)	Comments
Klear, Whizzies	Nitrite	Nitrite interferes with the GC/MS assay for tetrahydrocannabinol. The specimen may screen positive, but the marijuana metabolite, including the marijuana metabolite that the laboratory uses as an internal standard, cannot be detected by GC/MS. Consumption of certain foods (e.g., beef jerky) can cause urinary nitrite concentrations as high as 300 μg/mL. Nitrite is also associated with urinary tract infections. If the laboratory fails to recover the THC metabolite internal standard, it will test for nitirite by GC/MS. Urine nitrite concentration of greater than or equal to 500 μg/mL is used for determining the presence of nitrite as an adulterant.
Mary Jane's Super Clean 13	Alkylephoxysulfonate	Alkylephoxysulfonate is also used in Joy dishwashing detergent. When added in sufficient amount to urine, it can cause an apparent decrease in drug concentrations, especially of marijuana metabolites, when tested by immunoassay, particularly EIA.
Salt	Sodium and chloride	Sodium and chloride are normally found in urine but occur in especially high concentrations when salt has been added as an adulterant. High concentrations of salt can cause a decrease in the apparent concentrations of several drugs when tested by immunoassay, particularly EIA.
UrinAid	Glutaraldehdye	Glutaraldehyde interferes with the EIA and, to a lesser degree, other immunoassays. UrinAid is marketed for marijuana users

Table 4-4. Examples of Urine Adulterants (continued) ■

Adulterant	Test(s)	Comments
		but affects assays for each of the NIDA-5 drugs. When added to the urine specimen, it causes the immunoassay result to be either false-negative or uninterpretable. Glutaraldehyde does not interfere with GC/MS results, but because it interferes with screening the specimen, the specimen never reaches the stage of GC/MS testing. If the laboratory suspects glutaralde-hyde adulteration—for example, because materials have precipi-tated in the urine—it can test the specimen for glutaraldehyde. Glutaraldehyde is not found in nonadulterated urine.
Urine Luck	Pyridine	Urine Luck contains the salt pyridium chlorochromate, which dissociates in solution to form pyridine. The effect is similar to nitrite, as described above. If the laboratory fails to recover the THC metabolite internal stan-dard, it may test the specimen for pyridine by GC/MS.

a. *Dilute* if the creatinine is less than 20 mg/dL *and* the specific gravity is less than 1.003, unless the criteria for a *substituted specimen* are met.

b. *Substituted* (i.e., the specimen does not exhibit the clinical signs or charac-teristics associated with normal human urine) if the creatinine concentration is less than or equal to 5 mg/dL *and* the specific gravity is less than or equal to 1.001 or greater than or equal to 1.020.

c. *Adulterated* if the nitrite concentration is greater than or equal to 500 μg/mL.

d. *Adulterated* if the pH is less than or equal to 3 or if it is greater than or equal to 11.

e. *Adulterated* if an exogenous substance (i.e., a substance that is not a normal constituent of urine) is present in the specimen or an endogenous substance at a higher concentration than normal physiological range is present in the specimen.

The laboratory does not routinely report nitrite concentration, creatinine con-centration, specific gravity, or pH values, but will report them for specific specimens upon request by the MRO. If the laboratory has determined that a specimen has been adulterated or substituted, the laboratory reports neither a negative nor positive result. This eliminates the possibility that the employer will misinterpret "negative" results from such specimens.

The following sections define the above categories in further detail and address the laboratory's responsibilities in identifying such specimens. Chapter 5 addresses the actions the MRO takes if the laboratory has identified a specimen as dilute, substituted, or adulterated.

DILUTE SPECIMENS

If the specimen's specific gravity is less than 1.003 but greater than 1.001 and its creatinine concentration is less than 20 mg/dL but greater than 5 mg/dL, the laboratory prints "Dilute specimen" in the "Remarks" section of the CCF. The laboratory also prints the drug test result(s), whether negative or positive.

Urine specific gravity is normally 1.003 to 1.030; dilute urine is at the lower end of this range, and concentrated urine is at the upper end. The urine concentration of creatinine, a by-product of protein metabolism, is normally greater than or equal to 20 mg/dL and is related to the individual's muscle mass and state of hydration. A finding of dilute urine suggests that the donor put water in his or her specimen, drank a lot of fluids, used diuretics, or had a medical condition such as diabetes, kidney disease, or psychogenic polydipsia.

Water loading (ingesting large volumes of water) can dilute urine up to tenfold and thereby lower drug concentrations. Ingestion of 2 quarts of fluid can reduce creatinine and specific gravity values below 20 mg/dL and 1.003, respectively, and can reduce drug/metabolite concentrations below the cutoff concentrations for several hours [3]. Although the collection site can limit how much water it offers the donor, it cannot limit water consumption before arrival, and thus, in unannounced testing, employers should try to limit the interval between notifying donors and collecting their specimens. Diuretics, especially fast-acting prescription diuretics, increase urine flow and can also lower a urine drug concentration below a cutoff value.

TEST NOT PERFORMED: SPECIMEN SUBSTITUTED

If the urine's creatinine concentration is less than or equal to 5 mg/dL and the specific gravity is less than or equal to 1.001 or greater than or equal to 1.020, the laboratory report states "Test not performed" with the comment "Specimen substituted: Not consistent with normal human urine" printed in the remarks section of the CCF. The laboratory does not report the drug test result(s), whether negative or positive.

Tap water, apple juice, soft drinks, and other fluids have been submitted for human urine. Temperature and several other factors serve as obstacles to successfully submitting a substituted specimen. The donor may substitute his or her own urine specimen with urine from another person—one who is presumably drug-free. This specimen would have specific gravity and creatinine values consistent with human urine. If the donor claims that his or her positive result is from urine that was substituted for his or her own, it should be called to the donor's attention that he or she has signed a statement that the specimen was his or her own.

TEST NOT PERFORMED: SPECIMEN ADULTERATED

If the laboratory identifies a specific adulterant in the urine, or if the specimen's nitrite concentration or pH are out of range (see Figure 4-2), the "Test not performed" box is checked in Step 7 on the CCF, and one of the following statements is included on the "Remarks" line:

a. Specimen Adulterated: Nitrite is too high.
b. Specimen Adulterated: pH is too high (or too low).
c. Specimen Adulterated: Presence of _____ (specify) detected.

(Some laboratories use other phrases—for example, "Uncharacteristic of human urine"—to identify adulterated specimens.) The laboratory does not report the drug test result(s), regardless of whether they are negative or positive.

Adulterants are substances that can be added directly to urine in an attempt to destroy the drug/drug metabolite(s) or interfere with the assay(s). Effective adulterants generally act by disrupting the immunoassay reaction. Commercially sold adulterant products include Clean 'n Clear, Clear Choice Instant Purifying Additive, Klear, Mary Jane's SuperClean 13 (liquid soap), Purifyzit, Stealth, UrinAid, Urine Luck, and Whizzies (see Table 4-4). Some donors have added other household products and substances to urine samples. New adulterants continue to be introduced to the marketplace. Many are sold through direct mail and over the Internet. The manufacture, sale, and/or use of adulterants is a misdemeanor in Nebraska [Neb. Rev. Stat. §48-1909], Pennsylvania, and Texas [Tex. Health & Safety Code Ann. §481.133].

TEST NOT PERFORMED: SPECIMEN UNSUITABLE

If the laboratory is unable to complete the screening or confirmation analyses and the laboratory has not identified a specific adulterant or the presence of acid (pH $\leq$ 3) or base (pH $\geq$ 11), the laboratory report states "Test not

Figure 4-2. Laboratory Block for Primary Specimen ∎

STEP 7: TO BE COMPLETED BY THE LABORATORY - Specimen Bottle Seal(s) Intact: ☐ YES   ☐ NO, Explain in Remarks Below.

THE RESULTS FOR THE ABOVE IDENTIFIED SPECIMEN ARE IN ACCORDANCE WITH THE APPLICABLE INITIAL TEST AND CONFIRMATORY TEST CUTOFF LEVELS ESTABLISHED BY THE DHHS *MANDATORY GUIDELINES FOR FEDERAL WORKPLACE DRUG TESTING PROGRAMS*

☐ NEGATIVE ☐ POSITIVE, for the following: ☐ CANNABINOIDS as Carboxy-THC   ☐ COCAINE METABOLITES as Benzoylecognine   ☐ PHENCYCLIDINE

☐ OPIATES   ☐ AMPHETAMINES:

☐ TEST NOT PERFORMED   ☐ codeine   ☐ amphetamine   ☐ OTHER _____
☐ morphine   ☐ methamphetamine

REMARKS _____

TEST LAB (if different from above) _____   (___) _____
NAME   ADDRESS   PHONE NO.

I certify that the specimen identified by the laboratory accession number on this form is the same specimen that bears the specimen identification number set forth above, that the specimen has been examined upon receipt, handled and analyzed in accordance with applicable Federal requirements, and that the results set forth are for that specimen.

_____   _____   _____
(PRINT) Certifying Scientist's Name (First, MI, Last)   Signature of Certifying Scientist   Date (Mo. / Day / Yr.)

performed" with the comment "Specimen unsuitable: cannot obtain valid drug test result" printed in the remarks section of the CCF. Unsuitable specimens can occur if the absorbance in the immunoassay is too high or too low. Unsuitable specimens can be due to use of certain nonsteroidal anti-inflammatory medications or to the addition of adulterants that the laboratory may not have identified. Chapter 5 further discusses this.

Pills and Potions ■

Certain pills and potions are reputed to interfere with laboratory assays. One of these products, Golden Seal Tea, can cause false-negative opiate results on thin-layer chromatography (TLC), but few laboratories routinely use TLC for drug test assays. Other products include Clear Choice Herbal Detox Tea, Detoxify Carbo Clean, Eliminator, HealthTech Pre-Cleanse Formula, Naturally Klean Herbal Tea, Quick Tabs, Quick Flush Capsules and Tea, Ready-Clean, Test Free, Test Pure, THC Terminator Drink, and The Stuff. These products do not specifically interfere with the assays, but because they are supposed to be taken with large quantities of water, the urine may be diluted, thus lowering the urine drug concentration. Some products contain creatine to boost the urine creatinine value. Some contain vitamin B complex to make the urine more yellow.

Consumption of large amounts of vitamin C, vinegar, and acidic fruit juices can increase the excretion rate of amphetamines and phencyclidine, which are both basic compounds. This increases urine concentrations in the short term and decreases the duration of drug excretion.

Delivery of Laboratory Reports to the MRO ■

DHHS-certified laboratories must report test results to the MRO within an average of five working days after receipt of the specimen. The industry standard, however, is for reporting within one or two days for negatives and positives, respectively. DHHS-certified laboratories are not permitted to report results verbally, even if they are followed by written reports, because verbal reports are prone to misunderstanding, misdirection, and misrepresentation. Most laboratories provide electronically transmitted (e.g., modem, facsimile) results, similar to standard clinical laboratory reports. Some laboratories and software vendors offer systems that allow computer-to-computer data transfer and facilitate electronic reporting by MROs to employers. (Chapter 9 describes electronic reporting.)

Laboratories send, by mail or courier, original copies of the CCFs. Laboratories may fax the forms but must still send the originals. Laboratories must ensure that transmissions are reasonably confidential, and laboratories that fax results must first ask each MRO to certify that his or her fax machine is in a secure-access area.

Laboratories also print results on CCFs. Figure 4-2 shows the laboratory block from copies 1 and 2 of the federal CCF. The result of the primary specimen is printed here. Copy 3 of the federal CCF has a similar block, in which the result of the split specimen analysis, if performed, is printed. The laboratory sends CCF copy 2 and, if the split-specimen analysis was performed, CCF copy 3 to the MRO.

Specimen Storage ■

Negative specimens are discarded. Confirmed positive specimens are stored at minus 20° C or less for at least 12 months. In split specimen tests, Bottle B is discarded immediately if Bottle A is negative; but it is stored at minus 20° C for at least 60 days if Bottle A is positive and no request is made to analyze Bottle B. However, once analyzed, Bottle B is retained for one year. Laboratories will save specific specimens longer upon request—for example, because of a legal challenge.

Litigation Package ■

If a test result faces a legal challenge or the MRO has serious concerns about the validity of a test result, the employer or MRO may ask the laboratory for the complete set of analytical data, chain-of-custody records, and other administrative documents associated with that specimen. This information is generally referred to as a "full documentation package" or "litigation package." It should include copies of all results from the batch that contain the test result for the particular donor's specimen. It should also include internal and external chain-of-custody documents for the batch of specimens that contain the donor's specimen, and any other relevant information pertaining to the testing of the donor's specimen. Additional information can be obtained from the laboratory upon request—for example, a description of the laboratory's chain-of-custody procedures or a description of the laboratory's quality assurance program.

Performance Testing ■

In regulated programs, each employer must submit blind performance test samples to the drug testing laboratory at a 3-percent rate, that is, three blind quality control samples for every 100 employee specimens, up to a maximum of 100 blind samples per quarter. Blind performance testing programs help serve to:

■ Ensure accurate test results.
■ Detect laboratory testing problems.
■ Instill employee confidence in the program.
■ Demonstrate testing reliability if there are legal challenges to the program.

Employers with more than 2,000 covered employees must include, at a 20-percent or more rate, blind samples that contain one or more of the drugs tested. Positive samples should be distributed in approximately equal proportion to the drugs being tested. Drugs and drug metabolite concentrations in the spiked samples should exceed the cutoffs by at least 25 percent [4].

Submission of the samples should simulate real specimens, that is, they should be spread out over the year, and, if appropriate, over multiple collection sites.

The blind performance test samples must be certified by immunoassay and GC/MS, and stability data must verify their performance over time. SAMHSA maintains a list of companies that sell performance test samples and vendors who will purchase samples and arrange for their submission on behalf of their client companies. This list can be obtained by contacting SAMHSA's Division of Workplace Programs.

Performance test samples are sold in batches, distributed between blank and spiked samples, as requested by the purchaser. Most employers contract with vendors to purchase blind samples and have them submitted to laboratories as if they were real donor specimens. For each specimen, this requires completing a chain-of-custody form and properly labeling the bottle, including the name and identifiers of a fictitious donor. It is helpful if the collector notes that the specimen is a "performance test sample" where the donor would normally print his or her name. The laboratory copies of the CCF should not indicate that the specimen is a performance test sample. The program administrator may ask the collector to use specific names or numbers that will help identify the results, after receipt, as performance test samples.

As the recipient of the results, the MRO is well situated for decoding, tracking, and evaluating the results of the performance testing program. Variability of up to 20 percent in the concentration is considered acceptable. A false-negative result (i.e., the laboratory reports a negative result when a positive result was expected) can occur if a sample is prepared at a concentration just above the cutoff and the measured result is below the cutoff. Given a false-negative result, the MRO should ask the laboratory for the immunoassay value, even if it is below the cutoff. The laboratory cannot be asked to reanalyze the specimen, because the specimen will have already been discarded; however, other specimens that were prepared from the same batch of performance testing material may be available from the manufacturer, and these can be checked. False-negative results are considered a serious concern if they occur frequently. A false-positive result (i.e., the laboratory reports a positive result when a negative result is expected) is always serious and must be investigated. If the reanalysis confirms that the laboratory reported a false-positive result on a blind performance test sample, the MRO should contact the employer. The employer should then contact the appropriate regulatory office, which will conduct an investigation in an attempt to determine the cause of the false positive. In DOT-mandated testing, either DHHS or DOT investigates the discrepancy. When the specific cause is identified, the laboratory will be required to take corrective action to prevent recurrence of the error. The regulatory office will share the findings with the employer and the MRO.

Many DOT-covered employers are not in compliance with the performance testing requirements of the DOT Procedures. Providers of drug testing services have found it difficult to effectively market this service, especially to small- and moderate-size employers. On the other hand, only an investment in freezer space and purchase of some samples is required to get started.

References ∎

1. U.S. Department of Transportation. *Memorandum of Understanding Between the Department of Transportation of the United States of America and the Secretariat of Communications and Transport of the United Mexican States*. Washington, DC, June 10, 1998.
2. U.S. Department of Health and Human Services. *Guidance for Reporting Specimen Validity Results; Notice to DHHS Certified and Applicant Laboratories*. Rockville, MD, September 28, 1998.
3. Cone EJ, Lange R, Darwin WD. In vivo adulteration: excess fluid ingestion causes false-negative marijuana and cocaine urine test results. *J Anal Toxicol* 1998;22:460–73.
4. Report on laboratory certification issues. In: Finkle BS, Blanke RV, Walsh JM (eds), *Technical, Scientific and Procedural Issues of Employee Drug Testing*. Rockville, MD: National Institute on Drug Abuse, 1990. P 33.

Receiving and Reviewing Drug Test Results ∎

5

Receiving Forms and Laboratory Results ∎

In regulated programs, laboratories must send both negative and positive re-sults directly to the medical review officer (MRO). In some nonregulated pro-grams, employers and third-party administrators (TPAs) receive all laboratory results and send just the positive results to the MRO. While this reduces MRO expenses and expedites receipt of negative results, it also has several disad-vantages:

- If the employer receives negative results directly from the laboratory, the em-ployer can identify those laboratory-positive results reported as negative by the MRO following his or her medical review. Thus, the employer can determine which donors have alternative medical explanations; this information should remain off-limits to the employer.
- The MRO cannot adequately monitor and assure quality by handling only labo-ratory-positive tests. The MRO's role includes input into the handling and inter-pretation of specimens, both negative and confirmed positive, that are dilute, suspected of adulteration, or unsuitable for testing. The MRO cannot effectively identify, understand, and fix these problems if he or she handles just a small percentage of the tests.
- Laws in several states—including Florida, Hawaii, Louisiana, Montana, and New York—require laboratories to send all negative and positive workplace drug test results directly to MROs. New York State requires laboratories to send all drug test results to physicians.

Concentrations ∎

Certified laboratories are prohibited from routinely reporting concentrations for drugs other than morphine and codeine. The laboratory will routinely provide morphine and codeine concentrations for opiate-positive results if the MRO requests this in writing. Morphine and codeine concentrations can be used to guide the MRO's decision to order 6-AM analysis or a physical examination of the donor, or to ask about poppy seed use. They do not serve as clinical evidence of unauthorized or illicit opiate use (see Chapter 7).

If the MRO asks for the drug concentration(s) from a specific positive specimen, the laboratory will comply. The laboratory will also, upon request from the MRO, report the codeine concentration if present below the cutoff value in a morphine-positive specimen, or the amphetamine concentration if present below the cutoff in a methamphetamine-positive specimen.

In regulated programs, employers are authorized to receive concentration values only when test results are challenged in a legal or administrative procedure. The intent is to avoid misinterpretation and misuse of concentration data. A high concentration is not "more positive" than a low concentration. The concentration rarely provides the employer with meaningful information about the amount of drug used, the time or frequency of use, or the degree of impairment. Limited data have been published that correlate urine concentrations with dose and time of cocaine use [1]. No data have been published for the other drugs in the federal five-drug panel. The same dose will produce different concentrations and different effects in different people. Thus, urine concentrations cannot accurately be related to blood concentrations or impairment at the time of the urine specimen collection. The metabolism of alcohol and the interpretation of blood alcohol concentration (BAC) is better characterized. It is possible to estimate a previous BAC value based on a measured BAC value and an assumed metabolic rate, although this procedure also has limitations (see Chapter 11).

Urine concentrations can be helpful in monitoring an employee's progress after stopping drugs that have long half-lives, such as marijuana and benzodiazepines. If the urine concentration decreases over time, use of the drug has probably stopped. Small increases, however, do not prove new use. Concentrations can fluctuate slightly with normal analytic variation, changes in urine volume, diurnal changes, urine pH, and other factors [2]. One can adjust for urine flow changes by dividing the urine drug/metabolite concentration by the creatinine concentration and comparing adjusted values [3]. This is not a standard practice, and in regulated programs neither the employer nor the MRO can base a test's outcome on creatinine-adjusted values.

MINIMUM REQUIRED FORMS

MROs can review results based on faxed copies of custody-and-control forms (CCFs), but in regulated programs, MROs must make reasonable attempts to ensure receipt of "true" (original) copies. Many DHHS certified laboratories report test results electronically. The DOT and DHHS specifically prohibit the MRO from reporting test results to employers based on the electronic lab reports. The MRO must have received the appropriate copies of the CCF before reporting a test result to the employer.

- *If the result is laboratory negative,* before reporting the result, the MRO's office must have at least one copy of the CCF.
- *If the result is confirmed positive,* before reporting the result, the MRO must have at least two copies of the CCF: one copy with the donor's signature (which appears on copies 4 through 7) and one copy with the laboratory certifying scientist's signature (which appears on copies 1 and 2).

■ *If the result is for Bottle B of a split specimen test,* the MRO needs copy 3 from the laboratory that analyzed Bottle B. (Chapter 8 discusses split specimens further.)

The collection site sends copy 4 directly to the MRO (see Figure 3-1). If the MRO is far from the collection site, receipt of copy 4 can be a bottleneck that delays review and reporting of positive results. Programs that routinely send copy 4 to the laboratory for forwarding to the MRO are in violation of the federal rules, which are designed to prevent the laboratory from having any access to the donor's name and other personal data. While the routine routing of copy 4 through the laboratory is prohibited, the accidental routing of copy 4 to the laboratory, or the inadvertent labeling of a specimen bottle with the donor's name, is not grounds for canceling a test. DHHS-certified laboratories use numbers to identify the aliquots that are analyzed, so it is extremely unlikely that the donor's identity would be available to those who perform the analyses, even if it appears on the forms at accessioning.

Significant administrative effort goes into the sorting and collating of CCFs and drug test results. The MRO must usually sort through forms from the vast majority of negative results to find those corresponding to the small minority of positive results. This task is unavoidable and is among the reasons that MROs should charge for the handling and reporting of both negative and positive results.

Administrative Review ■

The MRO and laboratory have separate and independent responsibilities to perform an administrative review of the CCF. The laboratory accessioning staff checks the CCF against a list of potential errors. Each laboratory has developed its own list, which usually is based on guidelines issued by DOT (see Figure 5-1 [4]. Some errors can be corrected; others, especially discrepancies, cannot and are known as fatal flaws. If the laboratory identifies an error, it notes the error on the CCF and may also note it on the test report.

If the result is laboratory-negative, the MRO (or MRO's designate) performs an "administrative review" of the CCF to at least verify that the donor ID and specimen ID on the CCF match the donor ID and specimen ID on the laboratory report. The donor ID number on the CCF need not be the donor's actual ID number; for example, the donor might have entered an inaccurate number. It should be recognized, however, that the donor has been asked to sign a statement on the CCF attesting to the number's accuracy.

If the result is confirmed-positive, the MRO must personally verify that the chain-of-custody block is intact, the donor has signed Section 4, and the laboratory certifying scientist has signed Section 7. A missing donor's signature on a positive test can be recovered, too, if the donor is willing. The MRO (or collector, laboratory, or employer) would seek a corrective statement from the donor first; once corrected, the MRO would proceed with the review for alternative medical explanations.

Figure 5-1. DOT Test Cancellation Criteria ■

Correctable Flaws

1. Donor ID number is omitted from the CCF, unless the donor's refusal to provide the ID number is noted on the CCF.[a]

2. Incomplete chain-of-custody block (minimum requirement: two signatures and dates, shipping entry).

3. Collector's signature is omitted from the certification statement.

4. Donor's signature is omitted from the certification statement, unless the CCF elsewhere indicates that the donor refused to sign it.

5. Certifying scientist's signature is omitted on positive results.

Fatal Flaws

1. Specimen ID number is omitted from specimen bottle or does not match the specimen ID on the chain-of-custody form.

2. Specimen volume is below 30 mL. If the volume is between 27 and 30 mL, the specimen may be accepted if the laboratory can ensure that sufficient volume will be available for storage and for any necessary reanalyses for quality control or reconfirmation of results.[b]

3. Specimen bottle seal is broken or shows evidence of tampering.

4. Specimen shows obvious adulteration (i.e., color, foreign objects, unusual odor).

---

[a] The bottle and form are numerically coded to avoid disclosing the patient's name. It is essential that the codes on the bottle and form match, but it is not essential to use the donor's actual social security number or other identification number.

[b] In practice, the laboratory will accept the specimen with a volume less than 27 mL if the laboratory can ensure sufficient volume for storage and any necessary reanalyses.

MEMORANDUM FOR RECORD (CORRECTIVE STATEMENT)

If the error is potentially correctable, the laboratory attempts to obtain a Memorandum for Record (MFR), also known as a corrective statement, in which the person who erred, usually the collector, acknowledges the error. Figure 5-2 is an example of an MFR form. The laboratory may ask the MRO or employer to help obtain the MFR, especially if the collector reports directly to the MRO or employer, not the laboratory. The laboratory defers the analysis or the reporting of the result for at least five working days, until the MFR is received or until the MRO authorizes the analysis to be performed anyway (see "Test Not Performed"). After the MFR is received, the laboratory sends the result and a

---

Figure 5-2. Example of Memorandum for Record (MFR) ■

<Use an appropriate letterhead>

Date: <date>

From: <collector's printed name>

To: Drug Testing Laboratory   Medical Review Officer
           1234 Main Street   *or*   5678 Central Street
           City, State, Zip Code   City, State, Zip Code

Subject: Memorandum to Recover Missing Information (or insert an appropriate phrase
         that describes the issue)

Re: <specimen ID number>
         <donor SSN or other ID number>

On <collection date>, I served as the collector for the above specimen. While completing
the custody and control form, I forgot to <appropriate phrase that describes the omission,
e.g., mark the box in Step 2 on the CCF to indicate that the specimen temperature was
within the acceptable range>. I have reviewed the collection procedure and am certain
that I followed all other parts of the procedure <e.g., I looked at the temperature strip on
the collection container/specimen bottle > as required.

To ensure that this omission will not happen again, I am planning in future tests to review
the entire CCF before I separate the copies and seal the specimen bottle(s) and CCF in the
plastic bag.

                                               _____
                                            Collector's Signature

cc: <medical review officer or drug testing laboratory>

---

copy of the MFR to the MRO. The MRO then reports the result and is not required to inform the employer that an error occurred.

If the MRO finds a potentially correctable CCF error, caused either by the collector or the laboratory (for example, a missing certifying scientist's signature), the MRO should contact the person who caused the error and seek a corrective statement.

Adulteration and Dilution Remarks ■

The laboratory prints abnormal adulteration test findings, if any, on the printout and, in regulated testing, in the "Remarks" section of the CCF. The following sections discuss the actions that the MRO takes in response to laboratory reports of adulteration and dilution.

DILUTE

If the laboratory reports that the specimen was dilute, the MRO may report to the employer that the next time the donor is selected for a drug test, the employer may require the specimen to be collected under direct observation. The MRO may wish to report this information separately from the drug test report, because putting it on the report may call into question the report's validity. The outcome of the drug analyses, negative or positive, is valid even if the urine is dilute. In regulated testing, the employer is not authorized to retest the donor because his or her urine was dilute. Some companies retest anyway but do so under their own policy, not federal authority. Some companies take no action on dilute specimens, and, when this is the case, the MRO need not identify which specimens are dilute. The option for direct observation has been put into the federal rules to address the possibility of donors adding water to their specimens. In practice, it is difficult to track workers and indicate to collectors those who are due for observed collections. Also, direct observation does nothing to address the more common problem of donors diluting their urine by drinking large volumes of water.

"TEST NOT PERFORMED"

The laboratory issues the report "Test not performed" if the specimen's documentation or packaging has significant and uncorrected flaws, or if the specimen has been identified as substituted, adulterated, or unsuitable for analysis. The laboratory prints, on the "Remarks" line of the CCF and on the electronically generated printout, an explanation of why the test was not performed.

"Test Not Performed: Fatal flaw," or "Uncorrected flaw"
If an error in documentation or packaging has occurred, the laboratory may contact the MRO to ask if he or she wishes to authorize analysis of the specimen as a "nonforensic" or "non-chain-of-custody" specimen. The MRO may want a nonforensic analysis, for example, if he or she has a corrective statement and has not sent it to the laboratory, or if, in the MRO's opinion, the error is not significant enough to warrant cancellation of the test. If authorized by the MRO, the laboratory will proceed with the analysis and will print a disclaimer on the report that indicates the test did not meet forensic standards. The MRO must then be prepared to stand behind the test's validity.

If the laboratory reports that the test was not performed because of a fatal or uncorrected flaw, the MRO checks the "Test not performed" and "Test canceled" boxes in Step 8 of the CCF (see Figure 5-3) and enters "Fatal flaw, _____" (with the flaw stated), or "Uncorrected flaw, _____" (with the flaw stated), as appropriate, on the "Remarks" line. The MRO reports to the employer that no further action is required unless a negative test result is required (e.g., preemployment, return-to-duty, or follow-up testing).

Most canceled tests are identified by the laboratory and reported as such to the MRO, without a drug analysis report. If the laboratory has reported a negative or positive drug result and the MRO identifies an administrative error that invalidates the test, the MRO should report the test as canceled and should not disclose the drug result.

Figure 5-3. MRO Block for Primary Specimen ■

STEP 8: TO BE COMPLETED BY THE MEDICAL REVIEW OFFICER

I have reviewed the laboratory results for the specimen identified by this form in accordance with applicable Federal requirements. My determination/verification is:

☐ Negative   ☐ Positive   ☐ Test not performed   ☐ Test Cancelled

                        REMARKS _____

                                                                / /

     (PRINT) Medical Review Officer's Name (First, MI, Last)   Signature of Medical Review Officer   Date (Mo./Day/Yr.)

"Test Not Performed: Specimen Unsuitable: Cannot Obtain Valid Drug Test Result"
In response to "Specimen unsuitable," the MRO should:

1. Discuss the results directly with the certifying scientist or other responsible person at the laboratory to obtain more specific information. Is the problem a foreign substance or an interfering medication? What were the specific gravity, pH, and creatinine values? Based on the appearance and initial adulteration testing, does the laboratory recommend additional, specific tests?
2. Ask about alternative immunoassays. Most failures involve EMIT, a widely used immunoassay test. If the problems on immunoassay suggest interference from a medication, the laboratory may try one or more alternative immunoassays, for example, RIA, FPIA, or KIMS. The laboratory is not, however, permitted to neutralize or otherwise alter the specimen to try and obtain a valid immunoassay result.
3. Contact the donor and inform the donor that the specimen was not suitable for testing or contained an unexplained interferant. After explaining the limits of disclosure of medical information unrelated to the drug test result, the MRO should ask about medications the donor may have taken, and ask if the donor knows what may have caused the problem (i.e., admits to adulteration of the urine). Use of ciprofloxacin (Cipro), an antibiotic, metronidazole (Flagyl), an antiprotozoal and antibiotic, tolmetin (Tolectin), a nonsteroidal anti-inflammatory drug, and mefenamic acid (Ponstel), a nonsteroidal anti-inflammatory drug, have each been reported to interfere with the EMIT screening assay [5,6,7,8]. Use of fluorescein radiologic dye has been reported to interfere with the FPIA screening assay [9]. If the donor has finished taking a medication suspected of interfering with the test, and if a negative test result is required (for example, in a preemployment setting), the MRO should suggest that a new specimen be collected after several days have elapsed, to allow elimination of the medication.

If the donor gives an explanation that is acceptable to the MRO, the MRO checks the "Test not performed" and "Test canceled" boxes in Step 8 of the CCF and enters "Specimen unsuitable: cannot obtain valid drug test result" on the "Remarks" line. The MRO reports to the employer that the test is canceled, the reason for cancellation, and that no further action is required unless a negative test result is required (e.g., preemployment, return-to-duty, or follow-up testing).

If the donor is unable to provide an explanation and/or a valid prescription for one of the above medications but denies having adulterated the specimen, the MRO checks the "Test not performed" and "Test canceled" boxes in Step 8 of the CCF and enters "Specimen unsuitable: cannot obtain valid drug test result" on the "Remarks" line. The MRO reports to the employer that the test is canceled, the reason for cancellation, and that a second collection must take place immediately under direct observation.

"Test Not Performed—Specimen Substituted/Adulterated"

If the laboratory has identified the specimen as substituted or adulterated, the laboratory will not report the drug assay results, whether negative or positive. (Screening and confirmatory testing may take place even if the specimen is substituted or adulterated.) There is no requirement for the MRO to contact a donor about an adulterated or substituted specimen; however, the MRO may choose to do this to inform the donor of the outcome and ask if he or she substituted or adulterated the specimen. The MRO reports to the employer that the specimen was adulterated or substituted, either of which constitutes a refusal to test. The MRO checks the "Test not performed" box in Step 8 of the CCF and writes "Substituted" or "Adulterated," and writes "Refusal to test" on the "Remarks" line. The MRO also informs the employer that the donor's right to have the split specimen tested is withdrawn. Therefore, neither a test of the split specimen, nor a retest of the primary specimen, is offered to the donor.

Employers generally treat adulterated tests like positive tests. In DOT-regulated testing, an employee who submits an adulterated post-accident, random, reasonable suspicion, or follow-up drug testing sample must be referred to a substance abuse professional (SAP). For some employers, submission of an adulterated specimen is a more serious offense than a verified positive result, and the employer may be less likely to allow the person back into the workplace. (By contrast, in testing mandated by the Federal Aviation Administration [FAA], submission of an adulterated specimen can result in a less severe penalty than a second positive test, because a second positive test means a lifetime ban from that employee's safety-sensitive position.)

Contacting the Donor ■

Before declaring a result "verified positive," the MRO must give the donor an opportunity to speak directly with him or her and present alternative medical explanations. The MRO's staff can contact the donor and obtain information that allows the MRO to declare the result "negative," but the MRO cannot declare a result "positive" without first attempting to establish direct contact with the donor. If the MRO's assistant initiates the contact, the MRO should step in as soon as the donor has been reached and identified. The initial moments of contact can often provide enough information for decision making if the MRO is involved.

Most MROs call donors by telephone to discuss their positive results. The MRO-donor contact can be face-to-face, but telephone discussions are expedient, especially when the MRO and donor are located far apart. The donor's home and work telephone numbers should be written on copies 4 and 5 of the federal CCF. The MRO can usually also get the donor's phone number from the collection site (from their copy of the release and consent form or registration form) or from the employer representative. Reaching the donor at the work number is often more convenient but may prompt a confrontation between the donor and management that might be avoided by contacting the donor at home, thereby allowing him or her time to get composed. Calls at work are also prone to discovery by co-workers. Reaching the donor at home often entails after-hours calls, but these have the advantage of a higher rate of success in reaching the donor on the first attempt. Some large providers of MRO services increase their accessibility by having MROs on-call 24 hours a day, seven days a week, and by offering toll-free numbers.

If someone other than the donor answers the phone, the MRO (or MRO's assistant) should leave a brief message requesting that the donor return the call. If asked about the reason for the call, the MRO might explain that he or she is a physician who works for the donor's employer and that the call pertains to a recent examination. The MRO should be discrete and should not indicate that the call pertains to a drug test.

VERIFICATION CHECKLIST

Many MROs use a checklist, like that presented in Figure 5-4, for documenting the review process of each positive test result. Each attempt to contact the donor is logged in. Comments may include answering machines, messages, and disconnected or wrong telephone numbers. Thorough documentation of calls helps establish that the donor was given an opportunity to discuss the results. It also encourages consistency and provides a permanent record of the decision-making process for each positive result. The completed form is stored with the laboratory test result and CCF.

TIME FRAMES FOR CONTACT AND NONCONTACT POSITIVES

A first attempt to contact the donor should be made within hours of receiving the positive drug test report. If the MRO cannot reach the donor within a reasonable period, the MRO asks a designated employer's representative to help expedite contact. The MRO does not say that the donor tested positive. The employer's representative may suspect this is the case but should keep this suspicion confidential. Some employers remove a worker from duty pending an outcome report from the MRO; this action is neither authorized nor prohibited under the federal rules. If the donor is self-employed and hard to reach by phone, the MRO might send a fax, certified letter, or other traceable document to the donor, requesting a response.

The length of time that constitutes a reasonable period for contacting a donor varies, depending on the donor's job and job duties. For example, there is more urgency in contacting a cocaine-positive airline pilot than a codeine-positive receptionist. The employer's representative should be contacted promptly when results of preplacement testing are available, because applicants are sometimes hired even while their drug test results are pending, perhaps under an assumption that no news is good news. In general, there is little to be gained by not communicating with the employer's representative promptly.

Figure 5-4. Example of MRO Punchlist ■

Donor's Name _____ ID No. _____

❑ Negative
❑ Test not performed: ❑ Specimen substituted . . ❑ Specimen adulterated. . . . . . . "refusal to test"
                       ❑ Fatal flaw . . . . ❑ Uncorrected flaw . . . ."canceled"
              ❑ Specimen unsuitable (contact the donor) . . . . if it remains unsuitable: "canceled"

■ POSITIVE: Provide the donor with an opportunity to discuss positive test result(s). Note each
            attempt.

DATE	TIME	PHONE#	CONTACT	COMMENTS	INITIALS
____	____	( ) - _____	Y/N	_____	_____
____	____	( ) - _____	Y/N	_____	_____
____	____	( ) - _____	Y/N	_____	_____
____	____	( ) - _____	Y/N	_____	_____
____	____	( ) - _____	Y/N	_____	_____
____	____	( ) - _____	Y/N	_____	_____

(continue on the back of this page)

If unable to promptly contact the donor, ask for help from the employer's representative:

_____, _____
date   initials

If the donor has not contacted the MRO within five days of contact from the employer, report as
   positive.
If neither the MRO nor employer can contact the donor within 14 days of the lab report, report as
   positive.

INTERVIEW

✓ Identify yourself as a physician and medical review officer.
✓ Confirm the individual's identity, e.g., read five digits of their SSN and ask for the other four digits.
✓ Explain that fitness-for-duty information may be shared with the employer.
✓ Tell the donor the test results.
✓ Seek potential sources of the drug(s), e.g., legitimate medications, invasive procedures, poppy
   seeds.
✓ Ask the donor to help confirm that the prescription(s) is legitimate.
✓ If there is no alternative medical explanation, tell the donor that he/she has 72 hours to request a
   second analysis. (The bottom of this Punchlist addresses this further.)
✓ If the result is amphetamines positive and the donor reports using Vicks Inhaler during the three
   to four days before the collection, or the result is methamphetamine positive/amphetamine
   negative, order *d-* vs. *l-*isomers.
✓ Order if needed: ❑ Concentrations ❑ Reanalysis of the same specimen ❑ Additional adulterant tests
   Attach to this Punchlist a copy of the written request sent to the lab.
✓ If positive only for opiates, and not positive for 6-AM, attempt to establish clinical evidence of
   unauthorized opiate use.
✓ Consult with the laboratory's certifying scientist and/or other experts, as needed.

OUTCOME

❑ **Negative**   Reason: _____

❑ **Verified Positive**   _____

                   MRO's Signature: _____

If the donor requests a reanalysis of the same specimen or analysis of Bottle B (the split specimen),
complete the following:
Type of analysis: ❑ Reanalysis of the same specimen   ❑ Analysis of Bottle B
Date of the donor's request: _____/_____/_____
✓ Attach to this Punchlist only a copy of written requests sent to the lab.

If reasonable efforts to contact the donor fail, the MRO can report the result as verified positive without interviewing the donor, even if the result is opiate positive. In regulated programs, a noncontact verified positive is authorized in only three situations:

1. The donor has not contacted the MRO within five days after the employer has asked him or her to do so. These five days should be days that the MRO is accessible, for example, weekdays if the MRO is unavailable on weekends.
2. The donor expressly refuses to discuss the test.
3. Despite reasonable attempts, neither the employer nor the MRO can contact the donor within 14 days of the date on which the MRO received the positive result. (This most often occurs when the donor has not started working and is thus not readily available to the employer.)

When the MRO reports a positive result without having spoken with the donor, the employer should be informed of the circumstances of the noncontact. FHWA requires that MROs provide employers with documentation of efforts made to contact the driver in such cases [49 CFR §391.97(c)]. If the donor later demonstrates a serious illness or injury or other extenuating circumstances that prevented contact, the MRO must reopen the file and re-review the results.

The Interview ■

"Mr. Johnson, this is Dr. Welby at Industrial Medical in Beantown. I'm calling about a recent exam you had at our clinic. I have your chart in front of me, I believe this is yours. Let's see . . . your social security number is 1–3–3–5–5 . . . would you please help me with the last four numbers? . . . 8-7-6-6? Yes, that's the number. I'm calling because your drug test came back positive for marijuana. The company doesn't know this yet. I wanted to tell you first. If there are any medicines you took that could have caused this, we need to know so that we can clear this up."

The MRO needs the donor's cooperation in identifying alternative medical explanations and should approach the donor as his/her ally rather than accuser. The MRO is responsible for protecting the donor from false characterization as a drug abuser. Cooperation usually comes naturally because of public respect and trust for physicians. A professional, nonconfrontational approach helps sustain dialogue with the donor and reinforces the credibility of the process. The MRO should tell the donor at each step what will happen next, for example, "I will wait for you to call me back," or "I will notify your employer of the positive result tomorrow morning."

IDENTIFYING THE DONOR

The MRO does not initially know if the "John Doe" who answers the phone is John Doe Jr., John Doe Sr., or someone else. An attempt should be made to establish that the person contacted is, in fact, the donor. For example, the MRO can read the first part of the donor's ID (employee ID or social security number) and ask for the latter part. Alternatively, the MRO can ask for the donor's birth date or the name of his or her employer. The interchange in which identity is confirmed also serves to alert the donor that the MRO knows something about him or her and thus helps establish the MRO's legitimacy.

CONVEYING THE DONOR'S "MIRANDA RIGHTS"

The MRO should explain, at the start of each interview and before obtaining any medical information, that if medical information provided by the donor during the review process reveals a condition that may affect workplace safety or indicates that the donor is medically unqualified for his or her position (for example, as a driver or pilot), the employer will be notified. This process is analogous to reading the Miranda rights: "Anything you say can and will be used against you . . . "

REVIEWING THE COLLECTION PROCEDURE

The MRO may ask the donor about the collection process as another way of monitoring and verifying the test's integrity. If the donor describes a proper collection procedure—the specimen did not leave his or her sight until it was sealed with tape, initialed by the donor, and placed in a box or plastic bag— documentation of this conversation can be helpful if the test is later challenged. If the donor has signed the certification statement (see Figure 5-5) and there are no fatal flaws on the CCF, the test should generally be considered valid rather than canceled. However, if an issue is raised, the MRO should contact the collector to find out how the collection was performed. The MRO may also wish to contact the employer and offer an assessment of the test's integrity if the issue raises a significant possibility of a switched or contaminated sample.

ELICITING POTENTIAL MEDICAL EXPLANATIONS

The MRO seeks alternative medical explanations for each positive result. Alternative explanations are controlled medications that were prescribed or dispensed for the donor, and nonprescription medications that can account for positive results (see Table 5-1). If the result is positive for opiates, the MRO does not need to ask about poppy seed use, but instead must assume that poppy seeds are a possible explanation and can verify the result as positive only if there is corroborating clinical evidence of opiate abuse.

Figure 5-5. Donor Certification Statement ■

I certify that I provided my urine specimen to the collector; that I have not adulterated it in any manner; that each specimen bottle used was sealed with a tamper-evident seal in my presence; and that the information provided on this form and the label affixed to each specimen bottle is correct.

Table 5-1. Medications Sold in the United States That Can Cause Positive Drug Test Results ■

Medication	Nonprescription Medications	Prescription Medications
Amphetamines	l-methamphetamine Vicks Inhaler	l-amphetamine and l-methamphetamine Atapryl tablets Carbex tablets Eldepryl tablets Selegiline tablets d-amphetamine Adderall tablets (formerly known as Obetrol) Biphetamine capsules Dexedrine tablets and capsules Dextrostat tablets d-amphetamine and d-methamphetamine Desoxyn Gradumet tablets Didrex tablets
Barbiturates	none	amobarbital Tuinal pulvules butalbital Anolor 300 capsules Axocet capsules Bupap tablets Esgic and Esgic-Plus tablets and capsules Fioricet tablets and capsules Fiorinal tablets and capsules Medigesic capsules Pacaps capsules Phrenilin tablets and capsules Repan and Repan-CF tablets and capsules Sedapap tablets Tenake capsules pentobarbital Nembutal capsules, solution, and suppositories phenobarbital Arco-Lase Plus tablets Bellatal tablets Donnatal tablets, capsules, and elixir Quadrinal tablets secobarbital Seconal sodium capsules

Table 5-1. Medications Sold in the United States That Can Cause Positive Drug Test Results (continued) ■

Medication	Nonprescription Medications	Prescription Medications

Benzodiazepines	none	desmethyldiazepam
		    Centrax
		    Paxipam
		    Tranxene
		    Valium
		    Verstran
		
		diazepam
		    Diastat gel
		    Valium
		
		oxazepam
		    Centrax
		    Diastat gel
		    Paxipam
		    Restoril
		    Serax
		    Tranxene
		    Valium
		    Verstran

Cocaine	none	cocaine hydrochloride, Solution or viscous, used as a vasoconstrictive anesthetic, e.g., in otolaryngology, ophthalmology, and dentistry TAC (tetracaine, adrenaline, and cocaine mixture used in some emergency rooms as a topical anesthetic, e.g., before suturing) Brompton's Cocktail (contains an opiate—usually morphine or heroin—and cocaine and/or a phenothiazine. Used for pain control of the terminally ill.)

Marijuana	none	dronabinol
		    Marinol Capsules
		
		marijuana
		    (In the late 1990s, voters in several states approved referenda to allow use of marijuana for certain medical conditions under a physician's direction.)

Medication	Nonprescription Medications	Prescription Medications
Methaqualone	none	none

Opiates: codeine, Morphine	codeine
	  Ryna-C and Ryna-CX
	    liquid
		codeine
		  Acetaminophen and codeine
		  Brontex
		  Butalbital, aspirin, caffeine, and codeine
		    capsules
		  Capital and codeine suspension
		  Codimal PH syrup
		  Deconsal C expectorant and syrup
		  Dimetane-DC and Dimetane-DX cough
		    syrup
		  Fioricet with codeine capsules
		  Fiorinal with codeine capsules
		  Fiortal with codeine
		  Nucofed expectorant, syrup, and capsules
		  Pediacof cough syrup
		  Phenaphen with codeine capsules
		  Phenergan VC with codeine
		  Poly-Histine CS syrup
		  Promethazine hydrochloride and codeine
		    phosphate syrup
		  Robitussin A-C and Robitussin-DAC syrup
		  Soma compound with codeine
		  Triaminic expectorant with codeine
		  Tussar-2 and Tussar SF syrup
		  Tussi-Organidin NR and SNR liquid
		  Tylenol with codeine (#1,2,3,or 4)

	morphine
	  Amogel PG
	  Diabismul
	  Infantol Pink
	  Parepectolin suspension
		morphine
		  Astramorph/PF injection
		  Brompton's Cocktail (contains an opiate—
		    usually morphine or heroin—and
		    cocaine and/or phenothiazine. Used for
		    pain control of the terminally ill.)
		  Duramorph injection
		  Infumorph solution
		  Kadian capsules
		  MS Contin tablets
		  MSIR capsules, solution, and tablets
		  MS/L and MS/S
		  OMS concentrate
		  Oramorph SR tablets
		  Paregoric
		  RMS suppositories
		  Roxanol and Roxanol 100 solution

The MRO should tell the donor what drug(s) was detected and may ask the donor about illicit use of that drug. If the donor admits to illicit use of the drug, the MRO should verify the result as positive. Otherwise, the MRO should ask the donor about potential alternative sources for the positive result(s). The donor may not recall or recognize having used the drug. If the donor is positive for a drug that is found in prescription or over-the-counter medications, the MRO should ask the donor to identify medications taken before the collection. The MRO should consider the half-life of each drug and its metabolites, which is usually not more than a few days but can be much longer for some barbiturates and benzodiazepines.

Federal rules state that clinical evidence of unauthorized opiate abuse, such as an admission to the MRO of illicit use, supersedes an alternative medical explanation. It is reasonable to extend this approach to nonopiate drugs: If the donor has a prescription and admits to illicit use of the same drug, the MRO should verify the result as positive. If the donor admits to use of a drug that was not detected in the test, the MRO may alert the employer to a safety-sensitive issue. The MRO cannot, however, report a verified positive result for a drug that was not detected in the test.

Confirming the Explanation ■

Federal regulations require that the MRO review medical records provided by the donor to substantiate prescription medication(s) that could have caused the result. Beyond this, the verification process is left to the MRO's judgment.

The donor may have listed, before the analysis, medications that he or she recently took. These lists can be incomplete or inaccurate. The donor is not penalized for failing to record medications, nor should self-reports of medication use be accepted without independent corroboration. Corroboration is best obtained directly from the pharmacist or the prescribing medical provider. Less rigorous evidence (e.g., a prescription label or the donor's oral assurance) runs a risk of deception. Medical providers, understandably, may be reluctant to discuss their patients' medications with someone they do not know, particularly in the context of drug testing. In anticipation of this, the donor should be asked to authorize release of the information to the MRO. The donor can be asked to directly contact the medical provider and authorize the release; the donor should be instructed to notify the MRO once this contact is accomplished. The donor should receive reasonable deadlines for providing the information.

The corroborating information from the medical provider can be provided in person, in writing, or by telephone. A letter, especially if not on office letterhead, might prompt the MRO to make a follow-up telephone call to help confirm its authenticity. Calling the medical provider directly works well for MROs who are not always available to receive phone calls. Alternatively, the donor can be asked to have his or her medical provider call the MRO. If the MRO wants to corroborate that a physician is on the phone, he/she might ask for the physician's Drug Enforcement Administration (DEA) number; the second digit of the number should be the first letter of the physician's last name. Misrepresentation is possible, but an experienced MRO's instinct and good judgment can help reduce this possibility. If the health care provider does not recognize the donor's last name, this raises the possibility that the donor may have obtained the medicine using a different last name, for example, a maiden name.

If the MRO determines that prescribed medication was improperly used (e.g., too much was taken) or is tantamount to a safety risk when taken as prescribed, the test should be reported as negative and, if appropriate, the safety concerns reported to the employer.

Making a Determination ■

The MRO assigns each test to one of three outcomes: negative, positive, or test not performed (see Table 5-2). With the exception of opiates, a confirmed positive result becomes an MRO negative result only if the donor has an alternative medical explanation, i.e., the donor used or was administered a medication by a licensed health care professional that could account for the test result. The employer's policy may help define types of drug use that are unacceptable, for example, use of borrowed medications. Beyond this, the MRO's determination is based on professional judgment. The MRO makes a medical determination, not a legal judgment or employment decision. The MRO should not be influenced by the reason for the test or by the actions the employer may take on the basis of the test's outcome. Perceptions of the donor's honesty also should not critically influence the MRO's decisions. The forensic nature of workplace drug testing demands facts, not perceptions. A consistent approach helps assure fair and unbiased treatment of each donor.

After the MRO has reached a determination, a donor with a verified positive result may contact the MRO for additional discussion. The MRO should accept these calls within reason. A donor who feels he or she received inadequate attention may seek satisfaction by means of a lawsuit. When a donor is certain that the specimen is not his or hers, the MRO may want to ask the laboratory to pull the specimen from the freezer and describe, over the phone, the bottle's appearance—for example, the donor's two initials are printed on the seal, the label has the accessioning number, etc. The MRO can then offer this information to the donor, and read to the donor the statement that he or she signed on the CCF (see Figure 5-5).

Changing a Determination ■

Federal rules do not authorize the MRO to reopen a case if the donor reports flaws in the collection process or otherwise challenges the test's validity. In regulated testing, the MRO may reconsider and change his or her determination only if the donor provides a satisfactory, documented explanation that serious illness, injury, or something else unavoidably prevented contact with the MRO in a timely manner. In this situation, if the donor presents an alternative medical explanation, the MRO should consider the explanation, seek corroborating information as needed, and issue a revised report if an alternative medical explanation is corroborated.

Table 5-2. MRO Determinations

Laboratory Report	MRO	MRO's Report	Interpretation
Negative	→ →	→ Negative	1. Laboratory negative; 2. Confirmed positive and the donor has an alternative medical explanation; *or,* 3. Morphine or codeine positive, not 6-AM positive, and no clinical evidence of opiate abuse.
Positive	→ →	→ Positive	1. The donor refuses contact from the MRO; 2. The donor remains unreachable within the allotted time; 3. Confirmed positive for a drug/metabolite other than morphine or codeine, and the donor has no alternative medical explanation; 4. Confirmed positive for morphine or codeine, and clinical evidence of unauthorized opiate use; 5. 6-AM positive; *or,* 6. The donor admits illicit use.
Test not performed 1. Specimen substituted: not consistent with normal human urine	→ →	→ Test not performed; adulterated *or* substituted; refusal to test	1. An adulterant was identified in the specimen; *or,* 2. The specimen was substituted.
2. Specimen adulterated: nitrite is too high pH is too high (or too low) presence of _____ detected		→ Test not performed; Test canceled	1. The specimen was unsuitable for testing and no specific adulterant was identified; *or,* 2. The laboratory completed the test but the MRO determined that the specimen's integrity did not meet forensic criteria; *or,* 3. The split specimen failed to reconfirm the presence of the drug/metabolite.
3. Specimen unsuitable: cannot obtain valid confirmatory test result 4. Fatal flaw, _____ 5. Uncorrected flaw, _____			
Dilute	→ →	→ Dilute	The donor may undergo a directly observed collection at his/her next test.

References ■

1. Ambre J. The urinary excretion of cocaine and metabolites in humans: a kinetic analysis of published data. *J Anal Toxicol* 1985;9:241–5.
2. Cone EJ, Mitchell JM. Do consecutive urine catches differ in marijuana metabolite concentration? *J Anal Toxicol* 1993;17:186–7.
3. Huestis MA, Cone EJ. Predicting new marijuana use from creatinine normalized 11-nor-9-carboxy-delta-9-tetrahydrocannabinol (THCCOOH) concentrations: criteria development and validation. 1996 SOFT Meeting Abstracts. *J Anal Toxicol* 1997;21:82.
4. Knisely R. *Operating Guidance for DOT Mandated Drug Testing Programs*. Washington, DC.: U.S. Department of Transportation: May 29, 1991.
5. Lora-Tamayo C, Tena T, Rodriguez A. High concentration of ciprofloxacin in urine invalidates EMIT results. *J Anal Toxicol* 1996;20:334.
6. Lora-Tamayo C, Tena T. High concentration of metronidazole in urine invalidates EMIT results. *J Anal Toxicol* 1991;15:159.
7. Rollins DE, Jennison TA, Jones G. Investigation of the interference by nonsteroidal anti-inflammatory drugs in urine tests for abuse drugs. *Clin Chem* 1990;36:602–6.
8. Crane T, Badminton MN, Dawson CM, et al. Mefenamic acid prevents assessment of drug abuse with EMIT assays. *Clin Chem* 1993;39:549.
9. Inloes R, Clark D, Drobnies A. Interference of fluorescein, used in retinal angiography, with certain clinical laboratory tests. *Clin Chem* 1987;33:2126.

Special Issues for Medical Review Officers ■

Multiple Positive Results ■

If a specimen is confirmed positive for more than one drug, the medical review officer (MRO) should check for alternative medical explanations for each drug and inform the employer of each drug/metabolite that is verified positive. In testing mandated by the Department of Transportation (DOT), employers record data on multiple positive results in *Management Information System (MIS) reports*, required under the DOT rules.

DOT has advised MROs that, for a preemployment test and with the employer's concurrence, the MRO may report a verified positive result for one drug without continuing to seek verification for other confirmed positive results from the same specimen. In this situation, the MRO should use his or her judgment to determine if verification of the other drugs may be accomplished expeditiously. If the MRO verifies and reports only one of a multiple-positive result, the report to the employer should not mention the drug(s) that have not been verified. The MRO should document these nonverified positive results in his or her records as nonverified and nonreported results.

Medical Information Unrelated to the Drug Test ■

If the MRO learns of a medical condition or medication use that may pose a safety risk, the MRO is authorized under federal rules to alert the employer, appropriate federal safety agency, or physician who determines the donor's fitness for duty. At the start of the interview with the donor, the MRO is supposed to tell the donor that such information may be disclosed (see "Conveying the Donor's Miranda Rights" in Chapter 5). Disclosure is more of an obligation than an option, in part because of the potential repercussions of failure to disclose. However, for confidentiality and for liability reasons, the MRO should attempt to limit the amount of specific information disclosed to the employer and should disclose the information only to parties with an acceptable need to know. It is unnecessary to provide diagnoses or other specific medical information to nonmedical personnel. For example, the MRO could tell the employer that a safety condition was uncovered that requires a medical fitness-for-duty evaluation. The MRO could give more specific information to the physician who performs this evaluation.

While the MRO can disclose information incidental to the drug test result, the donor comes to the MRO only because of the drug test, not for a medical assessment. The MRO should therefore attempt to restrict the focus of each review to the specific drug(s) for which the donor tested positive.

Conditions that might prompt disclosure include the use of sedatives or stimulants and the presence of medical conditions that might lead to sudden incapacitation. Familiarity with federal-agency physical qualification standards, such as those of the Federal Highway Administration (FHWA) [49 CFR §391.41(b)] and FAA [14 CFR §67 Subpart A], will help the MRO recognize potentially unsafe conditions. The *FHWA Medical Standards for Commercial Drivers* states that an individual is not qualified to drive a commercial vehicle if he or she uses a "Schedule I drug or other substance identified in Appendix D to this subchapter, an amphetamine, a narcotic, or any other habit-forming drug" [49 CFR §391.41(b)(12)]. However, FHWA's *Regulatory Criteria for Evaluation* allows an exception if the drug has been prescribed by a licensed medical practitioner who is familiar with the driver's medical history and assigned duties, and who has advised the driver that the medication will not harm his or her ability to safely operate a commercial motor vehicle (CMV) [1]. Antidepressants, antihistamines, anxiolytics, skeletal muscle relaxants, and some blood pressure medications may cause drowsiness and make driving unsafe [2]. FHWA's 1987 Conference on Cardiac Disorders and Commercial Drivers recommended disqualification for use of coumadin and other anticoagulants, but FHWA has not adopted this recommendation, and medical examiners thus can determine the qualification of drivers who take coumadin on a case-by-case basis. Use of medications to control seizures and use of methadone are both disqualifiers, without exception, according to FHWA guidelines.

An employer can require workers to report the use of medications that may pose a safety risk but cannot require reporting of all medications without regard to safety risk [2]. Some companies provide their workers with lists of drugs that may pose safety risks, requesting that workers report use of such drugs.

Drug Tests and DOT Physicals ■

A *medical examiner* conducts a physical examination to determine if a driver is physically qualified to operate a CMV [49 CFR §391.43]. Any health care provider whose license permits him or her to perform medical examinations can be a medical examiner and perform DOT's commercial driver's license (CDL) examinations. In most states, this includes physicians, physician assistants, and nurse practitioners. The medical examiner keeps the physical examination form ("long form") and gives the Medical Examiner's Certificate ("the card") to the driver. The card appears on the bottom of the long form and can be detached and given to the driver, but most clinics instead use stand-alone cards that capture the same information.

The motor carrier is required to maintain a copy of the card and can do so by either maintaining a copy of the stand-alone card or, if the examiner has completed the bottom of the long form, a copy of the long form. Medical confidentiality is best served when the employer maintains just the card; the long form has personal medical information. Nevertheless, many motor carriers and even some local FHWA inspectors are under the impression that motor carriers must have the long forms. It is common for clinics to send long forms to motor carriers, and some carriers will not pay medical examiners until they receive the long forms.

A facsimile is as acceptable as an original signed form. The medical examiner usually makes the DOT's CDL certificate valid for a two-year period but may choose a shorter period if the examiner is concerned about compliance with medical treatment or deterioration of a chronic condition. If a driver with a nonexpired certificate changes jobs, he or she is subject to a preemployment drug test but is not required to undergo another DOT physical.

Drug tests and DOT physicals are considered separate events, even though both may occur at the same visit. DOT drug testing is intended for drug deterrence and not for assessing medical fitness for duty. The forms used for DOT physicals no longer reference FHWA's "Subpart H" drug testing rules [3]. References to drug testing appear on older versions of the long form and card, and, by selecting the comment "Controlled substance test not performed," a medical examiner could indicate that the drug test results were not considered in assessing a driver's medical qualification. While a medical examiner may feel that a drug or alcohol test is required to assess fitness for duty in selected instances, such testing is generally distinct from DOT drug testing and need not be limited to five drugs/drug classes and the DOT Procedures. The medical examiner should not keep the exam's outcome in pending status while waiting for a negative DOT drug test result. This kind of practice is prone to error. And, unless the same physician serves as medical examiner and MRO, it is often hard for the medical examiner to get the drug test result from the MRO. The employer is responsible for ensuring the potential driver is not allowed to operate its CMVs until the employer has received a negative drug test result from the MRO. Neither the medical examiner nor employer are obliged to retrieve, cancel, or otherwise nullify a DOT Medical Examiner's Certificate on the basis of a positive drug test result. If a driver has a positive drug test, the employer, not the MRO or medical examiner, is responsible for removing that driver from service for that employer.

Drug Tests and Impairment ■

The MRO does not determine, based on the drug test alone, if the person is impaired or if he/she is medically fit for duty. While the presence of a drug in the urine indicates past drug exposure and may suggest past pharmacologic effect, it does not prove current or past impairment [4]. (By contrast, alcohol impairment has a legal definition that is based on the blood alcohol concentration.) In some situations, the MRO may also be the physician who determines if an examinee is medically fit for duty. This is a separate and distinct task from drug testing. A drug test can be part of a medical fitness evaluation, but the physician is advised to treat routine workplace drug testing and medical fitness-for-duty examinations as separate items.

Passive Inhalation ■

Passive (bystander) inhalation of marijuana, cocaine, and perhaps other drugs can, in extraordinary circumstances, cause positive results, using the federal cutoffs. However, the intense exposure required to generate such concentrations makes it extremely unlikely that someone could test positive merely because others nearby smoked marijuana. In addition, passive inhalation of marijuana or cocaine cannot be construed as medically prescribed usage for therapy or a medical procedure. Therefore, the MRO cannot downgrade a positive result on that basis.

MARIJUANA

In the early 1980s, more than a dozen experimental studies on passive inhalation were published [5,6,7]. Researchers have generated occasional marijuana-positive immunoassay results, using the federal cutoff levels, but only when the exposures were extensive and unrealistic. Passive inhalation concerns resurfaced in the 1990s because larger cigarettes ("blunts") and more potent strains of marijuana came into use. On the other hand, immunoassays used in the 1990s have been less sensitive for cannabinoids and more specific for tetrahydrocannibinol (THC). The larger, more potent marijuana cigarettes and the less sensitive immunoassays have opposing effects on the likelihood of positive results by passive inhalation. Passive inhalation of marijuana remains a highly implausible explanation for a positive result.

COCAINE

Passive inhalation of cocaine vapor would not be expected to produce urine concentrations of benzoylecognine at or above the federal cutoff values. Under extensive exposure conditions, researchers have been able to generate peak urine benzoylecognine concentrations of 22–123 ng/mL for up to 7 hours after exposure [8]. Passive inhalation of cocaine is not an alternative medical explanation for a benzoylecognine-positive urine test.

METHAMPHETAMINE

No scientific studies have yet examined whether passive exposure to methamphetamine fumes can cause a positive urine test result for amphetamines. Passive exposure to methamphetamine cannot be construed as medically prescribed usage and thus is not an alternative medical explanation for a positive regulated test result.

Illicit Drugs in Food and Beverages ■

Ingestion of food or beverages laced with drugs can cause positive urine results. The donor may claim that the ingestion was unintentional, but intent is not the issue. Unintentional ingestion is not a prescribed use, nor is it a medical procedure. Therefore, the MRO cannot downgrade a laboratory-positive result on that basis.

Marijuana ingested orally (in brownies, for example) can produce psycho-active effects and THC-positive urine drug test results [9]. Food containing marijuana has a fibrous texture and often tastes bad. Food products containing hemp seeds or extracts became popular in the late 1990s, perhaps as much for their novelty as for their nutritional value or taste. Ingestion of hemp seed oil has been reported to result in THC-positive drug tests for several hours, using the federal cutoffs [10,11,12]. A variety of other hemp-containing food products contain traces of THC. DOT has advised MROs that hemp-containing food products are not an alternative medical explanation for THC-positive test results [13].

In the early 1980s, some health food stores sold an imported product called *Health Inca Tea (HIT)*. Its ingredients included "decocainized coca leaves." In 1986, it was reported that this tea contained detectable amounts of cocaine and could cause benzoylecognine-positive urine test results [14]. U.S. Customs inspectors have since become acutely aware of this issue and are thus better able to identify and confiscate this product. The tea is still sold in Bolivia, Columbia, and Peru and occasionally slips through Customs inspections and is brought into the United States. Consumption of Health Inca Tea can cause benzoylecognine-positive urine test results as high as 2,600–5,000 ng/mL [15,16]. The psychoactive effects of such ingestion are immediate and would not go unrecognized by the ingester.

Some recreational marijuana users and cancer and AIDS sufferers make tea from marijuana leaves, sometimes brewed with regular tea. Marijuana tea is more common among societies that accept marijuana—for example, the West Indies. Between 8 and 22 percent of the THC is released by boiling the marijuana leaves, and consumption of the tea can cause a THC-positive drug test [17,18].

DOT and DHHS have directed MROs *not* to reverse cocaine-positive results based on use of coca leaf tea. The same approach holds true for marijuana tea use. Neither is an alternative medical explanation for the presence of these drugs. The MRO is under no obligation to test the donor's food or beverage product for the suspected drug(s).

In the nonregulated setting, it is the employer's responsibility to decide how to handle issues of positive drug tests caused by inadvertent ingestion of hemp oil, coca leaf tea, and other food and beverages. The MRO who serve multiple clients may find it useful to alert them, by fax or letter, of the issues, current federal guidelines, and the MRO's approach to handling positive test results caused by inadvertent ingestion. Employers may want to warn their employees against using hemp oil and coca tea; thus, they may be on firmer ground if an employee challenges a verified positive result based on ingestion of these products.

Borrowed Medication ■

It is not uncommon for people to take drugs that are prescribed for family members, friends, and other acquaintances. This kind of use, sometimes referred to as *spousal use*, may appear medically indicated in some cases. The question is, should the MRO downgrade a laboratory-positive result based on use of a borrowed medication?

Federal rules require that prescriptions for controlled substances be labeled "Caution: Federal law prohibits the transfer of this drug to any person other than the patient for whom it was prescribed" [19]. Consistent with these rules, in 1990, DOT advised MROs: "An employee who acknowledges taking another individual's controlled substance prescribed medication has admitted unauthorized use of a controlled substance and the positive result should be verified positive" [20]. Many MROs are uncomfortable with this position and will consider borrowed medication as an alternative medical explanation, especially in nonregulated testing. Drug testing is not intended to deter use of borrowed medications. Furthermore, drug testing should be fair. MROs are often reluctant to label as "positive" test results due to use of borrowed medications because they do not feel the punishment (loss of employment) fits the crime.

Some employers' policies explicitly prohibit use of borrowed medications, and if this is the case, the MRO should verify as positive the result caused by use of borrowed medication. (Some employers reconsider such policies after contending with positive tests from valued employees who used their family member's medicine.) In the exceptional case in which it can be documented that a donor's physician advised the donor to use a borrowed medication and that medical use corresponds with the positive result, the MRO should declare the result "negative."

Some MROs opt to report each case of borrowed medication use as "positive" and, with the donor's permission, report the donor's explanation. The MRO may attempt to corroborate, with cooperation from the prescription's owner, that the prescription was valid. If the test is DOT-regulated, the employer can return the worker to safety-sensitive duties based on an SAP assessment, which, in the case of medically indicated use of someone else's medication, will generally be favorable.

Misuse of One's Own Prescription Medication ■

The MRO/donor interview or laboratory-reported drug concentration (if obtained) may suggest that the donor took too much of his or her own prescription medication or self-medicated for a new condition with an old prescription. Prescribed medications generally have no expiration dates, except for shelf life, nor are they limited to use for a specific diagnosis or condition. The most prudent course of action is for the MRO to corroborate the prescription's validity, report the test as "negative," and notify the employer if the donor needs further evaluation because of a safety-related concern.

Self-prescribing is common among physicians. Such use constitutes an alternative medical explanation, although, depending on the type of drug and nature of use, it may raise issues of fitness for duty.

Foreign Medications ■

Certain drugs—codeine, in particular—are available only by prescription in the United States but are dispensed over the counter in Mexico, Canada, and other countries. The acceptability of foreign medications as an explanation for a positive test result may depend on the individual employer's policy and any information the employer may have provided to employees concerning use of foreign medications. The FHWA has issued guidance for acceptability of Mexican and Canadian medications applicable to drug testing conducted under the North American Free Trade Agreement, and this guidance is expressed in the following paragraphs [21]:

USE ABROAD OF AN OVER-THE-COUNTER OR PRESCRIPTION MEDICINE

If a donor declares that he or she obtained and ingested an over-the-counter or prescription medicine abroad and can document presence in the foreign country within a few days prior to the specimen collection, the MRO may consider the over-the-counter medication an alternative medical explanation for the positive result. If the medication was issued by prescription, the donor should attempt to corroborate that a medical practitioner from the foreign country wrote the prescription.

USE IN THE UNITED STATES OF A MEDICINE OBTAINED ABROAD

Under U.S. federal law, U.S. domiciled residents may use controlled substances in the United States only if they have prescriptions from DEA-registered physicians. If a donor obtains a medication abroad, brings it into the United States, has had an opportunity to obtain a prescription for it in the U.S., and uses it without obtaining a prescription for it in the U.S., the MRO may consider the use "unauthorized."

DNA and Serologic Tests ■

Genetic marker analyses can help prove or disprove that a biologic specimen belongs to a specific individual. These tests target proteins, blood group antigens, and deoxyribonucleic acid (DNA). Genetic marker tests can refute, but not always prove, that a specific individual donated a specimen.

Genetic marker analyses work best with fresh urine. DNA markers are obtained from cells, which are more plentiful in female urine. Protein and DNA are often degraded in older specimens; this can be overcome to some extent by procedures that amplify (replicate) portions of the DNA. The analyses require approximately 20–50 mL of urine. If the laboratory can isolate protein or DNA markers, it will also analyze a blood or saliva sample from the suspected urine donor for the same markers. The tests take approximately six to eight weeks and cost $2000–$2500. The laboratory then reports one of two outcomes:

■ The individual cannot be excluded as a donor of the challenged urine. (The report also states the likelihood that the match is coincidental.)

or

■ The individual is not the donor of the challenged urine.

DOT's position is that, because its rules do not authorize these tests, they may be ordered only pursuant to a court order. Furthermore, DOT does not authorize reversal of a positive result based on genetic marker test results.

References ■

1. U.S. Department of Transportation. Federal Highway Administration. *Medical Advisory Criteria for Evaluation under 49 CFR part 391.41*. Washington, DC: Office of Motor Carriers. Updated April 8, 1998.
2. U.S. Department of Transportation. Federal Highway Administration. Conference on Psychiatric Disorders and Commercial drivers. Washington, DC: Office of Motor Carriers. Pub. No. FHWA-MC-91-006.
3. Federal Highway Administration. Commercial driver's license program and controlled substances and alcohol use testing; conforming and technical amendments. *Federal Register* 1997;62(July 11):37,150–3.
4. American Society for Clinical Pharmacology and Therapeutics. Scientific Consensus Conference: Clinical Pharmacologic Implications of Urine Screening for Illicit Substances of Abuse. San Diego, March 7–8, 1988.
5. Perez-Reyes M, Diguiseppi S, Mason AP, Davis KH. Passive inhalation of marijuana smoke and urinary excretion of cannabinoids. *Clin Pharmacol Ther* 1983;34:36–41.
6. Law B, Mason PA, Moffat AC, et al. Passive inhalation of cannabis smoke. *J Pharm Pharmacol* 1984;36:578–81.
7. Cone EJ, Johnson RE, Darwin M, et al. Passive inhalation of marijuana smoke: urinalysis and room air levels of delta THC. *J Anal Toxicol* 1987;11:89–96.
8. Cone EJ, Yousefilejad D, Hillsgrove MJ, et al. Passive inhalation of cocaine. *J Anal Toxicol* 1995;19:399–411.
9. Cone EJ, Johnson RE, Paul BD, et al. Marijuana-laced brownies: behavioral effects, physiologic effects, and urinalysis in humans following ingestion. *J Anal Toxicol* 1988;12:169–75.
10. Struempler RE, Nelson G, Urry FM. A positive cannabinoids workplace drug test following the ingestion of commercially available hemp seed oil. *J Anal Toxicol* 1997;21:283–5.
11. Callaway JC, Weeks RA, Raymon LP, et al. A positive THC urinalysis from hemp *(Cannabis)* seed oil. *J Anal Toxicol* 1997;21:319–20.
12. Costantino A, Schwartz RH, Kaplan P. Hemp oil ingestion causes positive urine tests for THC. *J Anal Toxicol* 1997;21:482–5.
13. U.S. Department of Transportation. Claims of Ingestion of Hemp Food Products; Interpretation. Washington, DC, December 1996.
14. Siegel RK, ElSohly MA, Plowman T, et al. Cocaine in herbal tea. *JAMA* 1986;255:40.
15. Floren AE, Small JW. Mate de Coca equals cocaine. *J Occup Med* 1993;35:95–6.
16. Jenkins AJ, Llosa T, Montoya I, et al. Identification and quantitation of alkaloids in coca tea. *Forensic Sci Int* 1996;177:179–89.
17. Mason AP. Marijuana tea: toxicological fact or fiction. *Proceedings of the 23rd Annual SOFT Meeting*. Phoenix, October 1993.
18. ElSohly MA, Jones AB. Drug testing in the workplace: could a positive test for one of the mandated drugs be for reasons other than illicit use of the drug? *J Anal Toxicol* 1995;19:450–8.
19. U.S. Food and Drug Administration. Controlled Substances. Drugs; Statement of required warning. 21 CFR §290.5.
20. U.S. Department of Transportation. *Medical Review Officer Guide*. Washington, DC, 1990.
21. U.S. Department of Transportation. Federal Highway Administration. Regulatory guidance for the Federal Motor Carrier Safety Regulations. *Federal Register* 1997;62(April 4):16,369–431.

Drugs: Classifications, Effects, and Pharmacology ■

7

Federal regulations require employers to test for:

- Amphetamines (amphetamine and methamphetamine).
- Cocaine.
- Marijuana.
- Opiates (codeine, morphine, and heroin).
- Phencyclidine.

Table 7-1 presents summary information about drugs in the federal five-drug panel and additional drugs and drug classes that are often included in nonregulated programs:

- Barbiturates.
- Benzodiazepines.
- Methadone.
- Methaqualone.
- Propoxyphene.

The following sections address issues specific to each drug.

Federal Five-Drug Panel ■

AMPHETAMINES: AMPHETAMINE AND METHAMPHETAMINE

d-Amphetamine and *d*-methamphetamine are stimulants and subject to abuse and are Schedule II controlled substances. They belong to a class of drugs known as amphetamines.

Therapeutic Uses
d-Amphetamine and *d*-methamphetamine have limited medical use: They are primarily for the treatment of narcolepsy, attention-deficit disorder, depression, and short-term treatment of obesity. Because of the abuse risk, many medical boards and organizations have taken the position that it is inappropriate to treat obesity with amphetamines for more than a few weeks.

Table 7-1. Uses and Effects of Drugs ■

	Amphetamine/ Methamphet- amine	Cocaine	Heroin	Marijuana/THC	Phencyclidine
DEA schedule	II	II	I	I (marijuana) II (THC)	I
Trade or other names	Crystal, Ice, Meth, Speed	Coke, Crack, Flake, Snow	Horse, Smack	Acapulco Gold, Bud, Grass, Pot, Reefer, Sinsemilla, Thai sticks	Angel Dust, Hog, Loveboat
Medical Uses	Attention-deficit disorder, narco- lepsy, weight control	Local anesthetic	None in United States	Dronabinol (Mar- inol) is prescribed to treat AIDS- related weight loss and as an anti- emetic for patients on chemotherapy. In 1997 and 1998 several states legalized medi- cal use of mari- juana	None
Physical dependence	Possible	Possible	High	Unknown	Unknown
Psychological dependence	High	High	High	Moderate	High
Duration of effect	2–4 hr	1–2 hr	3–6 hr	2–4 hr	1–2 days
Usual method	Injected, oral, smoked, snorted	Injected, smoked, snorted. Medical use as topical anesthetic	Injected, smoked, snorted	Oral, smoked	Oral, smoked
Possible effects	Increased alert- ness, excitation, euphoria, in- creased pulse rate and blood pressure, insom- nia, loss of appetite	Increased alert- ness, excitation, euphroia, in- creased pulse rate and blood pres- sure, insomnia, loss of appetite	Euphoria, drowsi- ness, respiratory depression, con- stricted pupils, nausea	Euphoria, relaxed inhibitions, in- creased appetite, disorientation	Illusions and hallucinations, altered perception of time and distance
Withdrawal syndrome	Apathy, long periods of sleep, irritability, depres- sion, disorienta- tion	Apathy, long periods of sleep, irritability, depres- sion, disorienta- tion	Watery eyes, runny nose, yawning, loss of appetite, irritability, tremors, panic, cramps, nausea, chills and sweating	Occasional re- ports of insomnia, hyperactivity, decreased appetite	Unknown
Maximum detection time in urine	2 days	3 days	8 hr as 6-AM; 4 days as mor- phine and codeine	Single dose of 1–2 joints: 3 days. Chronic use of more than 5 joints/ day: 18 days, rarely longer	Occasional use: 2 weeks. Chronic use: 30 days or more

Table 7-1. Uses and Effects of Drugs (continued) ■

Barbiturates	Benzodiazepines	Methadone	Methaqualone	Propoxyphene
II, III, IV	IV	II	I	IV
Barbs, Blue Devils, Downers, Red Devils, Tranks, Yellow jackets, Yellows	Tanks, Downers, Benzos, Ativan, Librium, Valium, Xanax	Dolophine	Ludes, Quaaludes, Sopors	Darvon, Darvocet
Anesthetic, anticonvulsant, sedative, hypnotic, veterinary euthanasia agent	Antianxiety, sedative, anticonvulsant, hynotic	Analgesic, treatment of dependence	None in United States	Analgesic
High to moderate	Low	High	Moderate	Moderate
High to moderate	Low	High	Moderate	High
5–8 hr (varies by agent)	4–8 hr (varies by agent)	12–72 hr	4–8 hr	2–4 hr
Oral, injected	Oral, injected	Oral, injected	Oral	Oral, injected
Slurred speech, disorientation, drunken behavior without odor of alcohol	Slurred speech, disorientation, drunken behavior without odor of alcohol	Euphoria, drowsiness, respiratory depression, constricted pupils, nausea	Slurred speech, disorientation, drunken behavior without odor of alcohol	Euphoria, drowsiness, respiratory depression, constricted pupils, nausea
Anxiety, insomnia, tremors, delirium, convulsions, possible death	Anxiety, insomnia, tremors, delirium, convulsions, possible death	Watery eyes, runny nose, yawning, loss of appetite, irritability, tremors, panic, cramps, nausea, chills and sweating	Anxiety, insomnia, tremors, delirium, convulsions, possible death	Watery eyes, runny nose, yawning, loss of appetite, irritability, tremors, panic, cramps, nausea, chills, and sweating
Short-acting: a few days. Phenobarbital: a week or more	Short-acting: 24 hr. Long-acting: 24 days. Long-acting, chronic user: weeks or months	3 days	3 days	3 days

Drugs: Classifications, Effects, and Pharmacology ■ 75

l-Methamphetamine is the active ingredient in Vicks Inhaler, an over-the-counter nasal decongestant; the manufacturer identifies it by the alternative name desoxyephedrine.

Illicit Uses

Amphetamines stimulate attention and prolong endurance. This makes them particularly subject to abuse by truck drivers, athletes, and students. A single therapeutic dose may enhance attention and performance, but exhaustion eventually occurs and performance deteriorates as the effects wear off. The worker on amphetamines is often nervous, suspicious, and hyperactive. He or she may appear to be a hard, aggressive worker, yet often is on the brink of collapse. Prolonged abuse of amphetamines can result in paranoia, delusions, and hallucinations ("amphetamine psychosis").

Methamphetamine use in the United States is most prevalent in large western and southwestern cities. The typical user is a 26- to 44-year-old male, who may take it in combination with alcohol, heroin, cocaine, or other drugs. Routes of administration include inhalation (smoking), intranasal (snorting), intravenous (IV) injection, and oral. An abuser may inject up to 1 g in a single intravenous dose. Unlike cocaine or marijuana, methamphetamine is easily manufactured from materials available in the United States and abroad.

Pharmacology

Amphetamine and methamphetamine are well absorbed from the gastrointestinal and respiratory tracts and distributed throughout the body. About 30 percent of an amphetamine dose appears in the urine unchanged, although this can increase up to 70 percent if the urine is acidic and can be as low as 1 percent if the urine is alkaline. Nearly half of a methamphetamine dose appears in the urine unchanged, and a small percentage is demethylated to amphetamine. Thus, after methamphetamine use, both amphetamine and methamphetamine appear in the urine, although not necessarily above the cutoff values.

When the urine is acidic, amphetamines are excreted more quickly in the urine and thus have less opportunity to undergo metabolism in the body. Some illicit drug users drink vinegar or cranberry juice to acidify their urine and "cleanse" themselves of amphetamines. A 10-mg dose of amphetamine or methamphetamine generally produces a positive urine for about 24 hours, depending on urinary pH and individual metabolic differences. High-dose abusers can have positive urines for two to four days after last use.

Amphetamine and methamphetamine exist as *d*- (dextro) and *l*- (levo) enantiomers, or stereoisomers. The designators, *d*- and *l*-, can be remembered as "drug" and "legal," but they actually indicate the direction in which each enantiomer rotates a beam of polarized light. The *d*-isomer of each substance has a strong stimulant effect on the central nervous system, while the *l*-isomer of each substance has primarily a peripheral action.

Several drugs are metabolized to amphetamine, methamphetamine, or both (Table 7-2). Some but not all drugs that have *amine* in their names are metabolized to methamphetamine and/or amphetamine. When metabolized, *d*- precursors form *d*- metabolites and *l*- precursors form *l*-metabolites. For example, selegiline has the *l*- configuration and is metabolized to *l*-methamphetamine and *l*-amphetamine.

Table 7-2. Prescription Drugs that Are Metabolized to Amphetamine and/or Methamphetamine ■

Drug	Metabolites	Medical Uses
benzphetamine (*US:* Didrex)	*d*-amphetamine, *d*-methamphetamine	Anorectic
clobenzorex (*Mex:* Asenlix, (*France:* Dinintel, *Spain:* Finedal)	*d*- and *l*-amphetamine	Anorectic
famprofazone (*Ger, Korea:* Geodowin)	*d*- and *l*-amphetamine *d*- and *l*-methamphetamine	Analgesic and antipyretic
fencamfamine (Altimine, Envitrol, Phencamine	*d*- and *l*-amphetamine *d*- and *l*-methamphetamine	Antidepressant
fenethylline (*Ger:* Captagon)	*d*- and *l*-amphetamine	A Schedule I drug in the United States. Used elsewhere to treat attention deficit disorder, narcolepsy, and depression
fenproporex (*Ger:* Appetizugler, *Spain:* Antiobes Retard, Dicel, Falagan, Grasmin, Tegisec)	*d*- and *l*-amphetamine	Anorectic
mefenorex (*Arg:* Doracil, *France:* Incital, *Ger:* Rondimen, *Switz,* Pondinil)	*d*- amphetamine	Anorectic
mesocarb (*Europe:* Sydnocarb)	amphetamine	
prenylamine (*Europe:* Segontin)	*d*- and *l*-amphetamine	Coronary vasodilator
selegiline (*Can:* Deprenyl, *Spain:* Plurimen, *US:* Atapryl, Carbex, Eldepryl)	*l*-amphetamine, *l*-methamphetamine	Parkinson's disease. May also have a role in the treatment of Alzheimer's disease

Laboratory Issues

Amphetamine/methamphetamine immunoassays are susceptible to false-positive results because of the wide variety of structurally similar chemicals contained in drugs. These include nonprescription drugs that contain ephedrine, pseudoephedrine, and phenylpropanolamine (e.g., Alka-Seltzer Plus, Dexatrim, Primatene Tablets, Triaminic); the prescription drug methylphenidate (Ritalin); and the prescription weight-loss drug combination Phen-Fen (phentermine and fenfluramine), which was removed from the market in September 1997. Use of these drugs can produce urine specimens that screen positive and fail to show amphetamine use upon confirmation testing.

Drugs: Classifications, Effects, and Pharmacology ■ 77

In 1990, it was reported that high concentrations of the nonprescription drugs ephedrine and psuedoephedrine could, under certain conditions, cause false-positive GC/MS test results for methamphetamine. It is unclear how this occurs. Some have hypothesized that the ephedrine mimics the pattern produced by methamphetamine or that the ephedrine is converted to methamphetamine. By contrast, methamphetamine taken as a medication would normally be metabolized to amphetamine so that both methamphetamine and amphetamine would be detected. In response to this issue, the Department of Health and Human Services (DHHS) has directed certified laboratories to report specimens as positive for methamphetamine only if amphetamine is also detected at a concentration at or above 200 ng/mL [1]. If the methamphetamine level is at or above 500 ng/mL and the amphetamine level is at or above 200 but less than 500, the laboratory report will be positive only for methamphetamine. The medical review officer (MRO) may contact the laboratory to confirm that amphetamine was present at a level between 200 and 500 ng/mL.

Interpreting Results

The laboratory report of an amphetamine-positive result generally does not indicate which enantiomer is present. While some immunoassays are more specific for d-, the laboratory procedure is set up to identify and quantify methamphetamine and amphetamine without regard to enantiomers. Optically selective derivitization procedures and chiral columns can definitively differentiate d- versus l-. Some laboratories do this routinely, some do it upon request, and some do not do it at all but instead send an aliquot from the specimen to a laboratory that has this capability. Federal drug testing rules do not require d- versus l- differentiation, but the MRO may nevertheless want this test performed to help distinguish between Vicks Inhaler and illicit and prescription forms of amphetamines. Because this test is expensive ($100) and it can take up to ten days to obtain results, some MROs order d- versus l- differentiation only in selected cases—for example, only if the donor provides a history of Vicks Inhaler use within several days before the test, or if the test is methamphetamine positive, amphetamine negative. Some MROs order d- and l-isomers routinely.

The assays that distinguish d- from l- are inexact, and thus a small percentage of d- may be "detected" when in fact only l- is present. Illegally manufactured amphetamine and methamphetamine often contain mixtures of the d- and l-isomers. The federal government has advised MROs to use an 80/20 guideline: If more than 80 percent of the methamphetamine is the l-isomer, this can be due to use of Vicks Inhaler and is not evidence of illicit drug use regardless of the total concentration [2]. Tests conducted after pure l-methamphetamine use generally detect 97–98 percent l-methamphetamine. The 80/20 guideline provides a margin of error that favors the donor. If 20 percent or more of the methamphetamine is the d- isomer, the MRO can safely conclude that the donor used a prescription or illicit drug.

COCAINE

Cocaine is present in the leaves of the coca plant, *Erythroxylon coca*. The commonly available white powder sold on the street contains cocaine hydrochloride (HCl). "Freebase" cocaine can be made by heating cocaine hydrochloride in water and adding a base, usually sodium bicarbonate. This mixture can be extracted with an organic solvent, usually diethyl ether, to recover the lipid-soluble alkaloid. Or, it can be dried to produce a chalky white solid. The solid is cut into chunks and sold as "crack," named for the crackling sound it makes when flame is applied to it in a pipe.

Cocaine is a Schedule II drug that is used medically as a local anesthetic. It is abused for its stimulant and euphoric properties. Large doses can cause mental confusion or paranoid delusions, and overdoses can cause seizures, respiratory depression, cardiac arrhythmias, and death. The drug is highly reinforcing: Repeated use of it tends to increase its use. Cocaine users often use it late at night and are exhausted at work. Chronic users become exhausted and lethargic. After repeated exposures, many patients say that although cocaine no longer produces much of a "high," they are unable to abstain. People withdrawing from cocaine experience moderate fatigue, increased appetite, vivid dreams, and mental depression. These symptoms last a few days to a few weeks.

Therapeutic Uses

Cocaine in solution is available for topical administration by physicians. It has anesthetic and vasoconstrictive, decongestant effects. Plastic surgeons, otolaryngologists, and ophthalmologists are among the specialists who are most likely to apply topical cocaine as a presurgical anesthetic. Emergency department physicians may apply a 4-percent cocaine solution before packing an intractable nose bleed. Some emergency physicians anesthetize lacerations, usually in children, by swabbing them with TAC—a solution of 0.5 percent tetracaine, 1/2,000 adrenaline, and 11.8 percent cocaine—before suturing. Administration of cocaine in dentistry is rare. Physicians and dentists must complete extensive documentation to obtain and administer cocaine in their practices.

Illicit Uses

Cocaine is usually taken by one of three routes: intranasal "snorting," inhalation of freebase or crack cocaine vapor, or intravenous injection. Approximately 75 percent of cocaine users snort it. As abuse progresses, addicts turn to smoking and intravenous use for its more intense effects. Cocaine addicts are often also dependent on marijuana, alcohol, heroin, or other drugs. In regulated testing, cocaine is the second most frequently detected illicit drug, after marijuana.

Pharmacology

Peak plasma cocaine concentrations occur approximately 5 minutes after intravenous or smoked use and approximately 30–40 minutes after intranasal use [3]. The immediacy and magnitude of effect make smoked cocaine particularly addictive.

Extensive contact of bare skin with cocaine can result in low urine concentrations of benzoylecognine. One study reports a peak concentration of 72 ng/mL in an individual 12 hours after the person handled money that had been immersed in coca paste [4].

The behavioral effects of cocaine reside primarily in the parent compound. Cocaine is rapidly and extensively metabolized by liver and plasma enzymes, primarily to benzoylecognine and ecgonine methyl ester. Both metabolites are excreted in the urine along with a fraction (< 1 percent) of nonmetabolized cocaine. The biologic half-lives of benzoylecognine, ecgonine methyl ester, and cocaine are 7.5 hours, 3.6 hours, and 1.5 hours, respectively [5]. Benzoylecognine can be detected in urine for up to three days after a single dose and does not significantly accumulate in the body.

Immunoassay screening procedures target benzoylecognine but respond to several cocaine metabolites. Confirmation procedures are specific for benzoylecognine. Thus, in regulated testing, the screening cutoff concentration (300 ng/mL) is set higher than the confirmation cutoff concentration (150 ng/mL).

When cocaine and alcohol are used together, cocaethylene is formed in the liver. This compound crosses the blood-brain barrier and may explain why so many cocaine users use alcohol; they apparently get a greater and longer high.

Interpreting Results

There are no prescription medications that contain cocaine. Medical use of cocaine as a topical anesthetic can lead to benzoylecognine-positive urine test results [6,7,8,9]. If cocaine is used, the physician performing the procedure documents its use in the donor's medical record. Topical "caine" anesthetics such as procaine (Novocain), lidocaine (Xylocaine), and benzocaine (cetacaine) have no structural similarity to cocaine or its metabolites and do not cause cocaine-positive drug test results. A small amount of cocaine is excreted in semen; however, exposure to semen from cocaine-using male partners does not cause positive drug test results when the federal cutoff values are used [10]. Chapter 6 addresses passive inhalation and cocaine in food and beverages.

MARIJUANA

Marijuana is the processed leaf material from the common hemp plant, *Cannabis sativa*. It contains a class of compounds known as cannabinoids.

Marijuana is a Schedule I drug; the federal government has determined that it has no legitimate medical use. It is a hallucinogen that produces euphoria, or a "high," which is commonly followed by drowsiness, especially when the user is alone. Users frequently report increased hunger, dry mouth and throat, dizziness, and increased visual and auditory awareness. Intoxication temporarily impairs concentration, learning, and perceptual-motor skills. Studies have shown impaired perception and motor coordination among pilots for 4–6 hours, and in some cases for up to 24 hours, after marijuana use [11]. Tolerance develops with chronic use of high doses. After such use, withdrawal can cause physical symptoms such as anorexia, nausea, diarrhea, insomnia, restlessness, irritability, and anxiety.

Therapeutic Uses

Dronabinol (Marinol) is chemically synthesized delta-9-tetrahydrocannabinol (THC), the principal psychoactive agent in marijuana. It is marketed as a capsule for oral administration, is FDA-approved for treatment of chemotherapy-induced nausea and for appetite stimulation in the treatment of AIDS-related anorexia, and is a Schedule II drug. (In 1998, the Drug Enforcement Administration issued a proposal to move dronabinol to Schedule III [12].) Patients who are prescribed Marinol should be warned not to drive, operate complex machinery, or engage in hazardous activities. Although smoking marijuana causes a temporary decrease in intraocular pressure in most users, it must be smoked continually to be effective for glaucoma, and this would lead to substantial systemic toxic effects [13]. A few individuals have been permitted by court order to use marijuana for the management of glaucoma; this marijuana is grown at the University of Mississippi and distributed by Research Triangle Park under strict federal supervision. From 1996 to 1998, voters in Alaska, Arizona, California, Colorado, the District of Columbia, Oregon, and Washington state approved referenda that legalized marijuana for certain medical reasons. The federal government has opposed these and similar initiatives.

Illicit Uses
After tobacco, alcohol and caffeine, marijuana is probably the most widely used drug in Western society. It is usually smoked in cigarettes; sometimes it is ingested with baked items or as a tea. "Blunts" are cigars in which the user has supplemented or replaced the tobacco with marijuana. "Fry" are marijuana cigarettes or cigars, sometimes mixed with phencyclidine (PCP), dipped in embalming fluid (formaldehyde).

Pharmacology
Cannabinoids are absorbed rapidly from the lungs and more slowly from the gastrointestinal tract. They enter the systemic circulation and, because they are lipophilic, are stored and can accumulate in adipose tissue. A person with no marijuana experience who smokes one marijuana cigarette may be positive for 11-nor-delta-9-tetrahydrocannabinol-9-carboxylic acid (THC-COOH) by CG/MS for one to three days, using a 15 ng/mL cutoff value [14]. A frequent, chronic marijuana user can be positive by immunoassay for more than four weeks after last use, depending on the cutoff value [15,16]. Prolonged excretion occurs by gradual release of cannabinoids that have accumulated in fat and other body compartments. Various estimates have placed the half-life of THC-COOH at anywhere from 18 hours to more than a few days, depending on the extent of use and other factors. Weight loss, i.e., a reduction in body fat, is not known to affect urine THC-COOH concentrations.

Laboratory Issues
Delta-9-tetrahydrocannabinol (THC), the primary psychoactive constituent of marijuana, is extensively metabolized in the liver, and its metabolites are primarily eliminated in feces and urine, with little or no parent compound being eliminated by either route. The metabolic profile varies from individual to individual and by level of use. THC-COOH is the metabolite that usually appears in the greatest concentration. While it has no pharmacologic activity, it is the target compound toward which both the screening and confirmation tests are directed. While the immunoassay has cross-reactivity with multiple

metabolites, GC/MS specifically identifies THC-COOH. Therefore, the federal cutoff concentrations for screening (50 ng/mL) and confirmation (15 ng/mL) differ significantly. Furthermore, because the ability of the antibodies to bind the various metabolites varies among manufacturers, a marijuana-positive urine specimen may yield different results when screened by different immunoassays. The results of repeated GC/MS analyses for THC-COOH, even when performed at different laboratories, should exhibit only normal laboratory variation.

In practice, people often refer to THC-COOH as "THC." The scientific literature more properly distinguishes between delta-9-tetrahydrocannabinol (THC) and 11-nor-delta-9-tetrahydrocannabinol (THC-COOH).

Interpreting Results

In regulated testing, use of dronabinol is the only alternative medical explanation for a THC-positive drug test result. The federal government has instructed MROs that, in federally regulated drug testing programs, "medical" marijuana use is not an acceptable explanation for a THC-positive result [17]. In nonregulated programs where local laws permit medical marijuana use and the donor presents this as an explanation for a THC-positive drug test, the MRO should check the employer's policy, because it may specifically prohibit marijuana use. If the employer offers no guidance on this issue, the MRO may wish to defer to the federal guidance as a standard of practice and verify the result as positive.

A ratio of 0.5 or greater between two creatinine-normalized positive cannabinoid tests can help differentiate new marijuana use from residual excretion [18].

Chapter 6 addresses passive inhalation of marijuana and ingestion of it in food and beverages.

OPIATES: CODEINE, MORPHINE, AND HEROIN

Opiates are products obtained or derived from the opium poppy plant. The more common opiates include codeine and morphine. Heroin (diacetylmorphine) can be produced through a reaction between morphine and acetic acid. Illicit heroin products contain small amounts of codeine because opium poppies contain codeine and because dealers often cut (adulterate) heroin with codeine. The term *narcotics* specifically refers to opiates but is generally used to refer to illicit drugs with sedative properties.

Heroin is a Schedule I drug; it has no legitimate medical use and is illegal in the United States. Morphine is a Schedule II drug and is used to treat moderate to severe pain. Codeine is a Schedule III, IV or V drug, depending on the concentration and preparation, and is used as an analgesic and cough suppressant.

Ingestion of low to moderate amounts of opiates produces a short-lived feeling of euphoria followed by several hours of physical and mental relaxation. Opiate intoxication may cause miosis (pinpoint pupils), a dull facies, confusion or mental dullness, slurring of speech, drowsiness, or partial ptosis (drooping of the upper eyelid). Opiates are physically and psychologically addictive. Opiate withdrawal is characterized by flu-like symptoms, such as watery eyes, nausea and vomiting, muscle cramps, and loss of appetite.

Therapeutic Uses
Morphine and codeine are used as analgesics. Codeine is used in prescription analgesics such as Tylenol #3, and prescription cough syrups such as Robitussin AC. Certain codeine preparations are sold over the counter in Canada (e.g., 222, AC&C) and Mexico. Several nonprescription, Schedule V antidiarrheal products contain opium, the plant extract that contains morphine and codeine.

Illicit Uses
Heroin users smoke it or use it intravenously. Morphine is usually used intravenously; if taken orally, it is less effective because of "first-pass" metabolism by the liver prior to systemic distribution.

Pharmacology
Codeine, morphine, and their metabolites can be detected in urine up to four days after use. After ingestion, codeine is rapidly absorbed and metabolized, primarily to codeine-6-glucuronide, a conjugated form. It is also demethylated (10–15 percent), forming morphine and norcodeine, principally in the form of conjugates. Thus, codeine, norcodeine, and morphine in free and conjugated forms appear in the urine after ingestion (see Figure 7-1). Codeine is rapidly cleared, with an elimination half-life of approximately 3.3 hours [19]. About 10 percent of the codeine dose is excreted in the urine as unchanged drug. After a time, the codeine is completely excreted or metabolized so that only morphine is detected in the urine. Thus, codeine use can lead to urine test results that are positive for codeine, morphine, or both.

Morphine is rapidly absorbed after oral administration. About 10 percent is excreted as morphine, and the rest is excreted as conjugated forms of morphine, primarily morphine-3-glucuronide. Morphine is not metabolized to codeine. Thus, ingestion of pure morphine cannot account for the presence of codeine in urine.

Heroin (diacetylmorphine) is rapidly deacetylated to 6-acetylmorphine (6-AM) also called 6-monoacetylmorphine (6-MAM), a metabolite that is specific for heroin. Heroin itself is rarely detected in the urine. 6-AM is rapidly deacetylated to morphine and, if detected at all, is found at very low concentrations after heroin use. After a single dose of heroin, 6-AM may be detectable in the urine for 2 to 8 hours at concentrations generally ranging from 10 to 250 ng/mL [20]. 6-AM is stable in urine refrigerated for up to ten days or frozen for up to two years. After heroin use, both morphine and codeine can be detected in urine. Morphine is a heroin metabolite, and codeine may occur when dealers cut heroin with codeine.

The synthetic and semisynthetic opiates—for example, hydromorphone (Dilaudid), hydrocodone (Hycodan), oxycodone (Percodan), propoxyphene (Darvon), methadone, meperidine (Demerol), and fentanyl (Sublimaze)—do not metabolize to codeine, morphine, or 6-AM and thus do not cause opiate-positive results in regulated testing.

Figure 7-1. Metabolism of Codeine to Morphine ■

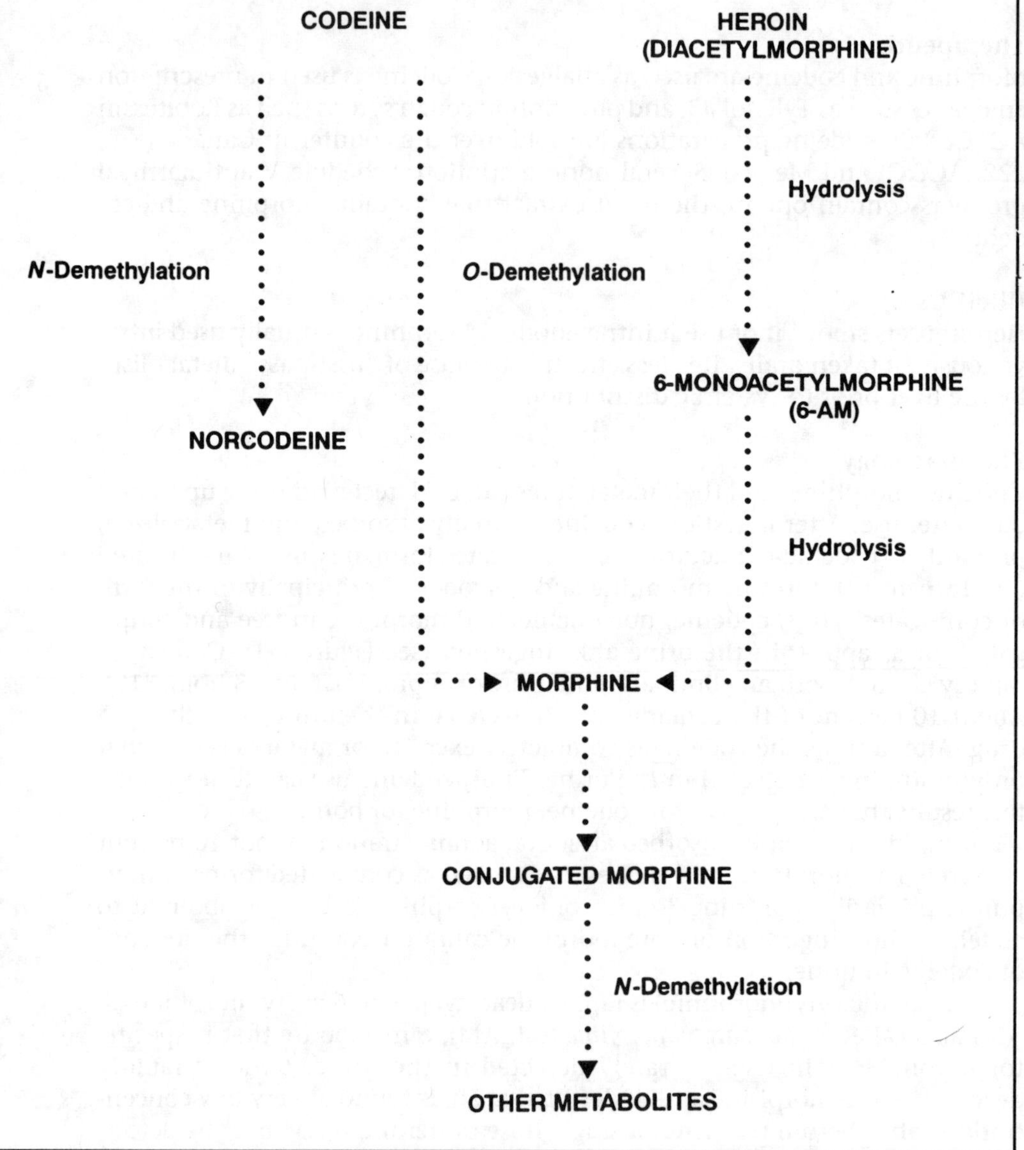

```
         CODEINE                          HEROIN
                                     (DIACETYLMORPHINE)


                                                        Hydrolysis

N-Demethylation        O-Demethylation


                                         6-MONOACETYLMORPHINE
                                                (6-AM)
        NORCODEINE


                                                        Hydrolysis




                          MORPHINE



                      CONJUGATED MORPHINE



                                         N-Demethylation



                       OTHER METABOLITES
```

Laboratory Issues

The opiate immunoassay is directed toward free morphine and has cross-reactivity with conjugated morphine, free and conjugated codeine, and the synthetic opiates hydrocodone, hydromorphone, and oxycodone. If the sample screening is positive for opiates, another aliquot is subjected to an acid or enzymatic hydrolysis procedure that liberates free morphine and, to a lesser extent, free codeine from their conjugated forms. The aliquot then undergoes GC/MS confirmation assays that are specific for morphine and codeine. The federal rules initially set the opiate screening and confirmation cutoff values at 300 ng/mL. In 1998, SAMHSA increased the opiate cutoffs to 2,000 ng/mL for screening and confirmation, and added 6-AM GC/MS analysis, with a 10 ng/mL cutoff, for each specimen with a morphine concentration at or above 2,000 ng/mL [21]. These increases made opiate testing more specific for heroin and less sensitive for codeine and poppy seeds. The military testing programs use opiate cutoff values of 2,000 ng/mL for screening, and 2,000 ng/mL and 4,000 ng/mL for confirmation of codeine and morphine, respectively. NRC requires 6-AM testing for opiate-positive specimens and has set no particular cutoff value for this test.

DHHS certified laboratories can routinely report codeine and morphine concentrations at or above the cutoff levels upon receipt of a written "blanket" request from the MRO. In addition, the MRO may request quantitative information on the presence of codeine below the cutoff value for specimens that have been reported positive for morphine only. These data can help guide MROs in their investigations.

Interpreting Results

Use of a number of prescription and nonprescription medications can result in drug tests that are positive for codeine and/or morphine (see Table 5-1). Urine codeine concentrations during typical use can be in the 10,000s of ng/mL [22]. If the donor says he or she took an opiate that was nonprescription, the MRO can verify this by contacting the pharmacy, which should have a bound record book that contains the name and address of the purchaser, the name and quantity of the product purchased, the date of the purchase, and the name or initials of the pharmacist who dispensed the product [21 CFR §1306.26(e)].

Some varieties of poppy seeds contain morphine and codeine. Poppy seeds are found in certain bagels, breads, sauces, cakes, and other foods. Ingestion of normal dietary amounts of poppy seeds can result in peak morphine concentrations of more than 4,000 ng/mL and peak codeine concentrations of more than 2,000 ng/mL [23]. Usually, poppy seeds produce urine codeine levels below 2,000 ng/mL, and because they contain more morphine than codeine, morphine-to-codeine ratios exceed 2:1. Codeine levels and morphine-to-codeine ratios are not infallible ways to distinguish codeine from morphine consumption [22]. There is no direct marker to establish whether opiate-positive urine results are due to poppy seeds or to drug use.

The MRO should not base a test outcome on whether or not the donor says he or she ate poppy seeds. Instead, poppy-seed ingestion is assumed, and the MRO can verify an opiate result as positive only if 6-AM is detected or if the MRO finds clinical evidence of recent unauthorized or illicit opiate use. The burden of proof shifts to the MRO: The donor need not present an alternative explanation; instead, the MRO must find 6-AM or clinical findings that corroborate the suspicion of opiate abuse. Clinical evidence can be either physiologic findings on a medical examination or the history provided by the donor. The clinical evidence is usually the donor's admission of unauthorized use of an opiate. Fresh needle-track marks and other physical findings are infrequently identified. Without detection of 6-AM or clinical evidence of opiate abuse, the test cannot be verified positive. With 6-AM or clinical evidence of opiate abuse, the MRO can verify the result as positive, even if the donor has a prescription or other alternative medical explanation.

6-AM is a metabolite of heroin and may be found, generally in low concentrations and for brief periods of time, only when heroin has been used. The absence of 6-AM does not rule out heroin use. Tests for 6-AM are most likely to be positive and physical examinations are most likely to yield clinical findings when the specimen's morphine concentration exceeds 5,000 ng/mL and the total-codeine-to-total-morphine ratio is less than 0.125 [24].

Clinical evidence is useful only if it correlates with the timing of the drug test. For example, old needle-track scars may suggest past use of heroin, but only fresh needle-track scars corroborate a recent opiate-positive drug test. Clinical evidence of abuse may come from the MRO's discussion with the donor—for example, the donor may admit to unauthorized use of an opiate product—or from a medical examination of the donor by the MRO or another clinician with appropriate expertise. The clinician need not be a specialist in addiction medicine. MROs can rely on other health care professionals to perform these evaluations. Observations by the donor's supervisors or by non-professional staff at the collection site are useful only if they supplement direct clinical evidence of recent use.

If the donor refuses a medical examination for clinical evidence of opiate abuse, the MRO should inform the donor that the refusal will lead to a verified positive result. If the donor still refuses, the MRO should report the outcome as positive. This approach is based on federal rules that authorize the MRO to verify a result as positive if the donor refuses to participate in the medical interview process.

Federal rules and guidelines do not require or recommend that the MRO conduct an examination or face-to-face interview of each donor whose urine is opiate-positive. Some MROs order physical examinations selectively, giving high priority to cases in which the laboratory data are consistent with heroin use and the logistics are reasonable. Clinical evidence can also be obtained through the telephone conversation if the donor admits to use of an unauthorized prescription medicine. The yield of clinical evidence from physical examinations of opiate-positive donors is low: If the donor used heroin intravenously, the MRO might find fresh needle tracks; if the donor snorted heroin, the examiner will find no needle tracks.

PHENCYCLIDINE

Phencyclidine (PCP) is a hallucinogen. It is a Schedule II drug and, in the United States, is used only for research purposes and as a drug standard.

PCP intoxication begins several minutes after ingestion and usually lasts 8 hours or more. PCP produces unpredictable side effects, such as psychosis, agitation and, occasionally, violent behavior. The most common physical findings are nystagmus (horizontal, vertical, or rotatory), hypertension, and tachycardia.

Therapeutic Uses
PCP was first synthesized in 1926. In the 1950s, physicians and veterinarians started administering it as a general anesthetic. In 1965, human use was dis-

continued because, as the anesthetic wore off, psychotic reactions were common. In 1978, commercial manufacturing of PCP in the United States ceased.

Illicit Uses
PCP first became popular as a drug of abuse in the 1960s, and its use resurged in the late 1970s and 1980s. During the 1990s, it accounted for approximately 1 percent of all laboratory-positive drug tests; many of these were laboratory proficiency testing samples. Illicit PCP is usually smoked but may be eaten, snorted, or injected intravenously. It is sometimes added to marijuana to produce more dramatic sensory distortions.

Pharmacology
PCP is well absorbed by any route. It is highly lipid soluble and accumulates in adipose tissue and in the brain [25]. About 10 percent of a PCP dose is excreted in the urine unchanged. Urine PCP levels decrease rapidly during the first nine days after use and then decrease more slowly. Most people who use PCP will have positive urine test results for less than two weeks; few will have positive results beyond 30 days [26]. PCP is a weak base. Urine acidification—for example, by drinking vinegar or cranberry juice—increases its elimination rate.

Interpreting Results
No medications approved for use in the United States contain PCP. Diphenhydramine (Benadryl) at urine concentrations of 50 to 1,200 µg/L may cause a urine specimen to screen positive for PCP by FPIA, but confirmatory testing of these specimens for PCP by GC/MS analysis does not produce positive results [27].

Other Drugs ■

The federal workplace programs—except those programs regulated by the Nuclear Regulatory Commission (NRC)—permit testing only for drugs and drug metabolites listed in the federal five-drug panel. Some employers test for additional drugs in nonregulated programs. DHHS does not certify or monitor laboratories for such tests.

BARBITURATES

Barbiturates are sedative-hypnotic agents. Various barbiturates fall in the Drug Enforcement Agency (DEA) Schedules II, III, and IV. At therapeutic doses, barbiturates do not noticeably affect simple motor performance but can impair performance on complex psychomotor and cognitive tasks. Withdrawal from barbiturates is characterized by anxiety, nervousness, tremor, progressive weakness, nausea and vomiting, loss of appetite and weight loss, and insomnia.

Therapeutic Uses
Barbiturates are prescribed for sedation, to prevent epileptic seizures, and as treatment for headaches. Phenobarbital in combination with theophylline

was sold in several over-the-counter preparations (Bronkolizer, Bronkotabs, Primatene-P, Tedrigen), but distribution of these drugs was discontinued after a 1995 FDA ruling against over-the-counter sales of theophylline [28].

Illicit Uses
Some illicit users take barbiturates to counteract the stimulant effects of amphetamines and potentiate the effects of heroin. The most commonly abused barbiturates are short- and intermediate-acting agents such as pentobarbital, secobarbital, and amobarbital.

Pharmacology
Barbiturates are rapidly and completely absorbed when taken orally and have a 10- to 60-minute onset of action. Long-acting barbiturates are excreted primarily as the parent drugs. Short- and intermediate-acting barbiturates are more extensively metabolized by the liver. Table 7-3 presents elimination half-lives of several common barbiturates. Ultra-short-acting barbiturates, such as thiopental, may be present in the urine for a day or less. Intermediate-acting barbiturates, such as secobarbital, may be detected for up to four days. Long-acting barbiturates, such as phenobarbital, can be detected for several weeks after chronic use [29]. Barbiturates, except for those with the shortest half-lives, can accumulate in the body with repeated use. Elimination rates increase with repeated use and are faster in younger people than older people.

Laboratory Issues
Immunoassays for barbiturates are generally designed to detect secobarbital but will cross-react with amobarbital, pentobarbital, butalbital, and other barbiturates if they are present. GC/MS analyses are generally targeted at a panel of barbiturates consisting of amobarbital, butalbital, pentobarbital, phenobarbital, secobarbital and, less often, butabarbital. The screening cutoff value is generally higher than the confirmatory cutoff—for example, 300 ng/mL for screening and 200 ng/mL for confirmation.

Interpreting Results
Most individuals who test positive for barbiturates have prescriptions. Like other commonly prescribed medications, use of borrowed barbiturates, especially butalbital, is often detected. If the donor has a prescription, the MRO will report the test as negative. If a safety-sensitive condition (e.g., seizure disorder) has been revealed the MRO may also alert the employer accordingly.

BENZODIAZEPINES

Benzodiazepines are minor tranquilizers and Schedule IV controlled substances. When used alone, benzodiazepines have a wide margin of safety, although they can impair task performance. Benzodiazepine overdoses can cause somnolence, hypotension, convulsions and, in the most severe cases, coma and respiratory depression. Chronic use of benzodiazepines can cause physical tolerance. If use suddenly stops, withdrawal symptoms such as vomiting, sweating, and convulsions may occur.

Table 7-3. Half-Lives of Common Barbiturates ■

Generic Name	Trade Name	Elimination Half-Life (hr)
Amobarbital	Amytal	8–42
Pentobarbital	Nembutal	15–48
Phenobarbital	Donnatal	24–140
Secobarbital	Seconal	19–34

Therapeutic Uses

Benzodiazepines are used as anti-anxiety agents, sedative-hypnotic agents, anticonvulsants, and muscle relaxants. Approximately 35 benzodiazepines are in clinical use in the United States or abroad. Triazolam (Halcion), lorazepam (Ativan), diazepam (Valium), and alprazolam (Xanax) are among the most widely used benzodiazepines. Physicians prescribe them for stress, anxiety-induced depression, panic disorders, sleep disorders, muscle spasms, alcohol withdrawal, and seizures.

Illicit Uses

People who abuse benzodiazepines frequently abuse other drugs as well. For example, addicts may use benzodiazepines to self-medicate opiate drug withdrawal or to manage the adverse effects of cocaine or methamphetamine. The benzodiazepine flunitrazepam (Rohypnol) is legally used only outside the United States and has gained notoriety because it has been used to lace drinks to sedate unsuspecting women for the purpose of obtaining nonconsensual sex.

Pharmacology

Benzodiazepines are usually taken by mouth and less often by injection. Metabolism by the liver produces active and inactive metabolites. The duration of effect is determined by the half-lives of the benzodiazepine and its active metabolites. For example, prazepam is long-acting because its metabolite, desmethyldiazepam, is pharmacologically active and has a half-life of 30–100 hours. Many benzodiazepines share common metabolic intermediates and urinary products. Table 7-4 lists the most commonly used benzodiazepines and their half-lives and major metabolites.

Laboratory Issues

Immunoassays for benzodiazepines are generally directed at nordiazepam, oxazepam, and/or conjugated metabolites of benzodiazepines. GC/MS analyses are usually targeted at a panel of four or five common benzodiazepine drugs and metabolites. These usually include the drugs diazepam and oxazepam and the metabolite nordiazepam. Laboratories will analyze for other benzodi-

Table 7-4. Benzodiazepine Pharmacology ■

Drug (D) or Metabolite (M)	Half-life (hr)	Metabolic Precursors
alprazolam (D) (Xanax)	10–15	
chlordiazepoxide (D) (Librium)	5–30	
clonazepam (D) (Clonopin)	18–50	
clorazepate (D) (Tranxene)	2 as clorazepate, 30–100 as nordiazepam	
demoxepam (M)		chlordiazepoxide
desalkylflurazepam (M)		flurazepam
diazepam (D) (Valium)	30–60 as diazepam, 30–100 as nordiazepam	
estazolam (D) (ProSom)	10–24	
flunitrazepam (D) (Rohypnol)	16–35	
flurazepam (D) (Dalmane)	50–100	
halazepam (D) (Paxipam)	14–16	
lorazepam (D) (Ativan)	10–25	
midazolam (D) (Versed)	1.3–2.5	
nordiazepam (M)	30–100	chlordiazepoxide, clorazepate, diazepam, halazepam, prazepam
oxazepam (D), (M) (Serax)	5–20	chlordiazepoxide, clorazepate, diazepam, halazepam, prazepam, temazepam
prazepam (D) (Centrax, Verstran)	0.6–2.0 as prazepam, 30–100 as nordiazepam	
quazepam (D) (Doral)	39–53	
temazepam (D) (Restoril)	3–13	
triazolam (Halcion)	1.5–5.5	

azepines upon request. The screening cutoff value is typically higher than the confirmatory cutoff. For example, a screening cutoff of 300 ng/mL and a GC/MS cutoff of 200 ng/mL could be used.

GC/MS is the preferred method for confirmation testing. Liquid chromatography is a reliable alternative that requires less sample preparation. Confirmation tests are difficult because there are many benzodiazepines, they share common metabolites, and their concentrations are often low.

Appreciable cross-reactivity occurs among benzodiazepines in screening tests. Oxaprozin (Daypro), a nonsteroidal anti-inflammatory drug, can cause false-positive results on benzodiazepine EIA, FPIA, and CMI immunoassays [30,31]. Some newer benzodiazepines are hard to detect because they are used at low doses, have short half-lives, and occur in urine at low concentrations.

Interpreting Results

Because of the many benzodiazepines and their metabolites, and because these drugs are commonly prescribed, interpretation of benzodiazepine-positive results can be particularly challenging.

Several nonprescription benzodiazepine-containing products are produced abroad. "Black pearls" (also known as Tung Shueh, Cows Head, and Chiufong Toukawan pills) are illegally imported from East Asia and are sold in some health food stores in the United States. Contrary to their labeling, "black pearls" contain diazepam; thus, their use can cause benzodiazepine-positive urine test results [32,33]. Case reports have described benzodiazepine-positive urine results after use of other products, too [34,35].

METHADONE

Methadone (Dolophine) is a Schedule II controlled substance. It is a synthetic opioid and is used clinically to treat severe pain and in maintenance programs for morphine and heroin addicts. Methadone is typically administered orally at daily doses of 30–100 mg. Patients on maintenance doses of methadone become more amenable to counseling, environmental changes, and support services and rarely show subjective intoxication or clinically detectable behavioral impairment. Nevertheless, many patients continue to use heroin and other drugs intermittently and to commit crimes, including the sale of take-home methadone. Guidelines for therapeutic use of methadone were issued by The National Institute on Drug Abuse. These guidelines can be obtained from the Food and Drug Administration, tel. (301)295-8020 [36].

Pharmacology

Methadone has a long half-life (15–72 hours) and slow onset of action and therefore a lower potential for abuse than short half-life, fast-acting opiates. Urine acidification can increase the rate of methadone excretion 5–22 percent [37].

Methadone is not metabolized to, and does not cross-react with commercial immunoassays for, codeine, morphine, or 6-AM. It therefore does not cause positive results in the federal five-drug panel.

Laboratory Issues
The laboratory assays used in workplace testing for methadone are targeted at the parent compound rather than its metabolites. Typical cutoff values are 100 ng/mL or 300 ng/mL for both the immunoassay and confirmation assays.

Interpreting Results
Most people who test positive for methadone are in methadone maintenance programs. If the methadone poses a safety risk at work, the MRO may wish to notify the employer. The Federal Highway Administration (FHWA) has advised medical examiners that an individual is not qualified to drive a commercial vehicle if he or she uses methadone [38].

METHAQUALONE

Methaqualone is a central nervous system depressant. In the 1970s, it became a popular drug of abuse because it was considered an aphrodisiac. In 1983, methaqualone was removed from the market and reclassified as a Schedule I controlled substance. It causes fatigue, dizziness, sluggishness, and paresthesias. High doses can cause delirium, convulsions, and coma.

Pharmacology
The elimination half-life of methaqualone is 10–42 hours. More than 99 percent of the drug is metabolized by the liver. The laboratory assays used in workplace drug testing are targeted at the parent compound rather than its metabolites. The typical cutoff value is 300 ng/mL for both the immunoassay and confirmation assay.

Interpreting Results
Methaqualone is no longer available by prescription in the United States and is difficult to manufacture in clandestine laboratories. It is rarely detected in workplace drug testing programs, and several large forensic drug testing laboratories stopped offering methaqualone tests in the late 1990s. The rare specimen that is methaqualone positive is usually a performance test sample rather than a real donor sample. If a real donor sample is methaqualone positive, after attempting to reach the donor, the MRO should verify the sample as positive.

PROPOXYPHENE

Propoxyphene is a widely used synthetic opioid that is prescribed for the treatment of mild to moderate pain. Its chemical structure is similar to methadone. Propoxyphene is approximately one-half to two-thirds as potent as codeine. It is usually formulated with aspirin or acetaminophen.

Propoxyphene by itself or in conjunction with other drugs, including alcohol, can be toxic and even fatal. Other reported toxic effects include pulmonary edema, cardiotoxicity, hallucinations, and convulsions. Propoxyphene is commonly prescribed and often abused. Because of accessibility, it is thought to be among the drugs more commonly abused by health care workers. Some propoxyphene abusers grind the tablets and inject them.

Pharmacology
The mean half-life of propoxyphene following ingestion is approximately 12 hours. Most laboratories target the parent drug, propoxyphene, rather than its primary metabolite, norpropoxyphene.

Interpreting Results
Most individuals who test positive for propoxyphene have prescriptions. If an individual's propoxyphene use poses a safety risk at work, the MRO should notify the employer.

References ■

1. Autry JH. *Notice to All DHHS/NIDA Certified Laboratories.* Rockville, MD: National Institute on Drug Abuse, December 19, 1990.
2. Autry JH. *Technical Advisory to All DHHS/NIDA Certified Laboratories.* Rockville, MD: National Institute on Drug Abuse, March 11, 1991.
3. Jones RT. The pharmacology of cocaine smoking in humans. In: Chiang CN, Hawks RL (eds), *Research Findings on Smoking of Abused Substances.* NIDA Research Monograph 99. Washington, DC: National Institute on Drug Abuse, 1990. Pp 30–41.
4. ElSohly MA. Urinalysis and casual handling of marijuana and cocaine. *J Anal Toxicol* 1991;15:46.
5. Ambre J. The urinary excretion of cocaine and metabolites in humans: a kinetic analysis of published data. *J Anal Toxicol* 1985;9:241–5.
6. Bralliar BB, Skarf B, Owens JB. Ophthalmic use of cocaine and the urine test for benzoylecognine. *N Engl J Med* 1989;320:1757.
7. Cruz OA, Patrinely JR, Reyna GS, et al. Urine drug screening for cocaine after lacrimal surgery. *Am J Ophthalmol* 1991;111:703–5.
8. Schwartz RH, Altieri M, Bogema S. Topical anesthesia using TAC (tetracaine, adrenalin, and cocaine) produces "dirty urine." *Otolaryngol Head Neck Surg* 1990;102:200–1.
9. Reichman OS, Otto RA. Effect of intranasal cocaine on the urine drug screen for benzoylecognine. *Otolaryngol Head Neck Surg* 1992;106:223.
10. Cone EJ, Kato K, Hillsgrove M. Cocaine excretion in the semen of drug users. *J Anal Toxicol* 1996;20:139–40.
11. Leirer VO, Yesavage JA, Morrow DG. Marijuana carry-over effects on aircraft pilot performance. *Aviat Space Environ Med* 1991;62:221–7.
12. Drug Enforcement Administration, Department of Justice. Schedules of controlled substances: rescheduling of synthetic dronabinol (Marinol) from Schedule II to Schedule III. *Federal Register* 1998;63(Nov. 5):59,751–59,759.
13. Green K. Marijuana smoking vs. cannabinoids for glaucoma therapy. *Arch Ophthalmol* 1998;116:1433–7.
14. Huestis MA, Mitchell JM, Cone EJ. Urinary excretion profiles of 11-nor-9-carboxy-delta-9-tetrahydrocannabinol in humans after single smoked doses of marijuana. *J Anal Toxicol* 1996;20:441–52.
15. Ellis GM, Mann MA, Judson BA, et al. Excretion patterns of cannabinoid metabolites after last use in a group of chronic users. *Clin Pharmacol Ter* 1985;38:572–8.
16. Dakis CA, Potlash ALC, Annito W, et al. Persistence of urinary marijuana levels after supervised abstinence. *Am J Psychiatry* 1982;139:1196–8.
17. Office of National Drug Control Policy. Administration response to Arizona Proposition 200 and California Proposition 215. *Federal Register* 1996;62(Feb. 11):6,164–6,166.
18. Huestis MA, Cone EJ. Differentiating new marijuana use from residual drug excretion in occasional marijuana users. *J Anal Toxicol* 1998;22:445–54.
19. Findlay JW, Butz RF, Welch RM. Codeine kinetics determined by radioimmunoassay. *Clin Pharmacol Ther* 1977;22:439.
20. Cone EJ, Welch P, Mitchell JM, et al. Forensic drug testing for opiates: I. Detection of 6-acetylmorphine in urine as an indicator of recent heroin exposure; drug and assay considerations and detection times. *J Anal Toxicol* 1996;20:541–6.
21. Department of Health and Human Services, Substance Abuse and Mental Health Services Administration. Revisions to the mandatory guidelines. *Federal Register* 1998;63(Nov 13):63483–4.

22. Cone EJ, Welch P, Paul BC, et al. Forensic drug testing for opiates: III. Urinary excretion rates of morphine and codeine following codeine administration. *J Anal Toxicol* 1991;15:161–6.

23. Selavka CM. Poppy seed ingestion as a contributing factor to opiate-positive urinalysis results: the Pacific perspective. *J Forensic Sci* 1991;36:685–96.

24. Fuller DC. A statistical approach to the prediction of verifiable heroin use from total codeine and total morphine concentrations in urine. *J Forensic Sci* 1997;42(4):685–9.

25. Cook CE, Brine DR, Jeffecote AR. Phencyclidine deposition after intravenous and oral doses. *Clin Pharmacol Ther* 1982;31:625–34.

26. Simpson GM, Khajawall AM, Alatorre E, et al. Urinary phencyclidine excretion in chronic abusers. *J Toxicol Clin Toxicol* 1982;19:1051–9.

27. Levine BS, Smith ML. Effects of diphenhydramine on immunoassay of phencyclidine in urine. *Clin Chem* 1990;36:1258.

28. Food and Drug Administration. Cold, cough, allergy, bronchodilator, and antiasthmatic drug products for over-the-counter human use. *Federal Register* 1995;60(July 27):38,635–38,642.

29. Hawks RL, Chiang CN. Examples of specific drug assays. In: Hawks RL, Chiang CN (eds), *Urine Testing for Drugs of Abuse.* (NIDA Research Monograph 73.) Rockville, MD: Department of Health and Human Services, 1986. P 109.

30. Pulini M. False-positive benzodiazepine urine test due to oxaprozin. *JAMA* 1995;273:1905–6.

31. Fraser AD, Howell P. Oxaprozin cross-reactivity in three commercial immunoassays for benzodiazepines in urine. *J Anal Toxicol* 1998;22:50–4.

32. Floren A, Fitter W. Contamination of urine with diazepam and mefenamic acid from an Oriental remedy. *J Occup Med* 1991;33:1168–9.

33. DuPont RL, Bogema SC. Benzodiazepines in a health-catalog product. *JAMA* 1990;264:695.

34. Fedoruk J, Lee L. Positive pre-employment urine drug screen caused by a foreign-manufactured vitamin formulation. *West J Med* 1991;55:663.

35. Ambre JJ, Rahmanian M. Prescription drugs in a mail order diet aid [letter]. *JAMA* 1988;260:925.

36. Section 291.501: Methadone in the maintenance treatment of narcotic addicts. Part 310: New drugs. Recodification of Methadone Regulations. Title 21: Food and Drugs. *Federal Register* 1977;42:46,698–710.

37. Chamberlain RT. *Methadone: In-Service Training and Continuing Education AACC/TDM.* Washington, DC: American Association for Clinical Chemistry, Inc., 1989;10(9):5–17.

38. U.S. Department of Transportation. Federal Highway Administration. *Medical Advisory Criteria for Evaluation under 49 CFR Part 391.41.* Washington, DC. Updated April 8,1998.

Reanalyses and Split Specimen Tests ■

8

In regulated testing, if the specimen result is verified positive, the donor or medical review officer (MRO) can request another analysis. When a single specimen has been collected, the reanalysis is conducted on a new aliquot from that specimen. When split specimens have been collected, the MRO can authorize a reanalysis of Bottle A and the donor can authorize analysis of an aliquot from Bottle B (see Table 8-1.) Split specimens are required by several of the Department of Transportation (DOT) modes (FAA, FHWA, FRA, and FTA) and are optional under the other DOT modes (USCG and RSPA) and under the DHHS and NRC rules.

- The second analysis must be performed at a different laboratory than the one that did the first analysis—preferably one owned by a different parent company. This offers a more independent verification of the first result.
- The laboratory looks only for the drug or metabolite found in the first analysis.
- The laboratory skips the screening assay and conducts only a confirmation assay. (The laboratory may first perform another immunoassay, but only to determine a dilution factor in preparation for the gas chromatography/mass spectrometry [GC/MS] assay.)
- The "cutoff" in the second analysis is the laboratory's limit of detection for that assay. Thus, if the second analysis detects the drug or drug metabolite at any concentration, whether above or below the original cutoff value, the second analysis has reconfirmed the first analysis.

A laboratory's "limit of detection" is the minimum concentration that it can identify with confidence. Limits of detection vary among laboratories and assays and are always much lower than the cutoff values used in regulated testing. The original cutoff values are not used in a reanalysis or split specimen analysis, because the assays have some degree of variance and because drug and metabolite concentrations normally decrease over time, owing to any of the following factors [1,2]:

- Drugs and their metabolites adsorb to the plastic container.
- Drugs and their metabolites degrade during freeze/thaw cycles.
- Bacterial growth causes pH changes.
- Adulterants, if present, can continue to affect the sample while it is stored.

Table 8-1. Reanalyses and Split Specimen Tests ■

	Collection Type	
	Single Specimen	**Split Specimen**
The donor can authorize:	Reanalysis of the single specimen	Analysis of Bottle B
The MRO can authorize:	Reanalysis of the single specimen	Reanalysis of Bottle A

Reanalyses on Behalf of the MRO or Employer ■

The MRO may want the specimen reanalyzed before deciding its outcome if there are concerns about the test's accuracy and validity. The MRO must have a sound basis for each reanalysis request and should not automatically request a reanalysis on every specimen [3]. The employer may want a specimen reanalyzed, for example, if the donor has formally challenged the result, and a second positive result may make the record appear stronger. The employer would notify the MRO, and the MRO authorizes each reanalysis. The donor's consent or request is not needed for a reanalysis on the employer's behalf. The test is not canceled based on insufficient urine volume remaining for a reanalysis on behalf of the MRO or employer.

Reanalyses and Split Specimen Tests on Behalf of the Donor ■

In regulated testing, if the specimen is verified positive, the MRO must tell the donor that he or she has 72 hours to request a reanalysis of the specimen (in single specimen programs) or a test of Bottle B (in split specimen programs). (RSPA, by exception, gives the donor up to 60 days to request a reanalysis of Bottle A if a split specimen collection was not performed.) The MRO reports the first positive result to the employer, who removes the employee from safety-sensitive functions; these actions take place without regard to the split specimen analysis.

The donor may request analysis of Bottle B only for reconfirmation of the detected drugs. He or she is not allowed to have Bottle B analyzed for other drugs or for adulterants or other chemical information. The donor forfeits his or her right to a reanalysis or split specimen analysis if an adulterant has been identified in Bottle A.

If the donor makes a timely request, the MRO arranges for the second analysis by transmitting written instructions to the laboratory. If the donor makes a request that is late but presents the MRO with information documenting a serious illness, injury, or another reason that prevented contact with the MRO, the MRO can accept this explanation and direct a second analysis. If there is any doubt, the MRO should honor the donor's request for a second analysis, because failure to do so can be perceived as tainting the first result. If the donor wants a particular laboratory to do the second analysis, the request should be accommodated, provided that laboratory is DHHS certified. Otherwise, the employer, MRO, or first laboratory (Lab A) can select the other laboratory (Lab B).

The MRO's written instructions to the laboratory should include:

1. MRO's name and address.
2. Names and addresses of Lab A and Lab B.
3. Specimen ID number.
4. Laboratory accession number, that is, the number assigned by Lab A to the specimen when it was received.
5. Request for a confirmatory test for the drug/metabolite reported by Lab A.

Split Specimen Procedures ■

Figure 8-1 depicts the procedure for handling of split specimens. In a split specimen collection, at least 45 mL is collected from a single void and divided by the collector into two portions, at least 30 mL for the primary (Bottle A) specimen and at least 15 mL for the split (Bottle B) specimen. The collector sends both bottles to Lab A as a pair. Lab A analyzes Bottle A. If the Bottle A result is negative, Lab A discards both specimens. If the Bottle A result is positive, Lab A freezes and stores Bottle A for at least 12 months and Bottle B for at least 60 days, or until the MRO requests analysis of Bottle B.

Upon receipt of the MRO's written request for analysis of Bottle B, Lab A sends the following items to Lab B:

1. A copy of the MRO's written request with the specimen ID number and the drug/metabolite to be reconfirmed.
2. Bottle B, with its seal intact.
3. Copy 3 of the custody and control form (CCF).

Lab B records receipt of the split specimen on the internal chain-of-custody form that Lab A sent with the split specimen. Lab B makes a copy of copy 3 of the CCF. (This copy is referred to as the "second original" of copy 3.) Lab B performs the GC/MS analysis for the drug/metabolite requested, testing to the limit of detection. The certifying scientist then completes and signs the "Results" section on both the original copy 3 of the CCF and the "second original" of copy 3. Lab B sends the signed "second original" of copy 3 and certified copies of any extensions or additional chain-of-custody forms to the requesting MRO. In regulated testing, Bottle B's result must be handled by the same MRO who handled Bottle A's result. Lab B reports the result to the MRO and saves Bottle B for at least 12 months.

The MRO files the Bottle B result with the test record and notifies the employer and the donor of the outcome:

■ Reconfirmed (with identification of the specific drug/drug metabolite).
■ Failed to reconfirm—Both tests canceled.
■ Failed to reconfirm—Adulterated, *or* failed to reconfirm—Substituted.
■ Test not performed—Both tests canceled.

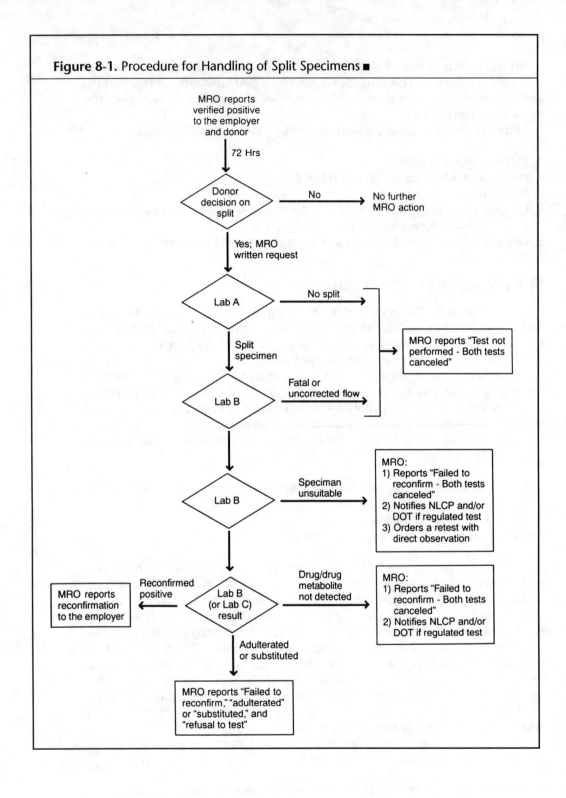

Figure 8-1. Procedure for Handling of Split Specimens ■

MRO reports
verified positive
to the employer
and donor

72 Hrs

Donor
decision on
split

No → No further MRO action

Yes; MRO
written request

Lab A — No split

Split
specimen

Lab B — Fatal or uncorrected flow

MRO reports "Test not performed - Both tests canceled"

Lab B — Speciman unsuitable

MRO:
1) Reports "Failed to reconfirm - Both tests canceled"
2) Notifies NLCP and/or DOT if regulated test
3) Orders a retest with direct observation

Reconfirmed positive ← Lab B (or Lab C) result → Drug/drug metabolite not detected

MRO reports reconfirmation to the employer

MRO:
1) Reports "Failed to reconfirm - Both tests canceled"
2) Notifies NLCP and/or DOT if regulated test

Adulterated or substituted

MRO reports "Failed to reconfirm," "adulterated" or "substituted," and "refusal to test"

The MRO can use Step 8 on copy 3 of the CCF (see Figure 8-2) or a separate form to report the outcome of the split analysis to the employer and the donor.

RECONFIRMED

The "Reconfirmed" and the specific drug/drug metabolite boxes are checked in Step 7 on copy 3 of the CCF when the laboratory confirms the presence of the drug/drug metabolite that was reported positive in Bottle A. The MRO checks the "Reconfirmed" box in Step 8 and indicates the specific drug/drug metabolite(s) detected on the "Remarks" line.

FAILED TO RECONFIRM—DRUG/DRUG METABOLITE NOT DETECTED

The laboratory checks the "Failed to reconfirm" box in Step 7 and prints "Drug/ drug metabolite not detected" on the "Remarks" line if the Bottle B result does not confirm the Bottle A result and no adulterant has been identified. The MRO checks the "Failed to reconfirm—Both tests canceled" box in Step 8 and reports to the employer that both tests must be canceled. Any personnel action the employer may have taken based on the Bottle A result is reversed. In regulated testing, the MRO must also notify the appropriate federal agency— DOT, DHHS, and so on—of each failure to reconfirm. The MRO notifies the National Laboratory Certification Program (a DHHS agency) and, if it is a DOT-mandated test, notifies DOT of the failure to reconfirm. Figure 8-3 is a sample form for reporting split-specimen cancellations to DOT.

Figure 8-2. Laboratory and MRO Blocks for Split Specimens ■

STEP 7: TO BE COMPLETED BY THE LABORATORY - Specimen Bottle Seal(s) Intact: ☐ YES ☐ NO, Explain in Remarks Below.

THE RESULTS FOR THE ABOVE IDENTIFIED SPECIMEN ARE IN ACCORDANCE WITH THE APPLICABLE PROCEDURES ESTABLISHED BY THE HHS MANDATORY GUIDELINES FOR FEDERAL WORKPLACE DRUG TESTING PROGRAMS

☐ RECONFIRMED for the following: ☐ CANNABINOIDS as Carboxy—THC   ☐ COCAINE METABOLITES as Benzoylecognine   ☐ PHENCYCLIDINE
☐ FAILED TO RECONFIRM   ☐ OPIATES: ☐ AMPHETAMINES:
☐ TEST NOT PERFORMED   ☐ codeine   ☐ amphetamine   ☐ OTHER _____
   ☐ morphine   ☐ methamphetamine

REMARKS _____

TEST LAB (if different from above) _____
NAME   ADDRESS   (   ) PHONE NO.

I certify that the specimen identified by the laboratory accession number on this form is the same specimen that bears the specimen identification number set forth above, that the specimen has been examined upon receipt, handled and analyzed in accordance with applicable Federal requirements, and that the results set forth are for that specimen.

_____ _____ / /
(PRINT) Certifying Scientist's Name (First, MI, Last)   Signature of Certifying Scientist   Date (Mo./Day/Yr.)

STEP 8: TO BE COMPLETED BY THE MEDICAL REVIEW OFFICER

I have reviewed the laboratory results for the specimen identified by this form in accordance with applicable Federal requirements. My determination/verification is:

☐ Reconfirmed   ☐ Failed to reconfirm -   ☐ Test not performed
   Both tests cancelled   Both tests cancelled   REMARKS _____

_____ _____ / /
(PRINT) Medical Review Officer's Name (First, MI, Last)   Signature of Medical Review Officer   Date (Mo./Day/Yr.)

Figure 8-3. MRO's Split Specimen Cancellation Report to DOT ■

Medical Review Officer (MRO)

Name:_____

Address:_____

_____

_____

_____

Specimen ID Number: _____

Lab Accession No.:_____

- - - - - - - - - - - - - - -

Laboratory for Primary (A) Specimen

Lab Name:_____

Address:_____

_____

_____

Telephone No.:_____

- - - - - - - - - - - - -

MRO Telephone No. _____

Fax No.: _____

Collection Site Name: _____

_____

_____

_____

Telephone No.:_____

Laboratory for Split (B) Specimen

Date Specimen Recd:_____

Lab Accession No.:_____

Lab Name:_____

Address:_____

_____

_____

Telephone No.:_____

Reason for Report

❏ Split failed to confirm for drug/metabolite _____ (Name of drug)

❏ Split was unavailable _____ (Explain in comments)

❏ Split did not contain adequate volume _____

❏ Split was untestable _____

❏ Other _____ (Explain in comments)

Note: Report is required only for those tests where donor requested test of the split.

Comments:_____

_____

Name and Telephone No. of Individual Submitting Report (if not MRO):_____

_____

Note: Please type or print information. This form is optional, provided all of the above information is submitted.

```
To:  U.S. DOT
Fax: (202) 366-3897
Initials:_____
```

FAILED TO RECONFIRM—SPECIMEN ADULTERATED/SUBSTITUTED

The laboratory checks the "Failed to reconfirm" box in Step 7 and prints one of the following comments on the "Remarks" line if the specimen has been determined to be adulterated or substituted:

- "Specimen adulterated: Nitrite is too high."
- "Specimen adulterated: pH is too high (or too low)."
- "Specimen adulterated: Presence of _____ (specify) detected."
- "Specimen substituted: Not consistent with normal human urine."

The MRO checks the "Failed to reconfirm" box, strikes out the accompanying phrase "Both tests canceled," replacing it with the entry "Adulterated" or "Substituted," and then enters "Refusal to test" on the "Remarks" line in Step 8. The MRO reports to the employer and the donor that the specimen was adulterated or substituted, either of which constitutes a refusal to test. Therefore, "refusal to test" becomes the final, single result for both tests.

A failure to reconfirm can occur if the specimen has been adulterated. When faced with a failure to reconfirm, Laboratory B must analyze the Bottle B specimen for pH and nitrites and may also analyze it for glutaraldehyde, surfactants, bleach, or other adulterants [4]. If the Bottle B specimen meets adulteration or substitution criteria (see Chapter 4), then Lab B reports the outcome as "Failed to reconfirm" and includes the remark "Specimen adulterated" or "Specimen substituted" with a further explanation on the "Remarks" line of the CCF. If Lab B does not have the capability to perform the desired adulteration test(s), the lab may, after receiving approval from the MRO, send an aliquot from the specimen to another DHHS certified laboratory (Lab C) that has that capability.

A failure to reconfirm may also occur if Lab B uses different GC/MS analytical procedures or GC/MS instruments than were used at Lab A. If Lab B thinks the drug/drug metabolite is present in the urine, but the confirmatory test results fail to satisfy the criteria established by Lab B to report a positive test result, Lab B may decide to continue testing the split specimen in an attempt to get a valid confirmatory test result. If it appears that Lab B may possibly use the entire split specimen in an attempt to get a valid confirmatory test result, Lab B must contact the MRO and explain the problem. Lab B and the MRO must decide if the remaining amount of the split specimen should be sent to another lab (Lab C) for the confirmatory test. If the decision is made to use another lab, Lab B sends the split specimen, using chain-of-custody procedures, to Lab C without reporting a result to the MRO.

TEST NOT PERFORMED—BOTH TESTS CANCELED

The laboratory checks the "Test not performed—Both tests canceled" box in Step 7 if the test for the drug/drug metabolite could not be completed successfully. The laboratory will print, on the "Remarks" line, one of the following explanations for the failure:

- "Fatal flaw, _____ (with the flaw stated)."
- "Uncorrected flaw, _____ (with the flaw stated)."

- "Specimen unsuitable: Cannot obtain valid confirmatory test result."
- "Insufficient specimen volume to complete testing."

When the laboratory reports a split specimen as "Test not performed," the MRO checks the "Test not performed—Both tests canceled" box in Step 8 of the CCF and provides the reason for the test not being performed on the "Remarks" line. The MRO reports to the employer and the donor that both tests must be canceled and the reason for the cancellation. In an effort to resolve the discrepancy created by a positive Bottle A and the inability to test Bottle B, the MRO must order an immediate collection of another specimen from the donor under direct observation. The MRO must inform the employer that no advanced notice should be given to the employee of the collection requirement, until immediately before the collection. In regulated testing, the MRO notifies the appropriate federal agency of the test not performed (see Figure 8-3).

Procedure for Missing Split Specimen ■

In DOT-mandated split specimen testing, if the donor requests analysis of the split specimen and no suitable split specimen is available, the MRO cancels the test, files a report with DOT, and orders an immediate collection of another specimen from the donor. (By contrast, under the DHHS rules, the donor is considered to have forfeited the right to a split analysis if he or she submits less than 45 mL, and thus the test is not canceled if no split has been collected.) In DOT-mandated testing, the laboratory is prohibited from informing the MRO that a suitable split specimen is unavailable until the MRO requests in writing that the split specimen be tested. If a split collection should have been performed but the collector indicated—for example, on the CCF— that only a single specimen was collected, the MRO should proceed with the review and cancel it only if the donor makes a proper request for analysis of his or her split specimen [4]. If the positive test is canceled because of the absence of a split specimen, the donor is required to undergo another split specimen collection procedure.

Payment for Reanalyses and Split Specimen Analyses ■

Federal policymakers feel no donor should be denied the right to a reanalysis or split specimen analysis because of cost. DOT takes the position that the costs of its programs and procedures are the employer's responsibility. "If the employee chooses not to pay 'up front' for the test of the split specimen, the employer must ensure, nevertheless, that the test takes place [5]."

MROs who manage laboratory contracts and pay laboratory fees are at financial risk if the employer, despite DOT's position, is unwilling to pay for the split analysis requested by the donor. The MRO should not delay the processing of the reanalysis or split specimen analysis while awaiting prepayment or assurance of payment from the donor or employer. Instead, the MRO should seek an agreement with the employer in which the employer accepts responsibility for costs associated with split analyses. In regulated testing, the donor should not pay the laboratory directly if doing so would divulge his or her identity.

References ■

1. Dugan S, Bogema S, Schwartz RW, et al. Stability of drugs of abuse in urine samples stored at -20° C. *J Anal Toxicol* 1994;18:391–6.
2. Levine B, Smith ML. Stability of drugs of abuse in biological specimens. *Forensic Sci Rev* 1990;2:147–56.
3. Vogl WF, Bush DM. *Medical Review Officer Manual for Federal Workplace Drug Testing Programs.* Rockville, MD: Substance Abuse and Mental Health Services Administration, 1997.
4. Stephenson RL. *Testing Split (Bottle B) Specimens for Adulterant.* Rockville, MD: Substance Abuse and Mental Health Administration, March 9, 1998.
5. Ashby RC. *Split Specimen Cancellation Report.* Washington, DC: U.S. Department of Transportation, October 11, 1994.
6. U.S. Department of Transportation. Procedures for transportation workplace drug and alcohol testing programs: insufficient specimens and other issues; final rule. *Federal Register* 1996;61(July 19):37,698.

Reporting, Record Keeping, and Data Management ■

9

Reporting Results

Medical review officers (MROs) and breath alcohol technicians (BATs) must send final individual test results directly to the employer as soon as the results are available. While results may be maintained by a consortium or third-party administrator (C/TPA), according to federal guidance, it is not appropriate for the MRO or BAT to send the results only to the C/TPA for subsequent transmittal to the employer.

Employers expect MROs to report drug test results as soon as they are reportable, especially for results that the MRO has verified as positive. The reports may be made by phone calls, thereby allowing the employer to initiate hiring or removal of workers, but the MRO should subsequently deliver hardcopy reports. MROs should report drug test results in writing because oral reports can be misunderstood and written reports are an enduring record, which can be important for medicolegal reasons. Reports can be transmitted by teleprinter, fax, and encrypted e-mail. Under Department of Health and Human Services (DHHS) [Section 2.6(h)] and Federal Highway Administration (FHWA) [§382.407] rules, the MRO must provide the employer with a signed report of his or her determination. FHWA requires that the MRO send a signed report to the employer within three days of completing the review and that each report include:

1. A statement that the test was performed according to 49 CFR, Parts 40 and 382.
2. The donor's name.
3. The kind of test (e.g., random, post-accident).
4. The collection date.
5. Identification of the collection site (i.e., clinic name and city).
6. Identification of the laboratory (i.e., laboratory name and city).
7. The MRO's name.
8. The test result and, if positive, the name of the drug.

Some MROs also put social security numbers on the reports because they are unique identifiers and are featured prominently in the drug testing proce-

Figure 9-1. Urine Drug Test Report ■

Donor's Name:_____, SSN: _____-_____-_____

Employer's Name: _____

Reason for Test: ❏ Preemployment   ❏ Random   ❏ Post-accident
❏ Return-to-duty ❏ Periodic   ❏ Reasonable   ❏ Other: _____
                                        suspicion   _____

Test Type: ❏ DOT (5-drug),   ❏ Non-DOT 5-drug   ❏ Non-DOT 10-drug
                   test performed   ❏ Other: _____
                   per 49 CFR §40

Collection Date: _____
                      Month   Day   Year

Collection Site: _____
                      Name   Location

Laboratory: _____
                      Name   Location

Test Result: ❏ Negative   ❏ Positive for:
                                           ❏ amphetamines
                                           ❏ cocaine
                                           ❏ marijuana
                                           ❏ opiates
                                           ❏ phencyclidine
                                           ❏ other: _____

❏ Test not performed (check one of the following):

–refusal to test: ❏ specimen substituted *or* ❏ specimen adulterated
                  or ❏ donor did not submit a specimen
                         (donor forfeits right to analysis of Bottle B or reanalysis of primary specimen)
–canceled: ❏ fatal or uncorrected flaw (describe: _____)
                  or ❏ specimen unsuitable with explanation
                         (no further action required unless a negative result is required)
                  or ❏ specimen unsuitable without explanation
                         (retest donor immediately under direct observation)

MRO's Name (print): _____ | To: _____
                                         |
MRO's Signature: _____ | Secure Fax#: _____
                                         |
Report Date: _____ | Initials: _____ Date:__/__/__

If this transmission is incomplete or illegible, please call us at (800)676-3784. This
communication is of a confidential nature. If it has been missdirected to you, or if this fax
machine is not in a secure access area, please call us immediately.

dures. Figure 9-1 presents a report form that is modeled after FHWA's reporting requirements. While one can put results from several tests on a single page, most employers find it more manageable to have separate reports for separate tests.

Step 8 of the federal custody and control (CCF) is a block in which the MRO can record the test's outcome. It is essential to record the outcome somewhere; however, the federal rules do not require completion of Step 8. The MRO can report the result to the employer by sending a photocopy of copy 4 of the CCF (assuming that the information on copy 4 is legible) with Step 8 filled out. The MRO should *not* send copies 1, 2, or 3 to the employer: These copies have the laboratory result, and sending them to the employer will reveal results that are confirmed positive but are MRO negative. Many MROs use a separate form—not the CCF—to report test results.

The MRO's report may include relevant comments provided by the donor, collector and/or laboratory as well as other information, such as documentation of attempts to contact the donor about a positive result or a statement of the donor's refusal to cooperate with the medical review process. Such additional information should not, however, reveal specific confidential medical information unless that information affects public safety or may make the donor medically unqualified for his or her position, or the donor has properly authorized release of that additional information.

If the donor has had both nonobserved and observed specimens collected at the same visit, either because of a cold or hot specimen or a documented attempt to adulterate a specimen, the MRO should inform the employer accordingly when reporting the result that is received first. Otherwise, if the first result is negative, the employer may hire an applicant without realizing that a second result, which could be positive, is pending.

In regulated testing, each negative test report must have either the MRO's original signature, or the MRO's signature stamp, and the initials of the MRO's staff person who reviewed the CCF. Each positive test report must have the MRO's original signature either on the CCF or the test report form.

Most MROs identify, on their reports, the drugs that have been verified positive. This is required in DOT testing and is common practice in non-DOT testing. Most employers want to know the drug(s) detected and, in DOT testing, need these data for preparation of annual statistical reports. Some MROs have been reluctant to identify the drugs because of confidentiality concerns. Nevertheless, employers legally have access to this information. In regulated testing, drug concentration data can be reported to the employer only if the donor has initiated an administrative or legal procedure concerning his or her test result.

Data Management Software ■

Drug-test software users can be grouped as follows:

- Internal (employer-based) program administrators.
- Small- to medium-size TPAs.
- Large TPAs who manage many programs, especially those with multiple sites.

The following text describes software capabilities in relation to the needs of each user group:

- *Internal program administrators.* Most commercially available software packages have been designed to meet the needs of internal (employer-based) program administrators. The packages generally provide modules for random sampling, test-result tracking, and audit reporting and tracking. Some can also produce reports of individual results.
- *Small- to medium-size TPAs.* Most drug-testing software packages support the administrative tasks that small- to medium-size MROs and consortia provide for employers. TPAs usually need software with robust reporting and invoicing capabilities. Summary reporting capabilities—for example, the ability to create management information system (MIS) reports according to DOT requirements—are also important.
- *Large TPAs.* Many off-the-shelf programs are inadequate for the needs of large TPAs. For example, many of these programs have limited options for formatting and transmission of drug test reports. Given these limitations, the largest administrators have custom-designed software systems with automated reporting, communications, and auditing features. Custom-designed systems require development and support staff for troubleshooting, modifications, and other maintenance.

Computer software can significantly reduce the staff size needed for reporting, reduce error rates, and streamline summary reporting. Custom-designed software typically includes automated fax, automated voice reporting, and electronic (computer-to-computer) reporting options.

- *Automated fax reporting.* The software can be set up to automatically generate and fax reports of a laboratory's negative results as soon as they are received. (*Note:* DOT requires an administrative review of the custody and control form at the MRO's office before negative results are reported.) Positive results reported by a laboratory are transmitted only after review by the MRO and, if appropriate, reclassification as "negative." Each test record must be matched to a reporting designate and fax number. The software sends reports by way of fax modem to these reporting designates. Automated fax reporting presents two particular challenges: (1) The user must maintain a complete and current list of reporting designates and fax numbers, and (2) the recipients should have secure (confidential) fax machines.
- *Automated voice reporting.* This method involves providing an automated voice system that verifies client identification (e.g., through use of a password) and reports data on cases entered into the system. After receiving the voice message, the client typically can request an automated fax report. Automated voice reporting has the advantage of confidentiality. Among its drawbacks, the client must initiate an inquiry into the system to determine if test results are available.
- *Electronic reporting.* The MRO or TPA can send test data to a client's printer or computer, can send a data file to an electronic mailbox for downloading by the client, or can e-mail results directly to the client. These technologies are useful only for clients who can receive electronic data, and require considerable technical support, as there are many pitfalls in establishing and then maintaining connections. Messages should be encrypted to help ensure confidentiality. Mes-

sages can be misdirected; thus, the sender needs a process that reliably ensures the accuracy of addresses. Electronic data can be altered without a trace; the sender and recipient should maintain data in a system that has audit capabilities. Electronic reporting offers the advantages of immediacy and direct transfer of data into the recipient's database systems.

Releasing Records ■

TO THE DONOR

If the donor wants his or her result sent elsewhere, the MRO should ask for the donor's authorization. The authorization must be a written, signed informed consent stating that the donor fully understands the intended use and disclosure of the test results. Specific items include the purpose of the release, specific test(s) to be released, and the party or parties to whom these data may be released. If the donor wants a copy of a positive drug test result, it is good practice for the MRO to inform the employer because the employer may have a procedure that employees should follow to obtain records and because each request represents a potential challenge.

TO A THIRD PARTY

The employer may release test records to a third party—for example, a DOT agency or other federal safety agency or an insurer, attorney, arbitrator, or judge—in the event of a lawsuit, unemployment or workers' compensation proceedings, grievance action, or other situation where the donor is seeking a benefit or challenging an action taken by an employer as a result of a drug test. The MRO should release only the test result report, copy of the CCF and, if the donor has brought action on the test result, quantitative levels. Interview notes, checklists, and other confidential information obtained by the MRO from the donor or medical practitioners should not be released unless demanded by court order.

If the donor is self-employed, the MRO sends the report to the donor and no one else. Exceptions are made under FAA and U.S. Coast Guard (USCG) rules. Under FAA rules, MROs also inform the Federal Air Surgeon (FAA/Drug Abatement Division [AAM-800]; 400 7th Street SW, Washington, DC 20590) of any person who holds a Part 67 airman medical certificate (e.g., a pilot) and who has a verified positive test result. Under USCG rules, marine employers must report positive tests to the Coast Guard for each person holding a Coast Guard license, Certificate of Registry, or Merchant Marine Document. MROs and TPAs often provide this reporting function on behalf of employers.

If a parent requests the drug test result of his or her child, and the child is a minor, the MRO should provide the result only with the minor's consent or if directed by a court of law.

Driver History Rule ■

Under FHWA rules, the employer must try to obtain information maintained over the preceding two-year period by the driver's previous employers concerning any violations of FHWA drug/alcohol rules prior to allowing that individual to perform a safety-sensitive function. This information comes from previous employers identified by the applicant and requires that the applicant provide written releases for the information. Employers should realize that applicants with unfavorable histories may provide incomplete employment histories.

Record Storage ■

The Substance Abuse and Mental Health Services Administration (SAMHSA) advises MROs to maintain records of federal agency drug tests for at least two years from the date of collection or as otherwise provided by law or contract with the employer [1]. Certified laboratories also retain drug testing records for two years. DOT-regulated employers must maintain records of positive results for at least five years and records of negative results for at least one year. MROs also are well advised to store records of positive results for five or more years, because challenges usually surface during this period.

Workplace drug testing records should be maintained separately from medical records. This helps preserve the distinction between drug tests and medical records. Also, by keeping them separately from medical records, the drug test records will not be inadvertently included when sending out copies of medical records. Also, keeping drug test records separate makes it easier to assemble them for copying, delivery, and statistical reporting. MROs without high volumes of tests may find it easiest to store the records chronologically— for example, in hanging files, clipped in folders (by month), or stacked in boxes. Some MROs with high volumes of tests use microfilm or electronic imaging techniques to reduce space requirements.

References ■

1. Vogl WF, Bush DM. *Medical Review Officer Manual for Federal Workplace Drug Testing Programs.* DHHS Publication No. (SMA) 97-3164. Rockville, MD: Department of Health and Human Services, 1997. P 62.

Alternative Drug Testing Technologies ■

10

Drug testing is an evolving technology. Existing methods are often improved and new methods emerge. While urinalysis is the state-of-the-art method for drug testing, it has some fundamental limitations, such as brief detection times and susceptibility to water loading and adulteration techniques. There are several alternative drug testing methodologies that are promising and significant adjuncts to laboratory-based urinalyses. Table 10-1 compares features of several of these methodologies.

On-Site Urine Tests ■

On-site urine tests, also known as point of care tests or quick tests, should be used only for screening. Specimens that screen positive should be sent to a laboratory for confirmation testing by GC or GC/MS. On-site assays can be less expensive and provide negative results more quickly than laboratory-based testing. Their disadvantages include increased demands on collection-site personnel, unacceptability for use in regulated testing, and the possibility that employers will act on unconfirmed positive test results. Collection sites should avoid identifying presumptive positive results, because employers may treat these as positives and fire or not hire the person. Employers should take no disciplinary action based on presumptive positive results, because some will fail to be confirmed as positive. Nevertheless, an employer faced with a presumptive positive result may want the employee removed from safety-sensitive tasks. If the employer removes the worker, this should be considered an administrative, not a disciplinary, action. Confidentiality is important but difficult to maintain in this situation.

More than a dozen products are commercially available for on-site urine drug testing. Each is self-contained, disposable, compact (about the size of a credit card), and uses an immunoassay that provides results in 2–10 minutes. Some devices identify one drug or metabolite; others identify several. In most devices, each assay result appears as a color or pattern change. Typically, a colored line appears for positives and no line appears for negatives, requiring some interpretation by the operator, especially if the change is borderline. In contrast, the large analytic instruments used by certified laboratories for

Table 10-1. Comparison of Drug Testing Methodologies ■

Method	Current Uses	Drugs Tested	Collection Methodology	Analytical Methodology
Urine-laboratory based	■ Used extensively in workplace drug testing programs and in treatment and correction programs	■ Regulated: marijuana, cocaine, amphetamines (amphetamine and meth-amphetamine), opiates (codeine and morphine), and phencyclidine ■ NRC and military may include other drugs, (barbiturates, benzodiazepines, LSD) ■ Nonregulated: barbiturates, benzodiazepines, LSD, methadone, methaqualone, propoxyphene	■ Nonobserved collection is common with provisions to limit substitution or adulteration ■ Custody-and-control forms document process ■ Split specimens are often obtained	■ Regulated testing requires immunoassay screening followed by G/MS confirmation at certified labs ■ Nonregulated tests may use other methodologies ■ Confirmation may not be included ■ Adulteration testing possible
Urine, on-site	■ Limited use in workplace programs ■ Treatment and correction programs	■ Single- and multiple-drug kits available ■ One commercial kit also tests for tricyclics ■ LSD, methaqualone tests unavailable	■ Similar to laboratory-based collection ■ Results are readily available to collector ■ Roche TesTcup uses collection device for testing ■ Split specimens are uncommon	■ Uses immunoassays and is not directly confirmed ■ Built-in controls may only monitor part of the testing process ■ Minimum space required ■ Some temperature dependent processes ■ Adulteration testing difficult
Hair	■ Used in the gaming industry for preemployment testing ■ Used in death investigations when other specimens are not available ■ Used in forensic investigations	■ Common drugs of abuse detected including heroin and 6-acetylmorphine ■ Can also be used to detect cocaethylene, which can occur after combined use of cocaine and alcohol	■ Cutting locks of hair near the scalp surface at the vertex of the head; root and tip of the hair lock are identified ■ Pubic, axillary, and arm hair also used	■ The parent drug is often present ■ Few laboratories perform hair analyses ■ Specifically adapted immunoassays for screening and G/MS for confirmation ■ Tandem MS-MS is required to increase sensitivity for marijuana testing
Blood	■ Postmortem death investigation ■ Driving under the influence of drugs ■ Post-accident investigation (e.g., NTSB, FRA) ■ Clinical, diagnostic, drug overdose purposes	■ Hundreds of drugs have been tested ■ Not generally available due to the complexity of testing ■ THC testing is particularly difficult	■ Venipuncture must be performed by trained medical personnel ■ Concern regarding the transmission of bloodborne diseases	■ Requires extensive sample preparation ■ Large database of methods, procedures, and experiences available ■ No specifically approved procedures exist ■ No standard methodology except for therapeutic drug monitoring
Sweat	■ Criminal justice system for monitoring parolees and prisoners ■ Interest in use by the treatment community	■ Drugs identified include cocaine, morphine, 6-acetylmorphine, codeine, amphetamine, methamphetamine, tetrahydrocannabinol, phencyclidine, methadone, alcohol, and nicotine	■ The "sweat patch" consists of an adhesive layer on a thin transparent film of surgical dressing to which an absorbent cellulose pad is attached ■ Worn for several days to several weeks ■ Placed in protective container and shipped to laboratory for analysis	■ Research limited until recently because of the difficulty in collection ■ Specific, immunoassay methods to detect the five DHHS drug classes ■ Confirmation is performed by G/MS ■ Parent drug detected
Saliva	■ No widespread use ■ Limited use by private sector for insurance evaluations	■ Alcohol, amphetamines, barbiturates, benzodiazepines (or their metabolites), cocaine, marijuana, heroin and other opiates, and phencyclidine	■ Commercial devices are available for collection (e.g., Salivette, Orasure, Epitope)	■ Parent drugs are frequently present ■ Immunoassay methods must be targeted toward parent drugs ■ Conventional confirmation procedures can be used (i.e., G/MS) at lower cutoff concentrations

Source: Caplan YH, Cone EJ. *Drug testing Advisory Board.* Rockville, MD: Substance Abuse and Mental Health Services Administration, April 1997.

Accuracy	Scientific Acceptability	Litigation Risk	Cost
■ Regulated testing essentially 100% accurate for positive results ■ Nonregulated testing may be equally accurate ■ Procedures using screening without confirmation are subject to false-positive results ■ Extensive performance-testing programs are available	■ Vast body of scientific literature addressing all aspects of urine testing ■ Properly conducted and evaluated urine tests are accepted and effectively utilized ■ Numerous court cases have upheld urine test results	■ Minimal if procedures are followed	■ $15–$25 for large clients and $25–$70 for small clients ■ Screening only performed at less than $10 ■ Confirmations $50–$100
■ Adequate procedures are not developed to ensure reliability ■ Determination of end-point is subjective in nature and subject to inter-individual differences ■ Kits vary as to detection end-points ■ Color-blindness and visual acuity are issues ■ Cutoff concentrations are not always accurate	■ Not generally used for forensic purposes ■ Not supported by court experience ■ Limited body of scientific literature	■ Higher than laboratory testing, unless tests confirmed	■ $2–$4 per analyte ■ Multiple analyte kits $15–$25 ■ Confirmations $50–$100
■ No performance-testing programs exist ■ Variation of analytical results because of nonuniform matrix ■ False-negative and false-positive results reported in National Institute of Standards Technology survey	■ Controversial aspects of hair testing remain unresolved ■ Possibility of drug entry from sweat and from the environment are issues ■ Interpretation of dose and time relationships not established ■ Possibility of ethnic bias related to melanin content ■ Feasibility of hair testing for marijuana use uncertain	■ High to moderate (depending on drug)	■ Screening and confirmation for the five DHHS drug classes $50–$100
■ Limited performance-testing programs exist ■ Most laboratories performing analyses are not accredited by SAMHSA	■ Scientific consensus available due to extensive literature base ■ Results have routinely been accepted by courts for criminal and civil litigation purposes	■ Minimal, if defined procedures are followed	■ Depending on the type and number of analyses, $50–$200
■ No performance-testing programs	■ Sweat patch methodology approved by FDA ■ Limited scientific evaluation	■ High; little judicial precedent	■ Sweat patch ($7), screening ($15), confirmation ($22)
■ No performance-testing programs	■ Numerous publications regarding testing ■ Mostly limited to specific instances involving forensic investigations	■ High; no judicial precedent	■ Similar to blood testing

screening give digital results and are not subject to operator variability in interpretation.

The requirements of the Clinical Laboratory Improvement Amendment of 1988 do not apply to on-site drug testing, except when the testing is part of a treatment program [42 CFR §493.3(b)(1)]. In on-site testing, two specimens should be processed using chain-of-custody procedures like those used for split specimens. (The Roche TesTcup is an exception; the cup is used to collect a single specimen that undergoes the on-site test and, if needed, the laboratory-based confirmation assay.) If the first specimen screens positive with the quick test, the other specimen is sent to a laboratory with a note on the chain-of-custody form, "Positive for [*drug name*], confirm only." If the specimen screens negative, both specimens may be discarded and the result is reported as negative. If the specimen is unsuitable for the quick test—for example, the indicator strips do not appear to work—it should be sent to a laboratory for screening and, if needed, adulteration testing. Some specimens that screen negative—approximately, 10 percent—should also be sent to the laboratory to monitor for false-negative results as a quality assurance measure.

The Nuclear Regulatory Commission (NRC) allows on-site testing for its programs. The Department of Transportation (DOT) and the Department of Health and Human Services (DHHS) do not. Among states that regulate on-site testing, some (Arkansas, Connecticut, Idaho, North Carolina, Oregon, Rhode Island, and Washington) allow it if positives are sent to a laboratory or confirmation testing, and some (Alaska, Arizona, Florida, Georgia, Hawaii, Iowa, Kansas, Louisiana, Maine, Maryland, Minnesota, Missouri, Oklahoma, and Vermont) limit or prohibit the use of on-site testing.

Products for on-site testing capture a small part of the workplace drug-test market. Some construction firms and offshore oil drillers use them because of requirements to put large numbers of people to work immediately. Fueled by increasing use in criminal justice and emergency room settings, manufacturers have continued to improve and sell more of these products. Manufacturers try to balance the sensitivity and specificity of the assays. Generally, if sensitivity is increased, specificity is decreased. The more sensitive the assay, the fewer false negatives; the less specific the assay, the more presumptive positives that fail to confirm.

Sweat Tests ■

PharmChem Laboratories of Menlo Park, California, markets the PharmChek patch, a device that collects sweat specimens for amphetamines, cocaine, phencyclidine (PCP), opiates, and tetrahydrocannabinol (THC) testing. The patch is a waterproof adhesive pad about the size of a playing card. A unique number is printed on the patch for use in chain of custody. After cleaning the skin with an isopropyl alcohol wipe, the patch is applied and worn like a bandage for approximately one week. If applied correctly, the patch is tamper evident—that is, one can tell if it has been removed. After the patch is worn, it is removed and sent to the laboratory, where about 2 mL of sample is extracted and tested for the presence of drugs and drug metabolites.

Sweat samples yield higher proportions of parent drug(s)—cocaine, heroin, marijuana, etc.—than corresponding urine samples. Because sweat tests detect drug use just before and during the period that the collection device is worn, they are potentially useful for monitoring workers' use of illicit drugs, for example, in return-to-work situations. Some courts use sweat tests to monitor persons on probation or parole.

Sweat tests provide a cumulative measure of drug use and therefore may provide a convenient means of assessing the amount of drug use by an individual. Establishing appropriate cutoff levels for sweat patch testing remains a significant issue. Also, individual variations in perspiration amounts make collection of adequate sweat volume a problem with some subjects. Sweat patches are subject to external contamination if the skin is not appropriately cleaned or if a hand that has touched drugs touches the patch.

Saliva Tests ■

Marijuana, cocaine, phencyclidine, opiates, barbiturates, amphetamines, and benzodiazepines (or their metabolites) have been detected in saliva by various analytical methods including immunoassay, GC/MS, and TLC. Saliva collection is less invasive than urine or blood collection and can be performed by nonmedical personnel in settings not suitable for blood or urine collection. To a large extent, it eliminates issues of adulteration. Disadvantages of saliva testing are the very low concentrations of drugs found in saliva—lower than in urine—and the possibility of saliva being contaminated with drug residues in the oral and nasal cavity [1]. For example, THC does not appear to be transferred from plasma to saliva but is instead sequestered in the buccal cavity during smoking and can be detected in saliva.

Blood Tests ■

In general, federal rules do not authorize blood testing for alcohol or drugs in the workplace. The U.S. Coast Guard (USCG) does allow blood alcohol testing in reasonable suspicion and post-accident circumstances. The Federal Railroad Administration (FRA) requires blood specimen analyses for drugs and alcohol in investigation of railroad accidents. The blood samples are analyzed at an FRA-designated laboratory, using limits of detection rather than standard federal cutoff levels and including tests for an expanded panel of psychoactive substances.

Some companies conduct blood testing under their own authority. Each blood specimen should be collected with chain-of-custody forms and procedures similar to those used for urine.

Detection windows in drug testing are shorter for blood than for urine and most other matrices. Formulas have been published that allow one to estimate time of marijuana use, based on plasma marijuana metabolite concentrations [2]. Blood levels of certain prescription drugs can be correlated with dosage, symptoms, or both [3]. Nevertheless, blood concentrations of illicit drugs are unreliable measures of impairment.

Hair Tests ■

Hair offers several advantages compared with other drug testing methods. Hair retains drugs for long periods and thus provides long windows of detection—weeks and months versus the two to three days during which rapidly eliminated drugs, such as cocaine or heroin, can be detected in blood or urine. The life span of a single hair ranges from about four months (eyelashes, axillary hair) to approximately four years (scalp hair). Because of the long time periods involved in the life of a hair, separate analyses of different sections of hair offer an opportunity to estimate the time period during which someone used drugs. Another advantage of hair testing is that hair-specimen collection does not involve the privacy issues associated with urine collection or the physical invasiveness of drawing blood. Hair testing has several major disadvantages: The tests are nearly twice as expensive as urine tests, hair testing does not detect alcohol and hair testing is less well accepted among the scientific and regulatory community [4]. The major scientific concerns, as listed in Table 10-1, include:

■ *Ethnic bias.* Hair from Hispanics, Native Americans, blacks, and people of other dark-haired races retains higher concentrations of cocaine, PCP, and certain other drugs than does hair from Caucasians. This is due to higher concentrations of melanin, which appears to increase the incorporation and retention of drugs. Approaches to addressing this concern have included (1) removing melanin during sample preparation and (2) considering the melanin concentration when interpretating the result. It is unclear if these approaches are effective.
■ *Environmental contamination.* Drug powders and smoke can contaminate hair. Some laboratories wash hair samples to remove obvious powder and residues, but it is unclear if this completely removes external contaminants without removing internal drug residues.
■ *Laboratory performance.* One laboratory, Psychemedics, performs virtually all workplace hair test analyses in the United States. The procedures used by this laboratory are proprietary and not fully available for public review. In contrast to urine testing, the laboratory analyses of hair specimens are not closely regulated or monitored through independent proficiency-testing programs. There is no consensus within the scientific community on cutoff levels or appropriate analytical procedures.

Federal drug testing rules do not authorize hair testing. There is variance in state laws on the subject of hair testing: Some prohibit it, some specifically allow it, and most do not address it [5]. Because hair testing generally provides a cumulative measure over a longer window of detection—a 3-cm sample can detect repeated use over a 60–90 day period—many employers find it preferable to urine testing. The longer detection time may raise Americans with Disabilities Act (ADA) issues. Current drug users are not afforded the protections of the ADA; however, employers may not discriminate in hiring applicants who have past substance abuse problems and are now drug-free. Hair testing advocates cite its increased deterrent value in random testing because of the increased detection times. Hair testing should not be used for post-accident or reasonable suspicion testing, because the results do not reflect use just before the incident. It is most effective in areas such as child protection, aftercare monitoring, and forensic cases in which a long window of detection is desirable.

References ■

1. Kato K, Hillsgrove M, Weinhold L, et al. Cocaine and metabolite excretion in saliva under stimulated and nonstimulated conditions. *J Anal Toxicol* 1993;17:338–41.
2. Huestis MA, Henningfield JE, Cone EJ. Blood cannabinoids: II. models for the prediction of time marijuana exposure from plasma concentrations of delta-9-tetrahydrocannabinol (THC) and 11-nor-9-carboxy-delta-9-tetrahydrocannabinol (THCCOOH). *J Anal Toxicol* 1992;16:283–90.
3. Ellenhorn MJ, Barceloux DG. *Medical Toxicology*. New York: Elsevier, 1988. P 579.
4. For a review of the scientific aspects of hair testing, see: Cone EJ, Welch MJ, Babecki MG (eds). *Hair Testing for Drugs of Abuse: International Research on Standards and Technology*. National Institute on Drug Abuse. NIH Publication No. 95-3727. Rockville, MD: Superintendent of Documents, U.S. Government Printing Office, 1995.
5. Summary of state hair testing restrictions and requirements. In: de Bernardo MA, Delogu NN, *Guide to State and Federal Drug-Testing Laws*. Washington, DC: Institute for a Drug-Free Workplace (updated and published annually).

Workplace Alcohol Testing ■

11

Saliva Alcohol Testing ■

Saliva testing for alcohol is a quick test process. The saliva sample is collected on a card or test strip, which is read after several minutes. The technician looks for a color or line change within the time limit identified by the manufacturer. Devices approved by the Department of Transportation (DOT) for use as saliva alcohol screening devices provide quantitative values in terms of blood alcohol concentration (BAC). Each device also has an expiration date and a built-in quality-control mechanism to help ensure the validity of results.

Saliva alcohol tests provide quick and accurate results for negative specimens. Each presumptive positive saliva alcohol test result should be confirmed with a blood alcohol test or, 15–30 minutes later, with an evidential breath alcohol test.

Blood Alcohol Testing ■

Blood testing is the best accepted forensic measure of alcohol impairment. Blood collection is a medical procedure performed by qualified professionals at suitable locations, such as medical clinics. The skin is cleaned with a nonethanol cleanser, for example, Betadine. If ethanol is used to clean the skin, it can contaminate the specimen, although the effect is usually negligible. The skin should not be cleaned with isopropyl alcohol, either, because the donor may (incorrectly) assume that it raises the blood alcohol concentration.

The blood specimen is collected in a tube that contains the preservatives sodium fluoride and potassium oxalate. Chain-of-custody and packaging procedures are similar to those for urine testing. The donor must stay with the specimen tube until it is labeled with a unique identification number and sealed. Security tape, initialed and dated, is put over the top and sides of the tube. If urine and blood specimens are collected at the same encounter, one chain-of-custody form can be used for both specimens if the tests are nonregulated. Since blood alcohol tests are not authorized by DOT for workplace testing, a federal custody and control form (CCF) cannot be used.

Most laboratories centrifuge samples before analysis so that the reported result is based on plasma rather than whole blood. A given volume of serum or plasma has 13–18 percent more water than the same volume of whole blood. In healthy subjects, the ratio of serum or plasma alcohol concentration to whole blood is 1.13:1.18 [1]. Thus, approximately 15–18 percent of the plasma alcohol value must be subtracted to determine the equivalent whole blood value. State and federal laws typically define driving-under-the-influence thresholds in terms of alcohol concentrations in whole blood.

Urine Alcohol Testing ■

Urine for alcohol testing should be collected by a two-sample procedure: The donor empties his or her bladder for the first sample (which is discarded) and waits 20–30 minutes before giving a second sample (which is analyzed). The BAC is estimated by dividing the urine alcohol concentration by 1.3.

A problem can occur among diabetics and other donors who may have glucose in their urine. If the urine contains glucose and is contaminated with various organisms, especially *Candida albicans*, it can undergo fermentation and generate ethanol if kept for several days at room temperature. For this reason, some laboratories also test the urine for glucose and, if it is detected, report that the results may be unreliable. Addition of the preservative sodium fluoride to the urine can eliminate this problem.

Breath Alcohol Testing ■

DOT rules require breath analysis to detect alcohol use because breath testing is noninvasive, provides immediate results, and is scientifically and legally acceptable. Breath alcohol testing is an on-site process. Breath alcohol tests are not covered under the requirements of the Clinical Laboratory Improvement Amendments (CLIA) of 1988, not even when conducted as part of a treatment program. A properly trained breath alcohol technician (BAT) instructs the examinee to blow into an evidential breath testing device. A successful test requires that the examinee provide a minimum breath pressure, continue blowing for a minimum time and, after the minimum time, continue blowing until the measured concentration appears constant, thereby indicating measurement of deep lung (alveolar) air. If the initial alcohol concentration is at or above 0.02 g/2,100 mL breath, the test is repeated 15–30 minutes later. The delay between screening and confirmation is to ensure that any alcohol residue in the subject's mouth is eliminated and not measured in the confirmation test. During the 15–30 minutes, the BAT stays with the examinee. If 30 minutes have elapsed and the test has not been performed, the BAT performs the confirmation test and documents the reason for the delay. If the repeat test result is 0.02 or above, the BAT immediately notifies the employer. In DOT-mandated testing, a breath alcohol concentration of 0.02–0.039 requires removal of the examinee from safety-sensitive duties for up to 24 hours; results of 0.04 or greater require removal from duty, evaluation by a substance abuse professional, and a return-to-duty breath alcohol test result of less than 0.02 prior to the examinee's resuming safety-sensitive duties.

The DOT program uses 0.02 g/2,100mL breath as an action level because the program is based on "zero tolerance" and 0.02 is the lowest concentration to which breath test devices are considered reliable and precise. The second threshold, 0.04, is the value at which impairment rises dramatically in people who are not alcohol tolerant. Employers with non-DOT alcohol testing programs may also use thresholds of 0.02 and 0.04 or other values. Some employer programs adopt their state driving-while-intoxicated (DWI) levels, which are generally 0.08 or 0.10. In some states, drivers with levels at or above 0.05 are also considered "under the influence" if there is corroborating evidence, for example, through a roadside sobriety test. The trend has been toward lower levels.

EVIDENTIAL BREATH TEST DEVICES   EBT

DOT requires that its confirmation alcohol tests be performed with evidential breath test devices (EBTs) listed on the National Highway Traffic Safety Administration's (NHTSA) "Conforming Products List" (CPL). A current CPL is published periodically in the *Federal Register,* and can be obtained by contacting NHTSA (400 Seventh Street SW, Washington, DC 20590; tel. [202]366-9825). EBTs listed in the CPL have passed a series of performance and calibration tests, including accuracy and precision, and noninterference by acetone. Acetone is an issue because people exhale acetone under certain conditions, such as fasting and diabetic ketoacidosis.

Most EBTs fall into one of three categories:

- *Fuel cells.* A fuel cell chemically oxidizes (burns) the breath sample, thereby producing an electric current in proportion to the alcohol concentration. Fuel cell units are compact and often portable and are the most common EBTs. They cost $1,700–$4,500.
- *Infrared spectrometry.* Infrared light passes through the breath sample in an infrared spectrometry unit. Alcohol, if present, absorbs the light at a characteristic wavelength in proportion to the alcohol concentration. These devices are generally larger and less portable than fuel cell devices. They cost $5,500–$7,000.
- *Gas chromatography.* These units are specific for ethyl alcohol. By contrast, isopropyl alcohol, methyl alcohol, and other alcohols can elevate the test results in fuel cells and infrared spectrometry, although to an insignificant extent. A gas chromatography (GC) unit requires compressed gas as a carrier, is not portable, and is a sensitive laboratory instrument. A unit costs approximately $7,000.

Most EBTs offer an option for purchase with personal computers (PCs), to which they can be connected. PCs offer enhanced interactive instructions for conducting tests and enhanced options for storing data and printing results. They also add expense and require additional skills to operate and maintain.

Breath testing sites should allow the employee some privacy so that bystanders will not know or infer the results. The BAT should use an alcohol test form to record data about the test subject, the EBT, and the test result. For DOT testing, the EBT must print three copies of the test result; the BAT affixes a copy to each of the three copies of the alcohol test form.

In DOT testing, if the screening test result is 0.02 g/2100 mL breath or greater, a confirmation test is done 15–30 minutes later. The delay between screening and confirmation is to ensure that any alcohol residue in the subject's mouth is eliminated and not measured in the confirmation test.

Under DOT rules, each approved EBT must have a quality-assurance plan that details the procedures for ensuring that EBT results are reliable and accurate. Checking the calibration of the EBT using a known alcohol standard in a compressed gas or liquid solution is the preferred method for ensuring the EBT's reliability. Most quality-assurance plans recommend conducting a calibration check after every confirmed positive result. The quality-assurance plan and calibration records are usually scrutinized in the event of a challenged test.

NONEVIDENTIAL TESTING DEVICES

DOT allows nonevidential devices listed on the CPL to be used for initial alcohol screening tests. Nonevidential testing devices do not provide printed results. Several nonevidential devices analyze saliva specimens, not breath. For example, the Q.E.D. Saliva Alcohol Test device (STC Diagnostics, Bethlehem, PA) displays a color change through a reaction with alcohol dehydrogenase on the swab. Nonevidential devices cost less than EBTs; however, because confirmatory tests must be performed using EBTs, an EBT must be readily accessible in case the screening result is positive. For this reason, most test sites purchase EBTs and use them for both screening and confirmatory tests.

DOT requires that nonevidential breath tests be performed only by qualified screening test technicians (STTs). DOT has a model curriculum for STT training like that for BATs. The course is approximately 4½ hours long. The U.S. Government Printing Office (GPO) sells the course manual. The Q.E.D. Saliva Alcohol Test devices have been granted waived status under CLIA.

BREATH ALCOHOL TECHNICIANS

Breath alcohol technicians (BATs) instruct and assist individuals in the alcohol testing process and operate EBTs. DOT requires that each BAT be trained for proficiency in the operation of the EBT he or she is using and DOT alcohol testing procedures. BAT training courses are taught with an instructor's curriculum and student handbooks:

BAT Instructor Training Curriculum $19.00; GPO Stock No. 050-000-00551-8. (includes *Student Handbook*.)

BAT Student Handbook (only) $7.50; GPO Stock No. 050 000-00550-0.

These can be ordered through any local GPO bookstore or by contacting:

Superintendent of Documents
U.S. Government Printing Office
Washington, DC 20402-9371
(202)783-3238, fax (202)512-2250

The DOT course is designed to take two days. Some EBT manufacturers, law enforcement officers, professional trainers, and health care providers train and certify BATs, typically for $300–$500 per student. Some EBT vendors offer training at no additional charge for their clients. DOT does not require refresher training for BATs.

INCOMPLETE BREATH ALCOHOL TESTS: "SHY LUNG"

If the donor is unable or alleges an inability to provide enough breath to permit a valid test, the BAT must immediately inform the employer. The employer then directs the donor to a licensed physician for a medical evaluation concerning the donor's inability to provide enough breath. If the physician indicates that there was a valid medical reason—for example, a severe asthma attack—for the inadequate amount of breath, the donor's failure to provide enough breath is not considered a refusal. If no valid medical reason is determined, the donor is deemed to have refused testing.

INTERPRETATION

Results of breath alcohol analysis are expressed in terms of grams of alcohol per 210 liters of breath. Each result is provided as a breath alcohol concentration, or BrAC, but is often interpreted as equivalent to a blood alcohol concentration, or BAC.

Alcohol test results undergo no medical review. The source of the alcohol—beverage versus cough syrup versus vanilla extract, and so on—does not mitigate the policy violation that occurs when the alcohol concentration is at or above the employer's cutoff value. Nonbeverage sources of alcohol are unlikely to significantly increase the alcohol concentration.

The alcohol test record should undergo an administrative review, especially if the result is positive, because the test's integrity depends on an adequate record. The breath alcohol test result should be canceled if the alcohol test form has significant errors or omissions (such as a missing EBT-printed confirmation test result), if the confirmation test result was obtained more than 30 minutes after the screening test, or if there is no EBT-printed confirmation test result.

FITNESS FOR DUTY

Under DOT rules, breath alcohol testing is only conducted just before, during, or immediately after performing safety-sensitive functions. Measurement of the alcohol concentration is used to determine a person's fitness to perform safety-sensitive functions as well as deter alcohol abuse. The NRC rules authorize licensees to conduct alcohol tests as a part of each employee's gaining access to a restricted site. Since alcohol testing is tied to safety-sensitive duties, there is reasonable support for the 0.02 and 0.04 levels as impacting safety and performance. Table 11-1 correlates BACs with stages of alcohol influence or intoxication and the corresponding clinical signs and symptoms.

A commercial motor vehicle driver is not required to undergo a physical examination and obtain a new Medical Examiner's Certificate if he or she violates the prohibitions on the use of alcohol. However, if the SAP determines that alcoholism exists, the driver is not qualified to drive a commercial motor vehicle in interstate commerce. The responsibility rests with the em-

Table 11-1. Stages of Acute Alcohol Influence/Intoxication ■

Blood Alcohol Concentration (g/100mL)	Stage of Alcohol Influence/Intoxication	Clinical Signs/Symptoms
0.01–0.05	Subclinical	No apparent influence. Behavior nearly normal by ordinary observation. Slight changes detectable by special tests.
0.03–0.12	Euphoria	Mild euphoria, sociability, talkativeness. Increased self-confidence; decreased inhibition. Diminution of attention, judgment, and control. Mild sensory-motor impairment. Slowed information processing. Loss of efficiency in finer performance tests.
0.09–0.25	Excitement	Emotional instability; loss of critical judgment. Impairment of perception, memory, and comprehension. Decreased sensory response; increased reaction time. Reduced visual acuity, peripheral vision, and glare recovery. Sensory-motor incoordination; impaired balance. Drowsiness.
0.18–0.30	Confusion	Disorientation, mental confusion, dizziness. Exaggerated emotional states (e.g., fear, rage, sorrow). Disturbances of vision (e.g., diplopia) and of perception of color, form, motion, dimensions. Increased pain threshold. Increased muscular incoordination, staggering gate, slurred speech. Apathy, lethargy.
0.25–0.40	Stupor	General inertia; approaching loss of motor functions. Marked muscular incoordination; inability to stand or walk. Vomiting; incontinence of urine and feces. Impaired consciousness; sleep or stupor.
0.35–0.50	Coma	Complete unconsciousness; coma; anesthesia. Depressed or abolished reflexes. Subnormal temperature. Incontinence of urine and feces. Impairment of circulation and respiration. Possible death.
0.45+	Death	Death from respiratory arrest.

Source: Dubowski KM. Alcohol determination in the clinical laboratory. *Am J Clin Pathol* 1980;74:747–50.

ployer to ensure the driver is medically qualified and to determine whether a new medical examination should be completed.

REPORTING

The BAT transmits the result of alcohol testing to the employer. In regulated testing, the Breath Alcohol Testing Form must not be routed to the employer by sending it with the urine specimen to the laboratory for forwarding to the employer; the form has employee identifiers on it, and sending it to the laboratory would disclose the test subject's identity. For results greater than or equal to 0.02, the BAT must inform the employer immediately, usually first by telephone and later by sending a copy of the result to the employer.

Supervisors and billing personnel with a "need to know" are permitted to have access to breath alcohol testing documentation. Access must be for a specific purpose and must be necessary for the employer's successful implementation of the program. Justifiable reasons for such access include review of the forms for completion, obtaining specific billing data from the forms, and filing the forms. Breath Alcohol Testing Forms should not be duplicated for purposes of supervision or billing: This would create additional files with potential problems of disclosure of confidential information. As an alternative, the BAT or other personnel could complete other forms that contain appropriate billing data and could be maintained as backup documentation.

EXTRAPOLATION OF ALCOHOL TEST RESULTS

While DOT procedures do not authorize physician interpretation of breath alcohol test results, the employer may ask the physician to verify the test's accuracy and interpret its results, especially if the test has been challenged. The test result is usually extrapolated to the time of the event that triggered the test, which may have been hours previously. DOT rules do not allow for back extrapolation of breath alcohol test results. Thus, alcohol test results cannot be used to identify employees who may have violated the "pre-duty abstinence" periods required of certain safety-sensitive employees.

Alcohol concentrations decrease from peak value at a fairly steady rate. The mean population rate of alcohol metabolism is in the range of 0.015–0.018 g/dL/hr. The rate of alcohol metabolism varies from person to person and even within the same person over time. Heavy drinkers usually have higher metabolic rates, for example, 0.018–0.024 g/dL/hr. Health conditions, age, sex, smoking history, and use of phenobarbital, oral contraceptives, and other drugs can also affect alcohol metabolism. One's alcohol concentration can increase after a given test, too, if there is alcohol in the stomach that has not yet been absorbed at the time of the test. Food in the stomach and drugs that slow gastric emptying time or reduce gastrointestinal transit time will decrease the rate, but not the extent, of absorption, leading to a lower peak ethanol concentration at a later period of time. References should be consulted for a more thorough review of the interpretation and extrapolation of blood alcohol results [2,3].

References ■

1. Caplan YH. Blood, urine and other fluids and tissue specimens for alcohol analyses. In: JC Garriott (ed), *Medicolegal Aspects of Alcohol*, 3rd Ed. Tucson, AZ: Lawyers & Judges Publishing, 1996.
2. Garriott JC (ed). *Medicolegal Aspects of Alcohol*, 3rd Ed. Tucson, AZ: Lawyers & Judges Publishing, 1996.
3. Jones AW. Measuring alcohol in blood and breath for forensic purposes—a historical review. *Forensic Sci Rev* 1996;8(1):13–43.

The Substance Abuse Professional ∎

12

DOT rules require that a donor who engages in prohibited drug- or alcohol-related conduct be informed of available resources to resolve substance abuse-related problems and be referred to a substance abuse professional (SAP) for assessment. Examples of prohibited conduct include positive drug tests and any refusal to submit to a post-accident, random, reasonable suspicion, or follow-up test. DOT rules do not require the employer to pay for the SAP assessment, nor do they state whether an employer should fire or not hire someone who has tested positive, or whether the employer must return that person to work after completion of treatment.

Qualifications and Restrictions ∎

DOT rules state that a SAP must be one of the following:

- A licensed physician with a medical doctor (MD) or doctor of osteopathy (DO) degree, with knowledge of, and clinical experience in, the diagnosis and treatment of alcohol and disorders related to substance abuse.
- A licensed or certified psychologist, social worker, or certified employee assistance professional (EAP) with knowledge of, and clinical experience in, the diagnosis and treatment of disorders related to alcohol and controlled substances.
- A counselor certified by the National Association of Alcohol and Drug Abuse Counselors or the International Certification Reciprocity Consortium.

The SAP should have experience in clinical assessment of substance abuse disorders, level of treatment criteria, and planning and monitoring of treatment. The SAP should have a working knowledge of the substance abuse disorders diagnostic criteria, as defined in the *Diagnostic and Statistical Manual of Mental Disorders (DSM-IV)*. Licensure as a clinical mental health professional is desirable because it establishes the SAP as a qualified independent practitioner of mental health services and thus lends clinical authority to the functions performed by the SAP and credibility to the SAP's decisions if challenged in court or arbitration proceedings. The SAP should be knowledgeable about insurance coverage and the availability and quality of local treatment programs.

∎ 127

The SAP should also understand the procedures and reliability of workplace drug and alcohol testing. This helps in responding to employees who blame the testing process for their positive results. Finally, the employer should verify that the SAP maintains adequate insurance coverage.

To avoid conflicts of interest, DOT rules prohibit SAPs from referring employees to treatment centers and resources in which they have financial involvement and from receiving referral fees in connection with their recommendations for assistance. Education and awareness services are included in this restriction because they are considered a form of treatment. DOT offers limited exceptions to this policy against self-referral so that SAPs can perform both the assessment and treatment functions if:

- There are no additional treatment resources other than the SAP or a facility with whom the SAP is affiliated in the employee's geographic area.
- The SAP is referring to a public treatment facility or service where the SAP is employed or performs contract services.
- The employer's policy provides for substance abuse assessment and treatment services by the same service provider.
- The employee's medical insurance coverage provides for treatment services from the same provider who serves as the SAP.

The MRO as Substance Abuse Professional ■

Medical review officers (MROs) can serve as SAPs if they have the aforementioned qualifications. MROs should understand that SAP assessments are done face-to-face with employees, not by telephone as many MRO interviews are done. Under Federal Aviation Administration (FAA) and U.S. Coast Guard (USCG) rules, MROs have roles in determining return-to-duty and follow-up testing schedules. Table 12-1 illustrates some of the differences among various DOT agencies as to their return-to-duty procedures if employees test positive for drugs or alcohol.

The employer may ask the MRO to oversee or manage the SAP process. This can take various forms: For example, the MRO may identify qualified SAPs for the employer and make referrals as part of his or her interviews with employees who have positive tests. Some employers ask MROs to review SAPs' findings and coordinate follow-up testing, including the selection of dates for testing. Some MROs provide SAPs with minimum standards for conducting the initial and follow-up assessments.

Although an employer may have questions about a SAP's performance and is free to select a different SAP to handle future cases, DOT prohibits employers from selecting a different SAP to provide a different assistance recommendation in a case that has already gone through an initial SAP assessment.

Duties ■

INITIAL EVALUATION

The initial evaluation is supposed to determine the extent of the employee's substance abuse problem and identify the kind of assistance or treatment that is needed. This is done through a face-to-face interview between the SAP and the employee. Adherence to standard operating procedures helps assure consistent evaluations and makes testimony based on these procedures more credible. SAP-conducted interviews should follow a standardized format that includes valid and reliable tools for assessing substance abuse. The SAP may also wish to interview family members, employers, and other outside sources who can comment on the employee's level of functioning. Interviews with outside sources should be structured and responses should be documented. Before contacting these people, the SAP needs the employee's written consent. If the employee refuses to consent, the SAP has the option of stopping the evaluation. The SAP should explain this to the employee, ideally at the first visit.

REFERRAL

Certain professional organizations—for example, the American Society of Addiction Medicine—have written criteria for levels of treatment for substance abuse disorders [1]. The treatment recommendations are among the most frequently challenged aspects of the SAP assessment process. SAPs must be able to justify each recommendation and show consistency in the decision-making process.

FOLLOW-UP EVALUATION

The purpose of the follow-up evaluation is to determine if the employee has complied with the SAP's recommendations at the initial evaluation and to provide recommendations to the employer concerning the employee's return to safety-sensitive duties. The employer makes the final decision regarding the employee's return to duty after a drug or alcohol violation.

Based on the initial evaluation, the SAP should identify a date to begin considering the employee's readiness for follow-up assessment. This is better than committing to a date for return to duty or even committing to a date on which to perform the follow-up assessment. One way to clarify this procedure is to give the employee a written statement at the initial evaluation that explains when the review process will begin and the basis of decision making, for example, discussion with treatment provider, test results, and program participation.

The employee is usually ready to return to work once he or she has met the treatment program's goals. The treatment provider should tell the SAP when this has happened. The SAP, in making a referral, may wish to send the treatment provider a letter that asks for a treatment summary and aftercare recommendations. The SAP should specifically ask about the employee's:

- Attendance.
- Attitude.
- Level of participation.
- Understanding of illness—cause (if known), course, symptoms, treatment, prognosis.
- Results of drug/alcohol tests during treatment.
- Family involvement.

Return-to-duty issues	Federal Aviation Administration		Federal Highway Administration	Federal Railroad Administration
	Drugs	Alcohol		
Who notifies the employee of available SAP resources?	MRO	Employer	Employer	Employer
Who determines what assistance is needed?	MRO (if qualified) or SAP	SAP	SAP	SAP
Who does the follow-up evaluation?	SAP	SAP	SAP	SAP
What is the purpose of the follow-up evaluation?	To determine if the employee has complied with the SAP's recommendations		To determine if the employee has complied with the SAP's recommendations	To determine if the employee has complied with the SAP's recommendations
Is an employee subject to follow-up testing even if treatment was not recommended?	Yes	No	No	Yes, up to 60 months, and at least six tests in the first 12 months following return to duty

The follow-up evaluation should be well structured and should include discussion with the employee concerning his or her:

■ Commitment to the aftercare plan.
■ Support systems at work and home.
■ Motivation to meet the employer's conditions for return to work.
■ Involvement in self-help programs.

Follow-up Testing ■

Follow-up testing is intended to encourage abstinence after treatment. As summarized in Table 12-1, the Federal Railroad Administration (FRA) and USCG

Federal Transit Administration	Research and Special Programs Administration		U.S. Coast Guard	
	Drugs	Alcohol	Drugs	Alcohol
Employer	Employers		MRO refers the employee to the employee assistance program. (The Coast Guard rule does not include use of a SAP.)	
SAP		SAP	MRO or employee assistance program	
SAP		SAP	MRO	Professional with experience in substance abuse and rehabilitation
To determine if the employee has complied with the SAP's recommendations	To determine if the employee has complied with the SAP's recommendations		To determine if the employee is at low risk to return to drug or alcohol misuse. (If the employee has had his or her Coast Guard license or Merchant Mariner's Document revoked because of drug or alcohol misuse, he or she must meet certain additional requirements for reinstatement.)	
No	Yes	No	Yes. USCG does not specify the duration or frequency.	

require follow-up testing for every employee in a return-to-duty status, and other DOT modes require it only if the SAP or MRO has recommended some form of assistance. The SAP or MRO—whoever does the follow-up evaluation—determines the frequency, type (drugs, alcohol, or both), and duration of follow-up testing. Federal rules authorize follow-up testing for the entire federal five-drug panel but not for other drugs/metabolites. DOT allows alcohol testing after drug misuse, and drug testing after alcohol misuse, as recommended by the SAP (or MRO) on a case-by-case basis. Under DOT rules, a follow-up testing program can last up to 60 months and must include at least six tests in the first 12 months following the individual's return-to-duty. Follow-up testing should be unannounced. It should be recognized as supportive to the employee's recovery, not punitive. Table 12-2 presents examples of time frames that can be applied to follow-up testing.

While the SAP is not required to monitor the worker's abstinence after return to work, this important task is a good opportunity for the SAP to expand his or her range of services.

Table 12-2. Suggested Time Frames for Follow-up Testing ■

Drug of Choice	Months					
	1–3	4–6	7–9	10–12	13–24	25–60
Cocaine	5 tests/mo	4 tests/mo	4 tests every 45 days	2 tests/mo	1 test/mo	1 test every 45 days
Alcohol and other water-soluble drugs	4 tests/mo	3 tests/mo	2 tests/mo	2 tests every 45 days	1 test/mo	1 test every 45 days
Marijuana and other fat-soluble drugs	3 tests/mo	2 tests/mo	2 tests/mo	2 tests every 45 days	1 test/mo	1 test/mo

Source: Stockman L. Employee assistance programs. In: Swotinsky RB (ed), *The Medical Review Officer's Guide to Drug Testing.* New York: Van Nostrand Reinhold, 1992. P 158.

Releasing Records ■

Information obtained by the SAP in assessment and evaluation of the employee is protected by strict confidentiality requirements. Before the MRO releases information to the SAP, the MRO should request the employee's consent to release the information to the SAP.

The SAP also has restrictions on the release of information about the evaluation, referral, and treatment recommendation. The SAP should obtain a written authorization from the employee to release any information to the employer or the MRO. Employers regulated by DOT rules must maintain documentation of the SAP assessment, assistance recommendations, and the employee's compliance with the SAP recommendations on all employees who return to safety-sensitive duties following a violation of DOT alcohol and drug rules. Prospective employers of an applicant who had a previous drug or alcohol-positive test may request information from the SAP to ensure that the employee is fully qualified to assume safety-sensitive duties. Again, the SAP should obtain a signed authorization from the applicant to release information.

Record Keeping ■

As mentioned earlier, the SAP should use some form of standard assessment interview. The interview notes, the SAP's diagnostic impression, psychometric test results (if any), and treatment plan, including where the employee was referred for further evaluation and/or treatment, should be documented and maintained. The treatment facility may ask the SAP for a diagnostic summary; the SAP should obtain the employee's consent before releasing this information.

The SAP's report to the employer or MRO about the initial assessment should contain the date of the assessment, the recommendation for assistance, if any, and pertinent referral information. It should not contain diagnoses, prescribed medications, information about testing conducted, or the prognosis. Likewise, written reports of the follow-up SAP assessment should be limited to information necessary for the employer to make a return-to-work decision. The employer, not the SAP, is responsible for making the return-to-work decision. The follow-up assessment report or letter should state the date of the follow-up evaluation, a statement that the employee has appropriately complied with the SAP's recommendations for assistance or treatment, the aftercare plan recommended by the treatment facility, and the SAP's decisions about follow-up testing (i.e., what kind of testing, how often, and over what period of time).

Reference ■

1. Mee-Lee D, Gartner L, Miller M, et al. *Patient Placement Criteria for the Treatment of Substance-Related Disorders* (PPC-2), 2nd ed. Annapolis Junction, MD: ASAM, 1998.

Information Sources ■

Books ■

Available from the National Clearinghouse for Alcohol and Drug Information (tel. 800-729-6686):

- SAMHSA. *Urine Specimen Collection Handbook for Federal Workplace Drug Testing Programs*. DHHS Publication No. (SMA) 96-3114.1996.
- SAMHSA. *Medical Review Officer Manual for Federal Workplace Drug Testing Programs*. DHHS Publication No. (SMA) 97-3164. 1997.

Available from the U.S. Department of Transportation's (DOT) fax-on-demand service (tel. 800-225-3784):

- DOT. *Urine Specimen Collection Procedures Guidelines*. Washington, DC, December 1994.
- DOT. *Substance Abuse Professional Procedures Guidelines*. Washington, DC, June 1995.

Available from the American Association of Clinical Chemistry (AACC) (tel. 800-892-1400):

- Liu RH, Goldberger BA (eds). *Handbook of Workplace Drug Testing*. Washington, DC: AACC Press, 1996. $49.

Available from the Institute for a Drug-Free Workplace (tel. 202-842-3914):

- *Guide to State and Federal Drug-Testing Laws*. Washington, DC. Published annually. $225.

Newsletter ■

Available from the American College of Occupational and Environmental Medicine, Arlington Heights, IL (tel. 847-228-6850).

■ Swotinsky RB (ed). *MRO Update.* (Ten issues per year. $220 for ACOEM members, $225 for nonmembers.)

Journal ■

Available from Preston Publications (tel. 847-647-2900):

■ Baselt RC (ed). *Journal of Analytical Toxicology.* Niles, IL: Ten issues per year, $305/yr.

Federal Agencies ■

Agency	Address	Telephone/Fax #
Drug and Alcohol Policy and Compliance	U.S. Department of Transportation 400 7th Street SW, Rm. 10317 Washington, DC 20590	tel. 202-366-3784 fax 202-366-3897
General Counsel	U.S. Department of Transportaton 400 7th Street SW, Rm. 10424 Washington, DC 20590	tel. 202-366-9306 fax 202-366-9313
Federal Aviation Administration	Drug Abatement Division 800 Independence Avenue SW, Rm. 803 Washington, DC 20590	tel. 202-267-8442 fax 202-267-5200
U.S. Coast Guard	Office of Investigations and Analysis and Analysis 2100 2nd Street SW, Rm. 2406 Washington, DC 20593-0001	tel. 202-267-1430 fax 202-267-1416
Federal Highway Administration	Office of Motor Carrier Safety and Technology 400 7th Street SW, Rm. 3419 Washington, DC 20590	tel. 202-366-6121 fax 202-366-7908
Research and Special Programs Administration	Office of Pipeline Safety 400 7th Street SW, Rm. 2335 Washington, DC 20590	tel. 202-366-6199 fax 202-366-4566
Federal Railroad Administration	Office of Safety 400 7th Street SW, Rm. 8314 Washington, DC 20590	tel. 202-632-3378 fax 202-632-3875
Federal Transit Administration	Office of Safety and Security 400 7th Street SW, Rm. 9301G Washington, DC 20590	tel. 202-366-2896 fax 202-366-3765
Substance Abuse and Mental Health Services Administration	Division of Workplace Programs 5600 Fishers Lane Rockwall 2 Bldg. Rm. 815 Rockville, MD 20857	tel. 301-443-6014 fax 301-443-3031
U.S. Nuclear Regulatory Commission	Office of Nuclear Reactor Regulation Division of Reactor Program Management Washington, DC 20555	tel. 301-415-2944 fax 301-415-1032

Professional Organizations ■

Organization	Address	Telephone/Fax #
American Association of Medical Review Officers (AAMRO)	P.O. Box 12873 Research Triangle Park, NC 27709	tel. 919-489-9588 fax 919-490-1010
American College of Occupational and Environmental Medicine (ACOEM)	55 W. Seegers Road Arlington Heights, IL 60005	tel. 847-228-6850 fax 847-228-1856
American Society of Addiction Medicine (ASAM)	4601 North Park Drive, Suite 101, Arcade Chevy Chase, MD 20815	tel. 301-656-3920 fax 301-656-3815
Medical Review Officer Certification Council (MROCC)	9950 West Lawrence Avenue Suite 106A Schiller Park, IL 60176	tel. 847-671-1829 fax 847-671-1931
Substance Abuse Program Administrators Association (SAPAA)	1550 South Coast Highway Suite 201 Laguna Beach, CA 92651	tel. 800-672-7229 fax 949-376-3456

The Medical Review Officer Certification Council ■

by Brian L. Compney, Executive Director, MROCC

The Council and Its Philosophy ■

The Medical Review Officer Certification Council (MROCC) was incorporated in 1992 to set a professional standard of excellence for medical review officers (MROs). This physician-based nonprofit organization is governed by a Board of Directors, with representation from the American Academy of Clinical Toxicology, American College of Medical Toxicology, American College of Occupational and Environmental Medicine (ACOEM), American Society of Addiction Medicine (ASAM), and College of American Pathologists, as well as the American Medical Association (AMA). The Council offers certification, by way of monitored written examinations, to licensed physicians who have had appropriate training in the duties and responsibilities of the MRO. Since its inception, MROCC has certified more than 3,000 physicians throughout the United States and Canada, as well as internationally, and continues to certify approximately 600 physicians each year.

The MROCC certification program promotes and preserves the highest professional standards of training and care among MROs. MROCC certification confirms to industry and to others the MRO's expertise in performing the essential duties of the MRO and provides the distinct recognition that he or she is up to date in the latest developments, techniques, and issues dealing with MRO work. MROCC's Board of Directors adheres to the philosophy that certification must go beyond the receipt of a diploma and that it is not enough to narrowly know rules and regulations. Certification should be a clear indication of a thorough understanding of the nature and the effects of both licit and illicit drugs and a genuine knowledge of the reliable methods available for identifying and responding to both industry and individual needs.

Why Certification? ■

The ramifications of workplace drug testing can be serious to both the employer and the employee. An employee who uses illegal drugs is a definite obstacle to the stability and safety of the workplace. However, proper evaluation of a test result in light of the employee's medical history, while protecting his or her privacy, is essential to avoid falsely accusing an employee of illicit drug use. For this reason, business, industry, and government agencies have seen a need for qualified MROs to evaluate work-related drug tests and to act as consultants and resources in achieving a drug-free workplace. Certification is a mark of an MRO's competency.

The certified MRO protects the donor from a false accusation of illicit drug use when there is an alternative medical explanation for the laboratory result. At the same time, the certified MRO acts as a valuable resource to protect the company, helping with policies and regulatory issues, as well as providing related services such as drug testing collections, breath alcohol testing services, coordination of laboratory services, laboratory performance testing, and preparation of summary reports for employers.

The Examination Process ■

MROCC offers its certification examination approximately eight times a year throughout the United States and in Canada in conjunction with MRO training courses sponsored by ACOEM and ASAM, and, perhaps in the future, those of other organizations. The certification examination is based on the federal requirements developed by the Department of Health and Human Services (DHHS) for federal drug testing programs. Each applicant for certification must meet specific eligibility requirements. These include graduation from an approved medical school or school of osteopathic medicine; a current medical license to practice medicine in a state, territory, or possession of the United States or a province of Canada (the board may consider applications from physicians practicing outside the United States or Canada who possess a valid license from the locale in which they reside and practice); and evidence of completion, during the 24 months preceding the certification examination, of a minimum of 12 category-1 continuing medical education (CME) credit hours of approved MRO training (six category-1 CME credit hours for recertification). The ongoing developments in the rapidly changing arena of workplace and alcohol testing require a certification time limit. Therefore, certification is valid only for a five-year period.

The Examination Content Areas ■

The examination items are developed and critically reviewed by nationally recognized leaders in drug testing drawn from the fields of occupational medicine, addiction medicine, forensic chemistry, toxicology, and the legal profession. In addition, leading experts in education measurement, evaluation, and psychometrics provide comprehensive guidance on the examination process in order to ensure relevance, validity, and reliability. The examination has been designed to measure the scope and knowledge and practical skills that the MRO applies in fulfilling the professional responsibilities in the evaluation of workplace drug tests.

Recognizing that drug testing is a multidisciplinary field which requires skills and knowledge in a variety of subject areas, the multiple-choice examination is divided into six categories: (1) chemical dependency, (2) regulatory issues and MRO responsibilities, (3) toxicology and pharmacology, (4) clinical aspects, (5) laboratory issues, and (6) collections and procedures.

Although the skills of the MRO may be quite different from those of the addictionist, the MRO will be called on to be a general resource for substance use issues. Therefore, knowledge in the area of chemical dependency enables the MRO to recognize chemical dependency as a primary disorder, to work effectively with a SAP in a workplace substance misuse prevention and control program, and to serve as a resource to the employer on issues of employees' drug misuse, aftercare monitoring, return-to-work, and medical qualifications for the performance of safety-sensitive tasks.

The MRO must stay current and be aware of new statutes and regulations, as these will impact a client's business. Planning is key to survival in business and the MRO must be able to help with the process. General knowledge in the area of regulatory issues and MRO responsibilities enables the MRO to advise employers and employees about the requirements of public and private sector drug-free workplace programs, policies and procedures as well as to make sure that regulatory and legal requirements are followed.

The MRO must be knowledgeable about the toxicology and pharmacology of drugs of abuse. Knowledge in this area enables the MRO to describe and recognize the clinical and toxic effects of drugs of abuse and alcohol as well as to recognize both trade names and generic names for substances that are likely to be presented to the MRO.

Familiarity with clinical issues related to drug use and testing, including medical explanations for positive or indeterminate tests and medical qualifications for performance safety-sensitive tasks, is essential in properly diagnosing, treating, and reporting the toxic effects of drugs of abuse. The MRO must recognize clinical evidence of drug use and the effects of withdrawal as well as evaluate the legitimacy of alternative medical explanations for positive test results.

While the MRO is not a laboratory director, he or she must know what goes on in the laboratory and how quality is assured. Knowledge in the area of laboratory issues not only allows the MRO to evaluate drug and alcohol laboratory testing services, but also enables him or her to recognize the appropriate analytical methods for drug and alcohol screening and confirmation and to properly interpret results, with consideration of limits of detection, sensitivity, specificity, interferences, cost, and availability.

Although the MRO does not routinely collect urine, he or she must thoroughly understand collection procedures and chain-of-custody issues as well as correctable and fatal flaws. Knowledge in the area of collections and procedures enables the MRO to describe and apply appropriate procedures for urine specimen collections, including unwitnessed, witnessed, split specimen and insufficient quantity collections, as well as assists the MRO to serve as a consultant to BATs, STTs, and employers on alcohol testing procedures.

Upon successful completion and passage of the MROCC examination, the certified MRO receives an individually numbered certificate stating that he or she has been found to possess special knowledge as a medical review officer and is listed in the annual MROCC directory and supplements supplied to Chambers of Commerce and SAHMSA Laboratories and to other agencies, clinics, and individuals in need of MRO services. A concise listing of

MROCC-certified physicians, as well as resources and links to assist the MRO in his or her duties, is also found online at the MROCC web site, *www.mrocc.com*.

Research Funding ■

In addition to its certification program, MROCC provides grants awards to fund research projects that have direct relevance to the work of the MRO and continue to advance this rapidly changing field. Grants have been awarded for such research on the topics of DNA typing of urine specimens, urine temperature and its effects on adulteration of specimens, and the concentration of marijuana metabolites in the urine following ingestion of hemp seed tea. MROCC also sponsored the development of this book, *The Medical Review Officer's Manual*.

Ethical Guidelines for Workplace Drug Testing ∎

The following features should be included in any program for the testing of employees and prospective employees for drugs [1]:

1. A written company policy and procedures concerning drug use and drug testing for the presence of drugs should exist and be applied impartially.
2. The reason for any requirement for testing for drugs should be clearly documented. Such reasons might include safety of the individual, other employees, or the public; security needs; or requirements related to job performance.
3. Affected employees and applicants should be informed in advance about the company's policy concerning drug use and testing. They should be made aware of their right to refuse such testing and the consequences of such refusal to their employment.
4. When special safety or security needs justify testing for drugs on an announced and possibly random, basis, employees should be made aware in advance that this will be done from time to time. Care should be taken to assure that such tests are done in a uniform and impartial manner for all employees in the affected group(s).
5. Written consent for testing and for communication of results to the employer should be obtained from each individual prior to testing.
6. Collection, transportation, and analysis of the specimens and the reporting of the results should meet stringent legal, technical, and ethical requirements.
7. A licensed physician who is qualified as a medical review officer (MRO) should evaluate positive results prior to a report being made to the employer. This may require the obtaining of supplemental information from the employer or applicant in order to ensure that a positive test does not represent appropriate use of prescription drugs, over-the-counter medication, or other substances that could cause a positive test.

    Training of the MRO should include the pharmacology of substances of abuse, laboratory testing methodology and quality control, forensic toxicology, pertinent federal regulations, legal and ethical requirements, chemical dependency illness, employee assistance programs, and rehabilitation.
8. The affected employee or applicant should be advised of positive results by the MRO and have the opportunity for explanation and discussion prior to

the reporting of results to the employer, if feasible. The mechanism for accomplishing this should be clearly defined.

9. After being informed of a drug abuse problem, the employee or applicant should be advised about appropriate treatment resources.

10. Any report to the employer should provide only the information needed for work-placement purposes or as required by government regulations. Identification to the employer of the particular drug(s) found and quantitative levels is not necessary, unless required by law. Reports to the employer should be made by a physician sensitive to the various considerations involved.

Reference ■

1. American College of Occupational Medicine. Drug screening in the workplace: ethical guidelines. *J Occup Med* 1991;33:651–2.

Controlled Substances Act, Schedules I–V ■

The drugs and drug products that come under the jurisdiction of the Controlled substances Act are divided into five schedules, as presented in 21 CFR §1308. Some examples in each schedule are outlined below [1]. For a complete listing of all the controlled substances, contact any office of the Drug Enforcement Administration.

Schedule I substances are those that have no accepted medical use in the United states and have high abuse potential. Some examples of Schedule I drugs are heroin, LSD, marijuana, mescaline, methaqualone, MDMA, and peyote.

Schedule II substances have a high potential for abuse, with a severe risk of psychic or physical dependence. Some examples of Schedule II drugs are amobarbital, amphetamine (Dexedrine), cocaine, dronabinol (Marinol), fentanyl (Sublimaze), hydromorphone (Dilaudid), meperidine (Demerol), methadone, methamphetamine (Desoxyn), methylphenidate (Ritalin), morphine, opium, oxycodone (Percodan), oxymorphone (Numorphan), pentobarbital, phencyclidine, and secobarbital. Amobarbital, codeine, secobarbital, and several other drugs appear in Schedule II at high doses and Schedule III at low doses.

Schedule III substances have a lesser abuse potential than those in Schedules I and II. Some examples of Schedule III drugs are anabolic steroids, benzphetamine, and paregoric. Codeine and several other drugs appear in Schedule III at low doses.

Schedule IV substances in this schedule have a lesser abuse potential than those listed in Schedule III and include such drugs as alprazolam (Xanax), barbital, chloral hydrate, chlordiazepoxide (Librium), clonazepam (Clonopin), clorazepate (Tranxene), dextropropoxyphene dosage forms (Darvon), diazepam (Valium), fenproporex, flurazepam (Dalmane), halazepam (Paxipam), lorazepam (Ativan), meprobamate (Equanil, Miltown), midazolam (Versed), oxazepam (Serax), paraldehyde, pentazocine (Talwin-NX), phenobarbital, phentermine, prazepam (Verstran), temazepam (Restoril), and triazolam (Halcion).

Schedule V substances have a lesser abuse potential than those listed in Schedule IV and consist primarily of preparations containing limited quantities of certain narcotic drugs generally used for antitussive, antidiarrheal, and analgesic purposes. Schedule V products are available over-the-counter but with restrictions—for example, they can be sold only by registered pharmacists, to individuals 18 years of age or older, and their sale must be recorded in bound ledgers.

Reference ∎

1. American College of Occupational Medicine. Drug screening in the workplace: ethical guidelines. *J Occup Med* 1991;33:651–2.

DOT Procedures, 49 CFR PART 40 ■

Code of Federal Regulations
Title 49—Transportation
Subtitle A—Office of the Secretary of transportation
PART 40—Procedures for Transportation Workplace Drug Testing Programs
Current through January 1, 1999; 63 FR 72352

SUBPART A—GENERAL

§40.1 Applicability.

This part applies, through regulations that reference it issued by agencies of the Department of Transportation, to transportation employers, including self- employed individuals, required to conduct drug and/or alcohol testing programs by DOT agency regulations and to such transportation employers' officers, employees, agents and contractors (including, but not limited to, consortia). Employers are responsible for the compliance of their officers, employees, agents, consortia and/or contractors with the requirements of this part.

§40.3 Definitions.

The following definitions apply to this part:

Air blank. A reading by an EBT of ambient air containing no alcohol. (In EBTs using gas chromatography technology, a reading of the device's internal standard.)

Alcohol. The intoxicating agent in beverage alcohol, ethyl alcohol or other low molecular weight alcohols including methyl or isopropyl alcohol.

Alcohol concentration. The alcohol in a volume of breath expressed in terms of grams of alcohol per 210 liters of breath as indicated by a breath test under this part.

Alcohol use. The consumption of any beverage, mixture or preparation, including any medication, containing alcohol.

Aliquot. A portion of a specimen used for testing.

Blind sample or blind performance test specimen. A urine specimen submitted to a laboratory for quality control testing purposes, with a fictitious identifier, so that the laboratory cannot distinguish it from employee specimens, and which is spiked with known quantities of specific drugs or which is blank, containing no drugs.

Breath Alcohol Technician (BAT). An individual who instructs and assists individuals in the alcohol testing process and operates an EBT.

Canceled or invalid test. In drug testing, a drug test that has been declared invalid by a Medical Review Officer. A canceled test is neither a positive nor a negative test. For purposes of this part, a sample that has been rejected for testing by a laboratory is treated the same as a canceled test. In alcohol testing, a test that is deemed to be invalid under §40.79. It is neither a positive nor a negative test.

Chain of custody. Procedures to account for the integrity of each urine or blood specimen by tracking its handling and storage from point of specimen collection to final disposition of the specimen. With respect to drug testing, these procedures shall require that an appropriate drug testing custody form (see §40.23(a)) be used from time of collection to receipt by the laboratory and that upon receipt by the laboratory an appropriate laboratory chain of custody form(s) account(s) for the sample or sample aliquots within the laboratory.

Collection container. A container into which the employee urinates to provide the urine sample used for a drug test.

Collection site. A place designated by the employer where individuals present themselves for the purpose of providing a specimen of their urine to be analyzed for the presence of drugs.

Collection site person. A person who instructs and assists individuals at a collection site and who receives and makes a screening examination of the urine specimen provided by those individuals.

Confirmation (or confirmatory) test. In drug testing, a second analytical procedure to identify the presence of a specific drug or metabolite that is independent of the screening test and that uses a different technique and chemical principle from that of the screening test in order to ensure reliability and accuracy. (Gas chromatography/mass spectrometry (GC/MS) is the only authorized confirmation method for cocaine, marijuana, opiates, amphetamines, and phencyclidine.) In alcohol testing, a second test, following a screening test with a result of 0.02 or greater, that provides quantitative data of alcohol concentration.

DHHS. The Department of Health and Human Services or any designee of the Secretary, Department of Health and Human Services.

DOT agency. An agency of the United States Department of Transportation administering regulations related to drug or alcohol testing, including the United States Coast Guard (for drug testing purposes only), the Federal Aviation Administration, the Federal Railroad Administration, the Federal Highway Administration, the Federal Transit Administration, the Research and Special Programs Administration, and the Office of the Secretary.

Employee. An individual designated in a DOT agency regulation as subject to drug testing and/or alcohol testing. As used in this part "employee" includes an applicant for employment. "Employee" and "individual" or "individual to be tested" have the same meaning for purposes of this part.

Employer. An entity employing one or more employees that is subject to DOT agency regulations requiring compliance with this part. As used in this part, employer includes an industry consortium or joint enterprise comprised of two or more employing entities.

EBT (or evidential breath testing device). An EBT approved by the National Highway Traffic Safety Administration (NHTSA) for the evidential testing of breath and placed on NHTSA's "Conforming Products List of Evidential Breath Measurement Devices" (CPL) and identified on the CPL as conforming with the model specifications available from the National Highway Traffic Safety Administration, Office of Alcohol and State Programs.

Medical Review Officer (MRO). A licensed physician (medical doctor or doctor of osteopathy) responsible for receiving laboratory results generated by an employer's drug testing program who has knowledge of substance abuse disorders and has appropriate medical training to interpret and evaluate an individual's confirmed positive test result together with his or her medical history and any other relevant biomedical information.

Screening test (or initial test). In drug testing, an immunoassay screen to eliminate "negative" urine specimens from further analysis. In alcohol testing, an analytic procedure to determine whether an employee may have a prohibited concentration of alcohol in a breath specimen.

Secretary. The Secretary of Transportation or the Secretary's designee.

Shipping container. A container capable of being secured with a tamper-evident seal that is used for transfer of one or more urine specimen bottle(s) and associated documentation from the collection site to the laboratory.

Specimen bottle. The bottle that, after being labeled and sealed according to the procedures in this part, is used to transmit a urine sample to the laboratory.

Substance abuse professional. A licensed physician (Medical Doctor or Doctor of Osteopathy); or a licensed or certified psychologist, social worker, or employee assistance professional; or an addiction counselor (certified by the National Association of Alcoholism and Drug Abuse Counselors Certification Commission or by the International Certification Reciprocity Consortium/Alcohol & Other Drug Abuse). All must have knowledge of and clinical experience in the diagnosis and treatment of alcohol and controlled substances-related disorders.

§§40.5 to 40.19 [Reserved]

SUBPART B—DRUG TESTING

§40.21 The drugs.

(a) DOT agency drug testing programs require that employers test for marijuana, cocaine, opiates, amphetamines and phencyclidine.

(b) An employer may include in its testing protocols other controlled substances or alcohol only pursuant to a DOT agency approval, if testing for those substances is authorized under agency regulations and if the DHHS has established an approved testing protocol and positive threshold for each such substance.

(c) Urine specimens collected under DOT agency regulations requiring compliance with this part may only be used to test for controlled substances designated or approved for testing as described in this section and shall not be used to conduct any other analysis or test unless otherwise specifically authorized by DOT agency regulations.

(d) This section does not prohibit procedures reasonably incident to analysis of the specimen for controlled substances (e.g., determination of pH or tests for specific gravity, creatinine concentration or presence of adulterants).

§40.23 Preparation for testing.

The employer and certified laboratory shall develop and maintain a clear and well-documented procedure for collection, shipment, and accessioning of urine specimens under this part. Such a procedure shall include, at a minimum, the following:

(a)(1) Except as provided in paragraph (a)(2) of this section, use of the drug testing form prescribed under this part.

(i) This form is found in Appendix A to this part.

(ii) Employers and other participants in the DOT drug testing program may not modify or revise this form, except that the drug testing custody and control form may include such additional information as may be required for billing or other legitimate purposes necessary to the collection, provided that personal identifying information on the donor (other than the social security number or other employee ID number) may not be provided to the laboratory.

(iii) Donor medical information may appear only on the copy provided the donor.

(2) Notwithstanding the requirement of paragraph (a)(1)(ii) of this section, employers and other participants may use existing forms that were in use in the DOT drug testing program prior to February 16, 1995, until June 1, 1995.

(b)(1) Use of a clean, single-use specimen bottle that is securely wrapped until filled with the specimen. A clean, single-use collection container (e.g., disposable cup or sterile urinal) that is securely wrapped until used may also be employed. If urination is directly into the specimen bottle, the specimen bottle shall be provided to the employee still sealed in its wrapper or shall be unwrapped in the employee's presence immediately prior to its being provided. If a separate collection container is used for urination, the collection container shall be provided to the employee still sealed in its wrapper or shall be unwrapped in the employee's presence immediately prior to its being provided; and the collection site person shall unwrap the specimen bottle in the presence of the employee at the time the urine specimen is presented.

(2) Use of a tamperproof sealing system, designed in a manner such to ensure against undetected opening. The specimen bottle shall be identified with a unique identifying number identical to that appearing on the urine custody and control form, and space shall be provided to initial the bottle affirming its identity. For purposes of clarity, this part assumes use of a system made up of one or more pre-printed labels and seals (or a unitary label/seal), but use of other, equally effective technologies is authorized.

(c) Use of a shipping container in which the specimen and associated paperwork may be transferred and which can be sealed and initialled to prevent undetected tampering. In the split specimen option is exercised, the split specimen and associated paperwork shall be sealed in a shipping (or storage) container and initialled to prevent undetected tampering.

(d) Written procedures, instructions and training shall be provided as follows:

(1) Employer collection procedures and training shall clearly emphasize that the collection site person is responsible for maintaining the integrity of the specimen collection and transfer process, carefully ensuring the modesty and privacy of the donor, and is to avoid any conduct or remarks that might be construed as accusatorial or otherwise offensive or inappropriate.

(2) A collection site person shall have successfully completed training to carry out this function or shall be a licensed medical professional or technician who is provided instructions for collection under this part and certifies completion as required in this part:

(i) A non-medical collection site person shall receive training in compliance with this part and shall demonstrate proficiency in the application of this part prior to serving as a collection site person. A medical professional, technologist or technician licensed or otherwise approved to practice in the jurisdiction in which the collection takes place is not required to receive such training if that person is provided instructions described in this part and performs collections in accordance with those instructions.

(ii) Collection site persons shall be provided with detailed, clear instructions on the collection of specimens in compliance with this part. Employer representatives and donors subject to testing shall also be provided standard written instructions setting forth their responsibilities.

(3) Unless it is impracticable for any other individual to perform this function, a direct supervisor of an employee shall not serve as the collection site person for a test of the employee. If the rules of a DOT agency are more stringent than this provision regarding the use of supervisors as collection site personnel, the DOT agency rules shall prevail with respect to testing to which they apply.

(4) In any case where a collection is monitored by non-medical personnel or is directly observed, the collection site person shall be of the same gender as the donor. A collection is monitored for this purpose if the enclosure provides less than complete privacy for the donor (e.g., if a restroom stall is used and the collection site person remains in the restroom, or if the collection site person is expected to listen for use of unsecured sources of water.)

§40.25 Specimen collection procedures.

(a) Designation of collection site.

(1) Each employer drug testing program shall have one or more designated collection sites which have all necessary personnel, materials, equipment, facilities and supervision to provide for the collection, security, temporary storage, and shipping or transportation of urine specimens to a certified drug testing laboratory. An independent medical facility may also be utilized as a collection site provided the other applicable requirements of this part are met.

(2) A designated collection site may be any suitable location where a specimen can be collected under conditions set forth in this part, including a properly equipped mobile facility. A designated collection site shall be a location having an enclosure within which private urination can occur, a toilet for completion of urination (unless a single-use collector is used with sufficient capacity to contain the void), and a suitable clean surface for writing. The site must also have a source of water for washing hands, which, if practicable, should be external to the enclosure where urination occurs.

(b) Security. The purpose of this paragraph is to prevent unauthorized access which could compromise the integrity of the collection process or the specimen.

(1) Procedures shall provide for the designated collection site to be secure. If a collection site facility is dedicated solely to urine collection, it shall be secure at all times. If a facility cannot be dedicated solely to drug testing, the portion of the facility used for testing shall be secured during drug testing.

(2) A facility normally used for other purposes, such as a public rest room or hospital examining room, may be secured by visual inspection to ensure other persons are not present and undetected access (e.g., through a rear door not in the view of the collection site person) is not possible. Security during collection may be maintained by effective restriction of access to collection materials and specimens. In the case of a public rest room, the facility must be posted against access during the entire collection procedure to avoid embarrassment to the employee or distraction of the collection site person.

(3) If it is impractical to maintain continuous physical security of a collection site from the time the specimen is presented until the sealed mailer is transferred for shipment, the following minimum procedures shall apply. The specimen shall remain under the direct control of the collection site person from delivery to its being sealed in the mailer. The mailer shall be immediately mailed, maintained in secure storage, or remain until mailed under the personal control of the collection site person.

(c) Chain of Custody. The chain of custody block of the drug testing custody and control form shall be properly executed by authorized collection site personnel upon receipt of specimens. Handling and transportation of urine specimens from one authorized individual or place to another shall always be accomplished through chain of custody procedures. Since specimens and documentation are sealed in shipping containers that would indicate any tampering during transit to the laboratory and couriers, express carriers, and postal service personnel do not have access to the chain of custody forms, there is no requirement that such personnel document chain of custody for the shipping container during transit. Nor is there a requirement that there be a chain of custody entry when a specimen which is sealed in such a shipping container is put into or taken out of secure storage at the collection site prior to pickup by such personnel. This means that the chain of custody is not broken, and a test shall not be canceled, because couriers, express carriers, postal service personnel, or similar persons involved solely with the transportation of a specimen to a laboratory, have not documented their participation in the chain of custody documentation or because the chain of custody does not contain entries related to putting the specimen into or removing it from secure temporary storage at the collection site. Every effort shall be made to minimize the number of persons handling specimens.

(d) Access to authorized personnel only. No unauthorized personnel shall be permitted in any part of the designated collection site where urine specimens are collected or stored. Only the collection site person may handle specimens prior to their securement in the mailing container or monitor or observe specimen collection (under the conditions specified in this part). In order to promote security of specimens, avoid distraction of the collection site person and ensure against any confusion in the identification of specimens, the collection site person shall have only one donor under his or her supervision at any time. For this purpose, a collection procedure is complete when the urine bottle has been sealed and initialled, the drug testing custody and control form has been executed, and the employee has departed the site (or, in the case of an employee who was unable to provide a complete specimen, has entered a waiting area).

(e) Privacy.

(1) Procedures for collecting urine specimens shall allow individual privacy unless there is a reason to believe that a particular individual may alter or substitute the specimen to be provided, as further described in this paragraph.

(2) For purposes of this part, the following circumstances are the exclusive grounds constituting a reason to believe that the individual may alter or substitute the specimen:

(i) The employee has presented a urine specimen that falls outside the normal temperature range (32degrees-38degrees C/90degrees-100degrees F), and

(A) The employee declines to provide a measurement of body temperature (taken by a means other than use of a rectal thermometer), as provided in paragraph (f)(14) of the part; or

(B) Body temperature varies by more than 1 <<degrees>> C/1.8 <<degrees>> F from the temperature of the specimen;

(ii) The last urine specimen provided by the employee (i.e., on a previous occasion) was determined by the laboratory to have a specific gravity of less than 1.003 and a creatinine concentration below .2g/L;

(iii) The collection site person observes conduct clearly and unequivocally indicating an attempt to substitute or adulterate the sample (e.g., substitute urine in plain view, blue dye in specimen presented, etc.); or

(iv) The employee has previously been determined to have used a controlled substance without medical authorization and the particular test was being conducted under a DOT agency regulation providing for follow-up testing upon or after return to service.

(3) A higher-level supervisor of the collection site person, or a designated employer representative, shall review and concur in advance with any decision by a collection site person to obtain a specimen under the direct observation of a same gender collection site person based upon the circumstances described in subparagraph (2) of this paragraph.

(f) Integrity and identity of specimen. Employers shall take precautions to ensure that a urine specimen is not adulterated or diluted during the collection procedure and that information on the urine bottle and on the urine custody and control form can identify the individual from whom the specimen was collected. The following minimum precautions shall be taken to ensure that unadulterated specimens are obtained and correctly identified:

(1) To deter the dilution of specimens at the collection site, toilet bluing agents shall be placed in toilet tanks wherever possible, so the reservoir of water in the toilet bowl always remains blue. Where practicable, there shall be no other source of water (e.g., shower or sink) in the enclosure where urination occurs. If there is another source of water in the enclosure it shall be effectively secured or monitored to ensure it is not used as a source for diluting the specimen.

(2) When an individual arrives at the collection site, the collection site person shall ensure that the individual is positively identified as the employee selected for testing (e.g., through presentation of photo identification or identification by the employer's representative). If the individual's identity cannot be established, the collection site person shall not

proceed with the collection. If the employee requests, the collection site person shall show his/her identification to the employee.

(3) If the individual fails to arrive at the assigned time, the collection site person shall contact the appropriate authority to obtain guidance on the action to be taken.

(4) The collection site person shall ask the individual to remove any unnecessary outer garments such as a coat or jacket that might conceal items or substances that could be used to tamper with or adulterate the individual's urine specimen. The collection site person shall ensure that all personal belongings such as a purse or briefcase remain with the outer garments. The individual may retain his or her wallet. If the employee requests it, the collection site personnel shall provide the employee a receipt for any personal belongings.

(5) The individual shall be instructed to wash and dry his or her hands prior to urination.

(6) After washing hands, the individual shall remain in the presence of the collection site person and shall not have access to any water fountain, faucet, soap dispenser, cleaning agent or any other materials which could be used to adulterate the specimen.

(7) The individual may provide his/her specimen in the privacy of a stall or otherwise partitioned area that allows for individual privacy. The collection site person shall provide the individual with a specimen bottle or collection container, if applicable, for this purpose.

(8) The collection site person shall note any unusual behavior or appearance on the urine custody and control form.

(9) In the exceptional event that an employer-designated collection site is not accessible and there is an immediate requirement for specimen collection (e.g., circumstances require a post-accident test), a public rest room may be used according to the following procedures: A collection site person of the same gender as the individual shall accompany the individual into the public rest room which shall be made secure during the collection procedure. If possible, a toilet bluing agent shall be placed in the bowl and any accessible toilet tank. The collection site person shall remain in the rest room, but outside the stall, until the specimen is collected. If no bluing agent is available to deter specimen dilution, the collection site person shall instruct the individual not to flush the toilet until the specimen is delivered to the collection site person. After the collection site person has possession of the specimen, the individual will be instructed to flush the toilet and to participate with the collection site person in completing the chain of custody procedures.

(10) The collection site person shall instruct the employee to provide at least 45 ml of urine under the split sample method of collection or 30 ml of urine under the single sample method of collection.

(i)(A) Employers with employees subject to drug testing only under the drug testing rules of the Research and Special Programs Administration and/or Coast Guard may use the "split sample" method of collection or may collect a single sample for those employees.

(B) Employers with employees subject to drug testing under the drug testing rules of the Federal Highway Administration, Federal Railroad Administration, Federal Transit Administration, or Federal Aviation Administration shall use the "split sample" method of collection for those employees.

(ii) Employers using the split sample method of collection shall follow the procedures in this paragraph (f)(10)(ii):

(A) The donor shall urinate into a collection container or a specimen bottle capable of holding at least 60 ml.

(B)(1) If a collection container is used, the collection site person, in the presence of the donor, pours the urine into two specimen bottles. Thirty (30) ml shall be poured into one specimen bottle, to be used as the primary specimen. At least 15 ml shall be poured into the other bottle, to be used as the split specimen.

(2) If a single specimen bottle is used as a collection container, the collection site person, in the presence of the donor, shall pour 15 ml of urine from the specimen bottle into a second specimen bottle (to be used as the split specimen) and retain the remainder (at least 30 ml) in the collection bottle (to be used as the primary specimen).

(C) Nothing in this section precludes the use of a collection method or system that does not involve the physical pouring of urine from one container or bottle to another by the collection site person, provided that the method or system results in the subdivision of the specimen into a primary (30 ml) and a split (at least 15 ml) specimen that can be transmitted to the laboratory and tested in accordance with the requirements of this Subpart.

(D) Both bottles shall be shipped in a single shipping container, together with copies 1,2, and the split specimen copy of the chain of custody form, to the laboratory.

(E) If the test result of the primary specimen is positive, the employee may request that the MRO direct that the split specimen be tested in a different DHHS-certified laboratory for presence of the drug(s) for which a positive result was obtained in the test of the primary specimen. The MRO shall honor such a request if it is made within 72 hours of the employee having been notified of a verified positive test result.

(F) When the MRO informs the laboratory in writing that the employee has requested a test of the split specimen, the laboratory shall forward, to a different DHHS-approved laboratory, the split specimen bottle, with seal intact, a copy of the MRO request, and the split specimen copy of the chain of custody form with appropriate chain of custody entries.

(G) The result of the test of the split specimen is transmitted by the second laboratory to the MRO.

(H) Action required by DOT agency regulations as the result of a positive drug test (e.g., removal from performing a safety-sensitive function) is not stayed pending the result of the test of the split specimen.

(I) If the result of the test of the split specimen fails to reconfirm the presence of the drug(s) or drug metabolite(s) found in the primary specimen, the MRO shall cancel the test, and report the cancellation and the reasons for it to the DOT, the employer, and the employee.

(iii) Employers using the single sample collection method shall follow the procedures in paragraph:

(A) The collector may choose to direct the employee to urinate either directly into a specimen bottle or into a separate collection container.

(B) If a separate collection container is used, the collection site person shall pour at least 30 ml of the urine from the collection container into the specimen bottle in the presence of the employee.

(iv)(A)(1) In either collection methodology, upon receiving the specimen from the individual, the collection site person shall determine if the specimen has at least 30 milliliters of urine for a single specimen collection or 45 milliliters of urine for a split specimen collection.

(2) If the individual has not provided the required quantity of urine, the specimen shall be discarded. The collection site person shall direct the individual to drink up to 40 ounces of fluid, distributed reasonably through a period of up to three hours, or until the individual has provided a new urine specimen, whichever occurs first. If the employee refuses to drink fluids as directed or to provide a new urine specimen, the collection site person shall terminate the collection and notify the employer that the employee has refused to submit to testing.

(3) If the employee has not provided a sufficient specimen within three hours of the first unsuccessful attempt to provide the specimen, the collection site person shall discontinue the collection and notify the employer.

(B) The employer shall direct any employee who does not provide a sufficient urine specimen (see paragraph (f)(10)(iv)(A)(3) of this section) to obtain, as soon as possible after the attempted provision of urine, an evaluation from a licensed physician who is acceptable to the employer concerning the employee's ability to provide an adequate amount of urine.

(1) If the physician determines, in his or her reasonable medical judgment, that a medical condition has, or with a high degree of probability, could have, precluded the employee from providing an adequate amount of urine, the employee's failure to provide an adequate amount of urine shall not be deemed a refusal to take a test. For purposes of this paragraph, a medical condition includes an ascertainable physiological condition (e.g., a urinary system dysfunction) or a documented pre-existing psychological disorder, but does not include unsupported assertions of "situational anxiety" or dehydration. The physician shall provide to the MRO a brief written statement setting forth his or her conclusion and the basis for it, which shall not include detailed information on the medical condition of the employee. Upon receipt of this statement, the MRO shall report his or her conclusions to the employer in writing.

(2) If the physician, in his or her reasonable medical judgment, is unable to make the determination set forth in paragraph (f)(10)(iv)(B)(1) of this section, the employee's failure to provide an adequate amount of urine shall be regarded as a refusal to take a test. The physician shall provide to the MRO a brief written statement setting forth his or her conclusion and the basis for it, which shall not include detailed information on the medical condition of the employee. Upon receipt of

this statement, the MRO shall report his or her conclusions to the employer in writing.

(11) After the specimen has been provided and submitted to the collection site person, the individual shall be allowed to wash his or her hands.

(12) Immediately after the specimen is collected, the collection site person shall measure the temperature of the specimen. The temperature measuring device used must accurately reflect the temperature of the specimen and not contaminate the specimen. The time from urination to temperature measure is critical and in no case shall exceed 4 minutes.

(13) A specimen temperature outside the range of 32°–38° C/90°–100° F constitutes a reason to believe that the individual has altered or substituted the specimen (see paragraph (e)(2)(i) of this section). In such cases, the individual supplying the specimen may volunteer to have his or her oral temperature taken to provide evidence to counter the reason to believe the individual may have altered or substituted the specimen.

(14) Immediately after the specimen is collected, the collection site person shall also inspect the specimen to determine its color and look for any signs of contaminants. Any unusual findings shall be noted on the urine custody and control form.

(15) All specimens suspected of being adulterated shall be forwarded to the laboratory for testing.

(16) Whenever there is reason to believe that a particular individual has altered or substituted the specimen as described in paragraph (e)(2) (i) or (iii) of this section, a second specimen shall be obtained as soon as possible under the direct observation of a same gender collection site person.

(17) Both the individual being tested and the collection site person shall keep the specimen in view at all times prior to its being sealed and labeled. As provided below, the specimen shall be sealed (by placement of a tamperproof seal over the bottle cap and down the sides of the bottle) and labeled in the presence of the employee. If the specimen is transferred to a second bottle, the collection site person shall request the individual to observe the transfer of the specimen and the placement of the tamperproof seal over the bottle cap and down the sides of the bottle.

(18) The collection site person and the individual being tested shall be present at the same time during procedures outlined in paragraphs (f)(19)- (f)(22) of this section.

(19) The collection site person shall place securely on the bottle an identification label which contains the date, the individual's specimen number, and any other identifying information provided or required by the employer. If separate from the label, the tamperproof seal shall also be applied.

(20) The individual shall initial the identification label on the specimen bottle for the purpose of certifying that it is the specimen collected from him or her.

(21) The collection site person shall enter on the drug testing custody and control form all information identifying the specimen. The collection site person shall sign the drug testing custody and control form certifying that the collection was accomplished according to the applicable Federal requirements.

(22)(i) The individual shall be asked to read and sign a statement on the drug testing custody and control form certifying that the specimen identified as having been collected from him or her is in fact the specimen he or she provided.

(ii) When specified by DOT agency regulation or required by the collection site (other than an employer site) or by the laboratory, the employee may be required to sign a consent or release form authorizing the collection of the specimen, analysis of the specimen for designated controlled substances, and release of the results to the employer. The employee may not be required to waive liability with respect to negligence on the part of any person participating in the collection, handling or analysis of the specimen or to indemnify any person for the negligence of others.

(23) The collection site person shall complete the chain of custody portion of the drug testing custody and control form to indicate receipt of the specimen from the employee and shall certify proper completion of the collection.

(24) The urine specimen and chain of custody form are now ready for shipment. If the specimen is not immediately prepared for shipment, the collection site person shall ensure that it is appropriately safeguarded during temporary storage.

(25)(i) While any part of the above chain of custody procedures is being performed, it is essential that the urine specimen and custody documents be under the control of the involved collection site person. If the involved collection site person leaves his or her work station momentarily, the collection site person shall take the specimen and drug testing custody and control form with him or her or shall secure them. After the collection site person returns to the work station, the custody process will continue. If the collection site person is leaving for an extended period of time, he or she shall package the specimen for mailing before leaving the site.

(ii) The collection site person shall not leave the collection site in the interval between presentation of the specimen by the employee and securement of the sample with an identifying label bearing the employee's specimen identification number (shown on the urine custody and control form) and seal initialed by the employee. If it becomes necessary for the collection site person to leave the site during this interval, the collection shall be nullified and (at the election of the employer) a new collection begun.

(g) Collection control. To the maximum extent possible, collection site personnel shall keep the individual's specimen bottle within sight both before and after the individual has urinated. After the specimen is collected, it shall be properly sealed and labeled.

(h) Transportation to Laboratory. Collection site personnel shall arrange to ship the collected specimen to the drug testing laboratory. The specimens shall be placed in shipping containers designed to minimize the possibility of damage during shipment (e.g., specimen boxes and/or padded mailers); and those containers shall be securely sealed to eliminate the possibility of undetected tampering with the specimen and/or the form. On the tape sealing the shipping container, the collection site person shall sign and enter the date specimens were sealed in the shipping container for shipment. The collection site person shall ensure that the chain of custody documentation is enclosed in each container sealed for shipment to the drug testing laboratory. Since specimens and documentation are sealed in shipping containers that would indicate any tampering during transit to the laboratory and couriers, express carriers, and postal service personnel do not have access to the chain of custody forms, there is no requirement that such personnel document chain of custody for the shipping container during transit. Nor is there a requirement that there be a chain of custody entry when a specimen which is sealed in such a shipping container is put into or taken out of secure storage at the collection site prior to pickup by such personnel. This means that the chain of custody is not broken, and a test shall not be canceled, because couriers, express carriers, postal service personnel, or similar persons involved solely with the transportation of a specimen to a laboratory, have not documented their participation in the chain of custody documentation or because the chain of custody does not contain entries related to putting the specimen into or removing it from secure temporary storage at the collection site.

(i) Failure to cooperate. If the employee refuses to cooperate with the collection process, the collection site person shall inform the employer representative and shall document the non-cooperation on the drug testing custody and control form.

(j) Employee requiring medical attention. If the sample is being collected from an employee in need of medical attention (e.g., as part of a post-accident test given in an emergency medical facility), necessary medical attention shall not be delayed in order to collect the specimen.

(k) Use of chain of custody form. A chain of custody form (and a laboratory internal chain of custody document, where applicable), shall be used for maintaining control and accountability of each specimen from the point of collection to final disposition of the specimen. The date and purpose shall be documented on the form each time a specimen is handled or transferred and every individual in the chain of custody shall be identified. Since specimens and documentation are sealed in shipping containers that would indicate any tampering during transit to the laboratory and couriers, express carriers, and postal service personnel do not have access to the chain of custody forms, there is no requirement that such personnel document chain of custody for the shipping container during transit. Nor is there a requirement that there be a chain of custody entry when a specimen which is sealed in such a shipping container is put into or taken out of secure storage at the collection site prior to pickup by such personnel. This means that the chain of custody is not broken, and a test shall not be canceled, because couriers, express carriers, postal service personnel, or similar persons involved solely with the transportation of a specimen to a laboratory, have not documented their participation in the chain of custody documentation or because the chain of custody does not contain entries related to putting the specimen into or removing it from secure temporary storage at the collection site. Every effort shall be made to minimize the number of persons handling specimens.

§40.27 Laboratory personnel.

(a) Day-to-day management.

(1) The laboratory shall have a qualified individual to assume professional, organizational, educational, and administrative responsibility for the laboratory's urine drug testing facility.

(2) This individual shall have documented scientific qualifications in analytical forensic toxicology. Minimum qualifications are:

(i) Certification as a laboratory director by a State in forensic or clinical laboratory toxicology; or

(ii) A Ph.D. in one of the natural sciences with an adequate undergraduate and graduate education in biology, chemistry, and pharmacology or toxicology; or

(iii) Training and experience comparable to a Ph.D. in one of the natural sciences, such as a medical or scientific degree with additional training and laboratory/research experience in biology, chemistry, and pharmacology or toxicology; and

(iv) In addition to the requirements in paragraph (a)(2) (i), (ii), or (iii) of this section, minimum qualifications also require:

(A) Appropriate experience in analytical forensic toxicology including experience with the analysis of biological material for drugs of abuse, and

(B) Appropriate training and/or experience in forensic applications of analytical toxicology, e.g., publications, court testimony, research concerning analytical toxicology of drugs of abuse, or other factors which qualify the individual as an expert witness in forensic toxicology.

(3) This individual shall be engaged in and responsible for the day-to-day management of the drug testing laboratory even where another individual has overall responsibility for an entire multi-specialty laboratory.

(4) This individual shall be responsible for ensuring that there are enough personnel with adequate training and experience to supervise and conduct the work of the drug testing laboratory. He or she shall assure the continued competency of laboratory personnel by documenting their in-service training, reviewing their work performance, and verifying their skills.

(5) This individual shall be responsible for the laboratory's having a procedure manual which is complete, up-to-date, available for personnel performing tests, and followed by those personnel. The procedure manual shall be reviewed, signed, and dated by this responsible individual whenever procedures are first placed into use or changed or when a new individual assumes responsibility for management of the drug testing laboratory. Copies of all procedures and dates on which they are in effect shall be maintained. (Specific contents of the procedure manual are described in §40.29(n)(1).)

(6) This individual shall be responsible for maintaining a quality assurance program to assure the proper performance and reporting of all test results; for maintaining acceptable analytical performance for all controls and standards; for maintaining quality control testing; and for assuring and documenting the validity, reliability, accuracy, precision, and performance characteristics of each test and test system.

(7) This individual shall be responsible for taking all remedial actions necessary to maintain satisfactory operation and performance of the laboratory in response to quality control systems not being within performance specifications, errors in result reporting or in analysis of performance testing results. This individual shall ensure that sample results are not reported until all corrective actions have been taken and he or she can assure that the tests results provided are accurate and reliable.

(b) Test validation. The laboratory's urine drug testing facility shall have a qualified individual(s) who reviews all pertinent data and quality control results in order to attest to the validity of the laboratory's test reports. A laboratory may designate more than one person to perform this function. This individual(s) may be any employee who is qualified to be responsible for day- to-day management or operation of the drug testing laboratory.

(c) Day-to-day operations and supervision of analysts. The laboratory's urine drug testing facility shall have an individual to be responsible for day-to-day operations and to supervise the technical analysts. This individual(s) shall have at least a bachelor's degree in the chemical or biological sciences or medical technology or equivalent. He or she shall have training and experience in the theory and practice of the procedures used in the laboratory, resulting in his or her thorough understanding of quality control practices and procedures; the review, interpretation, and reporting of test results; maintenance of chain of custody; and proper remedial actions to be taken in response to test systems being out of control limits or detecting aberrant test or quality control results.

(d) Other personnel. Other technicians or nontechnical staff shall have the necessary training and skills for the tasks assigned.

(e) Training. The laboratory's urine drug testing program shall make available continuing education programs to meet the needs of laboratory personnel.

(f) Files. Laboratory personnel files shall include: resume of training and experience, certification or license if any; references; job descriptions; records of performance evaluation and advancement; incident reports; and results of tests which establish employee competency for the position he or she holds, such as a test for color blindness, if appropriate.

§40.29 Laboratory analysis procedures.

(a) Security and chain of custody.

(1) Drug testing laboratories shall be secure at all times. They shall have in place sufficient security measures to control access to the premises and to ensure that no unauthorized personnel handle specimens or gain access to the laboratory process or to areas where records are stored. Access to these secured areas shall be limited to specifically authorized individuals whose authorization is documented. With the exception of personnel authorized to conduct inspections on behalf of Federal agencies for which the laboratory is engaged in urine testing or on behalf of DHHS, all authorized visitors and maintenance and service personnel shall be escorted at all times. Documentation of individuals accessing these areas, dates, and time of entry and purpose of entry must be maintained.

(2) Laboratories shall use chain of custody procedures to maintain control and accountability of specimens from receipt through completion of testing, reporting of results during storage, and continuing until final disposition of specimens. The date and purpose shall be documented on an appropriate chain of custody form each time a specimen is handled or transferred and every individual in the chain shall be identified. Accordingly, authorized technicians shall be responsible for each urine specimen or aliquot in their possession and shall sign and complete chain of custody forms for those specimens or aliquots as they are received.

(b) Receiving.

(1)(i) When a shipment of specimens is received, laboratory personnel shall inspect each package for evidence of possible tampering and compare information on specimen bottles within each package to the information on the accompanying chain of custody forms. Any direct evidence of tampering or discrepancies in the information on specimen bottles and the employer's chain of custody forms attached to the shipment shall be immediately reported to the employer and shall be noted on the laboratory's chain of custody form which shall accompany the specimens while they are in the laboratory's possession.

(ii) Where the employer has used the split sample method, and the laboratory observes that the split specimen is untestable, inadequate, or unavailable for testing, the laboratory shall nevertheless test the primary specimen. The laboratory does not inform the MRO or the employer of the untestability, inadequacy, or unavailability of the split specimen until and unless the primary specimen is a verified positive test and the MRO has informed the laboratory that the employee has requested a test of the split specimen.

(2) In situations where the employer uses the split sample collection method, the laboratory shall log in the split specimen, with the split specimen bottle seal remaining intact. The laboratory shall store this sample securely (see paragraph (c) of this section). If the result of the test of the primary specimen is negative, the laboratory may discard the split specimen. If the result of the test of the primary specimen is positive, the laboratory shall retain the split specimen in frozen storage for 60 days from the date on which the laboratory acquires it (see paragraph (h) of this section). Following the end of the 60-day period, if not informed by the MRO that the employee has requested a test of the split specimen, the laboratory may discard the split specimen.

(3) When directed in writing by the MRO to forward the split specimen to another DHHS-certified laboratory for analysis, the second laboratory shall analyze the split specimen by GC/MS to reconfirm the presence of the drug(s) or drug metabolite(s) found in the primary specimen. Such GC/MS confirmation shall be conducted without regard to the cutoff levels of §40.29(f). The split specimen shall be retained in long-term storage for one year by the laboratory conducting the analysis of the split specimen (or longer if litigation concerning the test is pending).

(c) Short-term refrigerated storage. Specimens that do not receive an initial test within 7 days of arrival at the laboratory shall be placed in secure refrigeration units. Temperatures shall not exceed 6° C. Emergency power equipment shall be available in case of prolonged power failure.

(d) Specimen processing. Laboratory facilities for urine drug testing will normally process specimens by grouping them into batches. The number of specimens in each batch may vary significantly depending on the size of the laboratory and its workload. When conducting either initial or confirmatory tests, every batch shall contain an appropriate number of standards for calibrating the instrumentation and a minimum of 10 percent controls. Both quality control and blind performance test samples shall appear as ordinary samples to laboratory analysts.

(e) Initial test.

(1) The initial test shall use an immunoassay which meets the requirements of the Food and Drug Administration for commercial distribution. The following initial cutoff levels shall be used when screening specimens to determine whether they are negative for these five drugs or classes of drugs:

Laboratory Analysis Procedures	Initial Test Cutoff levels (ng/ml)
Marijuana metabolites	50
Cocaine metabolites	300
Opiate metabolites	2,000
Phencyclidine	25
Amphetamines	1,000

(2) These cutoff levels are subject to change by the Department of Health and Human Services as advances in technology or other considerations warrant identification of these substances at other concentrations.

(f) Confirmatory test.

(1) All specimens identified as positive on the initial test shall be confirmed using gas chromatography/mass spectrometry (GC/MS) techniques at the cutoff levels listed in this paragraph for each drug. All confirmations shall be by quantitative analysis. Concentrations that exceed the linear region of the standard curve shall be documented in the laboratory record as "greater than highest standard curve value."

(2) These cutoff levels are subject to change by the Department of Health and Human Ser-

Confirmatory test	Confirmatory test cutoff levels (ng/ml)
Marijuana metabolites[1]	15
Cocaine metabolites[2]	150
Opiates:	
Morphine	2,000
Codeine	2,000
6-Acetylmorphine[4]	10
Phencyclidine	25
Amphetamines:	
Amphetamine	500
Methamphetamine[3]	500

[1] Delta-9-tetrahydrocannabinol-9-carboxylic acid.

[2] Benzoylecgonine.

[3] Specimen must also contain amphetamine at a concentration greater than or equal to 200ng/ml.

[4] Test for 6-AM when morphine concentration exceeds 2,000 ng/ml.

vices as advances in technology or other considerations warrant identification of these substances at other concentrations.

(g) Reporting results.

(1) The laboratory shall report test results to the employer's Medical Review Officer within an average of 5 working days after receipt of the specimen by the laboratory. Before any test result is reported (the results of initial tests, confirmatory tests, or quality control data), it shall be reviewed and the test certified as an accurate report by the responsible individual. The report shall identify the drugs/metabolites tested for, whether positive or negative, the specimen number assigned by the employer, and the drug testing laboratory specimen identification number (accession number).

(2) The laboratory shall report as negative all specimens that are negative on the initial test or negative on the confirmatory test. Only specimens confirmed positive shall be reported positive for a specific drug.

(3) The Medical Review Officer may request from the laboratory and the laboratory shall provide quantitation of test results. The MRO shall report whether the test is positive or negative, and may report the drug(s) for which there was a positive test, but shall not disclose the quantitation of test results to the employer. Provided, that the MRO may reveal the quantitation of a positive test result to the employer, the employee, or the decisionmaker

in a lawsuit, grievance, or other proceeding initiated by or on behalf of the employee and arising from a verified positive drug test.

(4) The laboratory may transmit results to the Medical Review Officer by various electronic means (for example, teleprinters, facsimile, or computer) in a manner designed to ensure confidentiality of the information. Results may not be provided verbally by telephone. The laboratory and employer must ensure the security of the data transmission and limit access to any data transmission, storage, and retrieval system.

(5) The laboratory shall send only to the Medical Review Officer the original or a certified true copy of the drug testing custody and control form (part 2), which, in the case of a report positive for drug use, shall be signed (after the required certification block) by the individual responsible for day-to-day management of the drug testing laboratory or the individual responsible for attesting to the validity of the test reports, and attached to which shall be a copy of the test report.

(6) The laboratory shall provide the employer an aggregate quarterly statistical summary of urinalysis testing of the employer's employees. Laboratories may provide the report to a consortium provided that the laboratory provides employer-specific data and the consortium forwards the employer-specific data to the respective employers within 14 days of receipt of the laboratory report. The laboratory shall provide the report to the employer or consortium not more than 14 calendar days after the end of the quarter covered by the summary. Laboratory confirmation data only shall be included from test results reported within that quarter. The summary shall contain only the following information:

(i) Number of specimens received for testing;

(ii) Number of specimens confirmed positive for—

(A) Marijuana metabolite

(B) Cocaine metabolite

(C) Opiates;

(D) Phencyclidine;

(E) Amphetamines;

(iii) Number of specimens for which a test was not performed.

Quarterly reports shall not contain personal identifying information or other data from which it is reasonably likely that information about individuals' tests can be readily inferred. If necessary, in order to prevent disclosure of such data, the laboratory shall not send such a report until data are sufficiently aggregated to make such an inference unlikely. In any quarter in which a report is withheld for this reason, or because no testing was conducted, the laboratory shall so inform the consortium/employer in writing.

(7) The laboratory shall make available copies of all analytical results for employer drug testing programs when requested by DOT or any DOT agency with regulatory authority over the employer.

(8) Unless otherwise instructed by the employer in writing, all records pertaining to a given urine specimen shall be retained by the drug testing laboratory for a minimum of 2 years.

(h) Long-term storage. Long-term frozen storage (-20° C or less) ensures that positive urine specimens will be available for any necessary retest during administrative or disciplinary proceedings. Drug testing laboratories shall retain and place in properly secured long-term frozen storage for a minimum of 1 year all specimens confirmed positive, in their original labeled specimen bottles. Within this 1-year period, an employer (or other person designated in a DOT agency regulation) may request the laboratory to retain the specimen for an additional period of time, but if no such request is received the laboratory may discard the specimen after the end of 1 year, except that the laboratory shall be required to maintain any specimens known to be under legal challenge for an indefinite period.

(i) Retesting specimens. Because some analytes deteriorate or are lost during freezing and/or storage, quantitation for a retest is not subject to a specific cutoff requirement but must provide data sufficient to confirm the presence of the drug or metabolite.

(j) Subcontracting. Drug testing laboratories shall not subcontract and shall perform all work with their own personnel and equipment. The laboratory must be capable of performing testing for the five classes of drugs (marijuana, cocaine, opiates, phencyclidine and amphetamines) using the initial immunoassay and confirmatory GC/MS methods specified in this part. This paragraph does not prohibit subcontracting of laboratory analysis if specimens are sent directly from the collection site to the subcontractor, the subcontractor is a laboratory certified by DHHS as required in this part, the subcontractor performs all analysis and provides storage required under this part, and the subcontractor is responsible to the employer for compliance with this part and applicable DOT agency regulations as if it were the prime contractor.

(k) Laboratory facilities.

(1) Laboratory facilities shall comply with applicable provisions of any State licensing requirements.

(2) Laboratories certified in accordance with DHHS Guidelines shall have the capability, at the same laboratory premises, of performing initial and confirmatory tests for each drug or metabolite for which service is offered.

(l) Inspections. The Secretary, a DOT agency, any employer utilizing the laboratory, DHHS or any organization performing laboratory certification on behalf of DHHS reserves the right to inspect the laboratory at any time. Employer contracts with laboratories for drug testing, as well as contracts for collection site services, shall permit the employer and the DOT agency of jurisdiction (directly or through an agent) to conduct unannounced inspections.

(m) Documentation. The drug testing laboratories shall maintain and make available for at least 2 years documentation of all aspects of the testing process. This 2 year period may be extended upon written notification by a DOT agency or by any employer for which laboratory services are being provided. The required documentation shall include personnel files on all individuals authorized to have access to specimens; chain of custody documents; quality assurance/quality control records; procedure manuals; all test data (including calibration curves and any calculations used in determining test results); reports; performance records on performance testing; performance on certification inspections; and hard copies of computer-generated data. The laboratory shall maintain documents for any specimen known to be under legal challenge for an indefinite period.

(n) Additional requirements for certified laboratories.—

(1) Procedure manual. Each laboratory shall have a procedure manual which includes the principles of each test preparation of reagents, standards and controls, calibration procedures, derivation of results, linearity of methods, sensitivity of methods, cutoff values, mechanisms for reporting results, controls criteria for unacceptable specimens and results, remedial actions to be taken when the test systems are outside of acceptable limits, reagents and expiration dates, and references. Copies of all procedures and dates on which they are in effect shall be maintained as part of the manual.

(2) Standards and controls. Laboratory standards shall be prepared with pure drug standards which are properly labeled as to content and concentration. The standards shall be labeled with the following dates: when received; when prepared or opened; when placed in service; and expiration date.

(3) Instruments and equipment.

(i) Volumetric pipettes and measuring devices shall be certified for accuracy or be checked by gravimetric, colorimetric, or other verification procedure. Automatic pipettes and dilutors shall be checked for accuracy and reproducibility before being placed in service and checked periodically thereafter.

(ii) There shall be written procedures for instrument set-up and normal operation, a schedule for checking critical operating characteristics for all instruments, tolerance limits for acceptable function checks and instructions for major trouble shooting and repair. Records shall be available on preventive maintenance.

(4) Remedial actions. There shall be written procedures for the actions to be taken when systems are out of acceptable limits or errors are detected. There shall be documentation that these procedures are followed and that all necessary corrective actions are taken. There shall also be in place systems to verify all stages of testing and reporting and documentation that these procedures are followed.

(5) Personnel available to testify at proceedings. A laboratory shall have qualified personnel available to testify in an administrative or disciplinary proceeding against an employee when that proceeding is based on positive urinalysis results reported by the laboratory.

(6) The laboratory shall not enter into any relationship with an employer's MRO that may be construed as a potential conflict of interest or derive any financial benefit by having an employer use a specific MRO.

§40.31 Quality assurance and quality control.

(a) General. Drug testing laboratories shall have a quality assurance program which encompasses all aspects of the testing process including but not limited to specimen acquisition, chain of custody security and reporting of results, initial and confirmatory testing and validation of analytical procedures. Quality assurance procedures shall be designed, implemented and reviewed to monitor the conduct of each step of the process of testing for drugs.

(b) Laboratory quality control requirements for initial tests. Each analytical run of specimens to be screened shall include:

(1) Urine specimens certified to contain no drug;

(2) Urine specimens fortified with known standards; and

(3) Positive controls with the drug or metabolite at or near the cutoff level.

In addition, with each batch of samples a sufficient number of standards shall be included to ensure and document the linearity of the assay method over time in the concentration area of the cutoff. After acceptable values are obtained for the known standards, those values will be used to calculate sample data. Implementation of procedures to ensure the carryover does not contaminate the testing of an individual's specimen shall be documented. A minimum of 10 percent of all test samples shall be quality control specimens. Laboratory quality control samples, prepared from spiked urine samples of determined concentration shall be included in the run and should appear as normal samples to laboratory analysts. One percent of each run, with a minimum of at least one sample, shall be the laboratory's own quality control samples.

(c) Laboratory quality control requirements for confirmation tests. Each analytical run of specimens to be confirmed shall include:

(1) Urine specimens certified to contain no drug;

(2) Urine specimens fortified with known standards; and

(3) Positive controls with the drug or metabolite at or near the cutoff level. The linearity and precision of the method shall be periodically documented. Implementation of procedures to ensure that carryover does not contaminate the testing of an individual's specimen shall also be documented.

(d) Employer blind performance test procedures.

(1) Each employer covered by DOT agency drug testing regulations shall use blind testing quality control procedures as provided in this paragraph.

(2) Each employer shall submit three blind performance test specimens for each 100 employee specimens it submits, up to a maximum of 100 blind performance test specimens submitted per quarter. A DOT agency may increase this per quarter maximum number of samples if doing so is necessary to ensure adequate quality control of employers or consortiums with very large numbers of employees.

(3) For employers with 2000 or more covered employees, approximately 80 percent of the blind performance test samples shall be blank (i.e., containing no drug or otherwise as approved by a DOT agency) and the remaining samples shall be positive for one or more drugs per sample in a distribution such that all the drugs to be tested are included in approximately equal frequencies of challenge. The positive samples shall be spiked only with those drugs for which the employer is testing. This paragraph shall not be construed to prohibit spiking of other (potentially interfering) compounds, as technically appropriate, in order to verify the specificity of a particular assay.

(4) Employers with fewer than 2000 covered employees may submit blind performance test specimens as provided in paragraph (d)(3) of this section. Such employers may also submit only blank samples or may submit two separately labeled portions of a specimen from the same non-covered employee.

(5) Consortiums shall be responsible for the submission of blind samples on behalf of their members. The blind sampling rate shall apply to the total number of samples submitted by the consortium.

(6) The DOT agency concerned shall investigate, or shall refer to DHHS for investigation, any unsatisfactory performance testing result and, based on this investigation, the laboratory shall take action to correct the cause of the unsatisfactory performance test result. A record shall be made of the investigative findings and the corrective action taken by the laboratory, and that record shall be dated and signed by the individual responsible for the day-to-day management and operation of the drug testing laboratory. Then the DOT agency shall send the document to the employer as a report of the unsatisfactory performance testing incident. The DOT agency shall ensure notification of the finding to DHHS.

(7) Should a false positive error occur on a blind performance test specimen and the error is determined to be an administrative error (clerical, sample mixup, etc.), the employer shall promptly notify the DOT agency concerned. The DOT agency and the employer shall require the laboratory to take corrective action to minimize the occurrence of the particular error in the future, and, if there is reason to believe the error could have been systemic, the DOT agency may also require review and reanalysis of previously run specimens.

(8) Should a false positive error occur on a blind performance test specimen and the error is determined to be a technical or methodological error, the employer shall instruct the laboratory to submit all quality control data from the batch of specimens which included the false positive specimen to the DOT agency concerned. In addition, the laboratory shall retest all specimens analyzed positive for that drug or metabolite from the time of final resolution of the error back to the time of the last satisfactory performance test cycle. This retesting shall be documented by a statement signed by the individual responsible for day-to-day management of the laboratory's urine drug testing. The DOT agency concerned may require an on-site review of the laboratory which may be conducted unannounced during any hours of operation of the laboratory. Based on information provided by the DOT agency, DHHS has the option of revoking or suspending the laboratory's certification or recommending that no further action be taken if the case is one of less serious error in which corrective action has already been taken, thus reasonably assuring that the error will not occur again.

§40.33 Reporting and review of results.

(a) Medical review officer shall review confirmed positive results.

(1) An essential part of the drug testing program is the final review of confirmed positive results from the laboratory. A positive test result does not automatically identify an employee/applicant as having used drugs in violation of a DOT agency regulation. An individual with a detailed knowledge of possible alternate medical explanations is essential to the review of results. This review shall be performed by the Medical Review Officer (MRO) prior to the transmission of the results to employer administrative officials. The MRO review shall include review of the chain of custody to ensure that it is complete and sufficient on its face.

(2) The duties of the MRO with respect to negative results are purely administrative.

(b) Medical review officer—qualifications and responsibilities.

(1) The MRO shall be a licensed physician with knowledge of substance abuse disorders and may be an employee of a transportation employer or a private physician retained for this purpose.

(2) [Reserved]

(3) The role of the MRO is to review and interpret confirmed positive test results obtained through the employer's testing program. In carrying out this responsibility, the MRO shall examine alternate medical explanations for any positive test result. This action may include conducting a medical interview and review of the individual's medical history, or review of any other relevant biomedical factors. The MRO shall review all medical records made available by the tested individual when a confirmed positive test could have resulted from legally prescribed medication. The MRO shall not, however, consider the results or urine samples that are not obtained or processed in accordance with this part.

(c) Positive test result.

(1) Prior to making a final decision to verify a positive test result for an individual, the MRO shall give the individual an opportunity to discuss the test result with him or her.

(2) The MRO shall contact the individual directly, on a confidential basis, to determine whether the employee wishes to discuss the test result. A staff person under the MRO's supervision may make the initial contact, and a medically licensed or certified staff person may gather information from the employee. Except as provided in paragraph (c)(5) of this section, the MRO shall talk directly with the employee before verifying a test as positive.

(3) If, after making all reasonable efforts and documenting them, the MRO is unable to reach the individual directly, the MRO shall contact a designated management official who shall direct the individual to contact the MRO as soon as possible. If it becomes necessary to reach the individual through the designated management official, the designated management official shall employ procedures that ensure, to the maximum extent practicable, the requirement that the employee contact the MRO is held in confidence.

(4) If, after making all reasonable efforts, the designated management official is unable to contact the employee, the employer may place the employee on temporary medically unqualified status or medical leave.

(5) The MRO may verify a test as positive without having communicated directly with the employee about the test in three circumstances:

(i) The employee expressly declines the opportunity to discuss the test;

(ii) Neither the MRO nor the designated employer representative, after making all reasonable efforts, has been able to contact the employee within 14 days of the date on which the MRO receives the confirmed positive test result from the laboratory;

(iii) The designated employer representative has successfully made and documented a contact with the employee and instructed the employee to contact the MRO (see paragraphs (c)(3) and (c)(4) of this section), and more than five days have passed since the date the employee was successfully contacted by the designated employer representative.

(6) If a test is verified positive under the circumstances specified in paragraph (c)(5) (ii) or (iii) of this section, the employee may present to the MRO information documenting that serious illness, injury, or other circumstances unavoidably prevented the employee from being contacted by the MRO or designated employer representative (paragraph (c)(5)(ii) of this section) or from contacting the MRO (paragraph (c)(5)(iii) of this section) within the times provided. The MRO, on the basis of such information, may reopen the verification, allowing the employee to present information concerning a legitimate explanation for the confirmed positive test. If the MRO concludes that there is a legitimate explanation, the MRO declares the test to be negative.

(7) Following verification of a positive test result, the MRO shall, as provided in the employer's policy, refer the case to the employer's employee assistance or rehabilitation program, if applicable, to the management official empowered to recommend or take administrative action (or the official's designated agent), or both.

(d) Verification for opiates; review for prescription medication. Before the MRO verifies a confirmed positive result for opiates, he or she shall determine that there is clinical evidence—in addition to the urine test—of unauthorized use of any opium, opiate, or opium derivative (e.g., morphine/codeine). (This requirement does not apply if the employer's GC/MS confirmation testing for opiates confirms the presence of 6-monoacetylmorphine.)

(e) In a situation in which the employer has used the single sample method of collection, the MRO shall notify each employee who has a confirmed positive test that the employee has 72 hours in which to request a reanalysis of the original specimen, if the test is verified positive. If requested to do so by the employee within 72 hours of the employee's having been informed of a verified positive test, the Medical Review Officer shall direct, in writing, a reanalysis of the original sample. The MRO may also direct, in writing, such a reanalysis if the MRO questions the accuracy or validity of any test result. Only the MRO may authorize such a reanalysis, and such a reanalysis may take place only at laboratories certified by DHHS. If the reanalysis fails to reconfirm the presence of the drug or drug metabolite, the MRO shall cancel the test and report the cancellation and the reasons for it to the DOT, the employer and the employee.

(f)(1) In situations in which the employer uses the split sample method of collection, the MRO shall notify each employee who has a confirmed positive test that the employee has 72 hours in which to request a test of the split specimen, if the test is verified as positive. If the employee requests an analysis of the split specimen within 72 hours of having been informed of a verified positive test, the MRO shall direct, in writing, the laboratory to provide the split specimen to another DHHS-certified laboratory for analysis. If the analysis of the split specimen fails to reconfirm the presence of the drug(s) or drug metabolite(s) found in the primary specimen, or if the split specimen is unavailable, inadequate for testing or untestable, the MRO shall cancel the test and report cancellation and the reasons for it to the DOT, the employer, and the employee.

(2) If the analysis of the split specimen is reconfirmed by the second laboratory for the presence of the drug(s) or drug metabolites(s), the MRO shall notify the employer and employee of the results of the test.

(g) If an employee has not contacted the MRO within 72 hours, as provided in paragraphs (e) and (f) of this section, the employee may present to the MRO information documenting that serious illness, injury, inability to contact the MRO, lack of actual notice of the verified positive test, or other circumstances unavoidably prevented the employee from timely contacting the MRO. If the MRO concludes that there is a legitimate explanation for the employee's failure to contact the MRO within 72 hours, the MRO shall direct that the reanalysis of the primary specimen or analysis of the split specimen, as applicable, be performed.

(h) When the employer uses the split sample method of collection, the employee is not authorized to request a reanalysis of the primary specimen as provided in paragraph (e) of this section.

(i) Disclosure of information. Except as provided in this paragraph, the MRO shall not disclose to any third party medical information provided by the individual to the MRO as a part of the testing verification process.

(1) The MRO may disclose such information to the employer, a DOT agency or other Federal safety agency, or a physician responsible for determining the medical qualification of the employee under an applicable DOT agency regulation, as applicable, only if—

(i) An applicable DOT regulation permits or requires such disclosure;

(ii) In the MRO's reasonable medical judgment, the information could result in the employee being determined to be medically unqualified under an applicable DOT agency rule; or

(iii) In the MRO's reasonable medical judgment, in a situation in which there is no DOT agency rule establishing physical qualification standards applicable to the employee, the information indicates that continued performance by the employee of his or her safety-sensitive function could pose a significant safety risk.

(2) Before obtaining medical information from the employee as part of the verification process, the MRO shall inform the employee that information may be disclosed to third parties as provided in this paragraph and the identity of any parties to whom information may be disclosed.

§40.35 Protection of employee records.

Employer contracts with laboratories shall require that the laboratory maintain employee test records in confidence, as provided in DOT agency regulations. The contracts shall provide that the laboratory shall disclose information related to a positive drug test of an individual to the individual, the employer, or the decisionmaker in a lawsuit, grievance, or other proceeding initiated by or on behalf of the individual and arising from a certified positive drug test.

§40.37 Individual access to test and laboratory certification results.

Any employee who is the subject of a drug test conducted under this part shall, upon written request, have access to any records relating to his or her drug test and any records relating to the results of any relevant certification, review, or revocation-of-certification proceedings.

§40.39 Use of certified laboratories.

(a) Except as provided in paragraph (b) of this section, employers subject to this part shall use only laboratories certified under the DHHS "Mandatory Guidelines for Federal Workplace Drug Testing Programs," April 11, 1988, and subsequent amendments thereto.

(b) Employers subject to this part may also use laboratories located outside the United States if—

(1) The Department of Transportation, based on a written recommendation from DHHS, has certified the laboratory as meeting DHHS laboratory certification standards or deemed the laboratory fully equivalent to a laboratory meeting DHHS laboratory certification standards; or

(2) The Department of Transportation, based on a written recommendation from DHHS, has recognized a foreign certifying organization as having equivalent laboratory certification standards and procedures to those of DHHS, and the foreign certifying organization has certified the laboratory, pursuant to those equivalent standards and procedures.

SUBPART C—ALCOHOL TESTING

§40.51 The breath alcohol technician.

(a) The breath alcohol technician (BAT) shall be trained to proficiency in the operation of the EBT he or she is using and in the alcohol testing procedures of this part.

(1) Proficiency shall be demonstrated by successful completion of a course of instruction which, at a minimum, provides training in the principles of EBT methodology, operation, and calibration checks; the fundamentals of breath analysis for alcohol content; and the procedures required in this part for obtaining a breath sample, and interpreting and recording EBT results.

(2) Only courses of instruction for operation of EBTs that are equivalent to the Department of Transportation model course, as determined by the National Highway Traffic Safety Administration (NHTSA), may be used to train BATs to proficiency. On request, NHTSA will review a BAT instruction course for equivalency.

(3) The course of instruction shall provide documentation that the BAT has demonstrated competence in the operation of the specific EBT(s) he/she will use.

(4) Any BAT who will perform an external calibration check of an EBT shall be trained to proficiency in conducting the check on the particular model of EBT, to include practical experience and demonstrated competence in preparing the breath alcohol simulator or alcohol standard, and in maintenance and calibration of the EBT.

(5) The BAT shall receive additional training, as needed, to ensure proficiency, concerning new or additional devices or changes in technology that he or she will use.

(6) The employer or its agent shall establish documentation of the training and proficiency test of each BAT it uses to test employees, and maintain the documentation as provided in §40.83.

(b) A BAT-qualified supervisor of an employee may conduct the alcohol test for that employee only if another BAT is unavailable to perform the test in a timely manner. A supervisor shall not serve as a BAT for the employee in any circumstance prohibited by a DOT operating administration regulation.

(c) Law enforcement officers who have been certified by state or local governments to conduct breath alcohol testing are deemed to be qualified as BATs. In order for a test conducted by such an officer to be accepted under Department of Transportation alcohol testing requirements, the officer must have been certified by a state or local government to use the EBT or non- evidential alcohol screening device that was used for the test.

§40.53 Devices to be used for breath alcohol tests.

(a) For screening tests, employers shall use only EBTs. When the employer uses for a screening test an EBT that does not meet the requirements of paragraphs (b) (1) through (3) of this section, the employer shall use a log book in conjunction with the EBT (see §40.59(c)).

(b) For confirmation tests, employers shall use EBTs that meet the following requirements:

(1) EBTs shall have the capability of providing, independently or by direct link to a separate printer, a printed result in triplicate (or three consecutive identical copies) of each breath test and of the operations specified in paragraphs (b) (2) and (3) of this section.

(2) EBTs shall be capable of assigning a unique and sequential number to each completed test, with the number capable of being read by the BAT and the employee before each test and being printed out on each copy of the result.

(3) EBTs shall be capable of printing out, on each copy of the result, the manufacturer's name for the device, the device's serial number, and the time of the test.

(4) EBTs shall be able to distinguish alcohol from acetone at the 0.02 alcohol concentration level.

(5) EBTs shall be capable of the following operations:

(i) Testing an air blank prior to each collection of breath; and

(ii) Performing an external calibration check.

§40.55 Quality assurance plans for EBTs.

(a) In order to be used in either screening or confirmation alcohol testing subject to this part, an EBT shall have a quality assurance plan (QAP) developed by the manufacturer.

(1) The plan shall designate the method or methods to be used to perform external calibration checks of the device, using only calibration devices on the NHTSA "Conforming Products List of Calibrating Units for Breath Alcohol Tests."

(2) The plan shall specify the minimum intervals for performing external calibration checks of the device. Intervals shall be specified for different frequencies of use, environmental conditions (e.g., temperature, altitude, humidity), and contexts of operation (e.g., stationary or mobile use).

(3) The plan shall specify the tolerances on an external calibration check within which the EBT is regarded to be in proper calibration.

(4) The plan shall specify inspection, maintenance, and calibration requirements and intervals for the device.

(5) For a plan to be regarded as valid, the manufacturer shall have submitted the plan to NHTSA for review and have received NHTSA approval of the plan.

(b) The employer shall comply with the NHTSA-approved quality assurance plan for each EBT it uses for alcohol screening or confirmation testing subject to this part.

(1) The employer shall ensure that external calibration checks of each EBT are performed as provided in the QAP.

(2) The employer shall take an EBT out of service if any external calibration check results

in a reading outside the tolerances for the EBT set forth in the QAP. The EBT shall not again be used for alcohol testing under this part until it has been serviced and has had an external calibration check resulting in a reading within the tolerances for the EBT.

(3) The employer shall ensure that inspection, maintenance, and calibration of each EBT are performed by the manufacturer or a maintenance representative certified by the device's manufacturer or a state health agency or other appropriate state agency. The employer shall also ensure that each BAT or other individual who performs an external calibration check of an EBT used for alcohol testing subject to this part has demonstrated proficiency in conducting such a check of the model of EBT in question.

(4) The employer shall maintain records of the external calibration checks of EBTs as provided in §40.83.

(c) When the employer is not using the EBT at an alcohol testing site, the employer shall store the EBT in a secure space.

§40.57 Locations for breath alcohol testing.

(a) Each employer shall conduct alcohol testing in a location that affords visual and aural privacy to the individual being tested, sufficient to prevent unauthorized persons from seeing or hearing test results. All necessary equipment, personnel, and materials for breath testing shall be provided at the location where testing is conducted.

(b) An employer may use a mobile collection facility (e.g., a van equipped for alcohol testing) that meets the requirements of paragraph (a) of this section.

(c) No unauthorized persons shall be permitted access to the testing location when the EBT remains unsecured or, in order to prevent such persons from seeing or hearing a testing result, at any time when testing is being conducted.

(d) In unusual circumstances (e.g., when it is essential to conduct a test outdoors at the scene of an accident), a test may be conducted at a location that does not fully meet the requirements of paragraph (a) of this section. In such a case, the employer or BAT shall provide visual and aural privacy to the employee to the greatest extent practicable.

(e) The BAT shall supervise only one employee's use of the EBT at a time. The BAT shall not leave the alcohol testing location while the testing procedure for a given employee (see ¤§40.61 through 40.65) is in progress.

§40.59 The breath alcohol testing form.

(a) Each employer shall use the breath alcohol testing form prescribed under this part. The form is found in appendix A to this subpart. Employers may not modify or revise this form, except that a form directly generated by an EBT may omit the space for affixing a separate printed result to the form.

(b) The form shall provide triplicate (or three consecutive identical) copies. Copy 1 (white) shall be transmitted to the employer. Copy 2 (green) shall be provided to the employee. Copy 3 (blue) shall be retained by the BAT. Except for a form generated by an EBT, the form shall be 8 1/2 by 11 inches in size.

§40.61 Preparation for breath alcohol testing.

(a) When the employee enters the alcohol testing location, the BAT will require him or her to provide positive identification (e.g., through use of a photo I.D. card or identification by an employer representative). On request by the employee, the BAT shall provide positive identification to the employee.

(b) The BAT shall explain the testing procedure to the employee.

§40.63 Procedures for screening tests.

(a) The BAT shall complete Step 1 on the Breath Alcohol Testing Form. The employee shall then complete Step 2 on the form, signing the certification. Refusal by the employee to sign this certification shall be regarded as a refusal to take the test.

(b) An individually-sealed mouthpiece shall be opened in view of the employee and BAT and attached to the EBT in accordance with the manufacturer's instructions.

(c) The BAT shall instruct the employee to blow forcefully into the mouthpiece for at least 6 seconds or until the EBT indicates that an adequate amount of breath has been obtained.

(d)(1) If the EBT does not meet the requirements of §40.53(b)(1) through (3), the BAT shall ensure, before a screening test is administered to each employee, that he or she and the employee read the sequential test number displayed on the EBT. The BAT shall record the displayed result, test number, testing device, serial number of the testing device, and time in Step # of the form.

(2) If the EBT does not meet the requirements of §40.53(b)(1) through (3), the BAT and the employee shall take the following steps:

(i) Show the employee the result displayed on the EBT. The BAT shall record the displayed result, test number, testing device, serial number of the testing device, time and quantified result in Step 3 of the form.

(ii) Record the test number, date of the test, name of the BAT, location, and quantified test result in the log book. The employee shall initial the log book entry.

(3) If the EBT provides a printed result, but does not print the results directly onto the form, the BAT shall show the employee the result displayed on the EBT. The BAT shall then affix the test result printout to the breath alcohol test form in the designated space, using a method that will provide clear evidence of removal (e.g., tamper-evident tape).

(4) If the EBT prints the test results directly onto the form, the BAT shall show the employee the result displayed on the EBT.

(e)(1) In any case in which the result of the screening test is a breath alcohol concentration of less than 0.02, the BAT shall date the form and sign the certification in Step 3 of the form. The employee shall sign the certification and fill in the date in Step 4 of the form.

(2) No further testing is authorized. The BAT shall transmit the result of less than 0.02 to the employer in a confidential manner, and the employer shall receive and store the information so as to ensure that confidentiality is maintained as required by §40.81.

(3) If the employee does not sign the certification in Step 4 of the form for a test, it shall not be considered a refusal to be tested. In this event, the BAT shall note the employee's failure to sign in the "Remarks" section of the form.

(4) If a test result printed by the EBT (see paragraph (d)(3) or (d)(4) of this section) does not match the displayed result, or if a sequential test number printed by the EBT does not match the sequential test number displayed by the EBT prior to the screening test (see paragraph (d)(1) of this section), the BAT shall note the disparity in the "Remarks" section. Both the employee and the BAT shall initial and sign the notation. In accordance with §40.79, the test is invalid and the employee shall be so advised.

(f) If the result of the screening test is an alcohol concentration of 0.02 or greater, a confirmation test shall be performed as provided in §40.65.

(g) If the confirmation test will be conducted by a different BAT, the BAT who conducts the screening test shall complete and sign the form and log book entry. The BAT will provide the employee with Copy 2 of the form.

(h) If the confirmation test will be conducted at a different site from the screening test, the employer or its agent shall ensure that—

(1) The employee is advised against taking any of the actions mentioned in the first sentence of §40.65(b) of this Part;

(2) The employee is advised that he or she must not drive, perform safety-sensitive duties, or operate heavy equipment, as noted in Block 4 of the alcohol testing form; and

(3) The employee is under observation of a BAT, STT, or other employer personnel while in transit from the screening test site to the confirmation test site.

§40.65 Procedures for confirmation tests.

(a) If a BAT other than the one who conducted the screening test is conducting the confirmation test, the new BAT shall follow the procedures of §40.61.

(b) The BAT shall instruct the employee not to eat, drink, put any object or substance in his or her mouth, and, to the extent possible, not belch during a waiting period before the confirmation test. This time period begins with the completion of the screening test, and shall not be less than 15 minutes. The confirmation test shall be conducted within 30 minutes of the completion of the screening test. The BAT shall explain to the employee the reason for this requirement (i.e., to prevent any accumulation of mouth alcohol leading to an artificially high reading) and the fact that it is for the employee's benefit. The BAT shall also explain that the test will be conducted at the end of the waiting period, even if the employee has disregarded the instruction. If the BAT becomes aware that the employee has not complied with this instruction, the BAT shall so note in the "Remarks" section of the form. If the BAT conducts the confirmation test more than 30 minutes after the result of the screening test has been obtained, the BAT shall note in the "Remarks" section of the form the time that elapsed between the screening and confirmation tests and the reason why the confirmation test could not be conducted within 30 minutes of the screening test.

(c)(1) If a BAT other than the one who conducted the screening test is conducting the confirmation test, the new BAT shall initiate a new Breath Alcohol Testing form. The BAT shall complete Step 1 on the form. The employee shall then complete Step 2 on the form, signing the certification. Refusal by the employee to sign this certification shall be regarded as a refusal to take the test. The BAT shall note in the "Remarks" section of the form that a different BAT conducted the screening test.

(2) In all cases, the procedures of §40.63 (a), (b), and (c) shall be followed. A new mouthpiece shall be used for the confirmation test.

(d) Before the confirmation test is administered for each employee, the BAT shall ensure that the EBT registers 0.00 on an air blank. If the reading is greater than 0.00, the BAT shall conduct one more air blank. If the reading is greater than 0.00, testing shall not proceed using that instrument, which shall be taken out of service. However, testing may proceed on another instrument. Any EBT taken out of service because of failure to perform an air blank accurately shall not be used for testing until a check of external calibration is completed and the EBT is found to be within tolerance limits.

(e) Before the confirmation test is administered for each employee, the BAT shall ensure that he or she and the employee read the sequential test number displayed by the EBT.

(f) In the event that the screening and confirmation test results are not identical, the confirmation test result is deemed to be the final result upon which any action under operating administration rules shall be based.

(g)(1) If the EBT provides a printed result, but does not print the results directly onto the form, the BAT shall show the employee the result displayed on the EBT. The BAT shall then affix the test result printout to the breath alcohol test form in the designated space, using a method that will provide clear evidence of removal (e.g., tamper-evident tape).

(2) If the EBT prints the test results directly onto the form, the BAT shall show the employee the result displayed on the EBT.

(h)(1) Following the completion of the test, the BAT shall date the form and sign the certification in Step 3 of the form. The employee shall sign the certification and fill in the date in Step 4 of the form.

(2) If the employee does not sign the certification in Step 4 of the form, it shall not be considered a refusal to be tested. In this event, the BAT shall note the employee's failure to sign in the "Remarks" section.

(3) If a test result printed by the EBT (see paragraph (g)(1) or (g)(2) of this section) does not match the displayed result, or if a sequential test number printed by the EBT does not match the sequential test number displayed by the EBT prior to the confirmation test (see paragraph (e) of this section), the BAT shall note the disparity in the "Remarks" section. Both the employee and the BAT shall initial and sign the notation. In accordance with §40.79, the test is invalid and the employee shall be so advised.

(i) The BAT shall transmit all results to the employer in a confidential manner.

(1) Each employer shall designate one or more employer representatives for the purpose of receiving and handling alcohol testing results in a confidential manner. All communications by BATs to the employer concerning the alcohol testing results of employees shall be to a designated employer representative.

(2) Such transmission may be in writing (the employer copy (Copy 1) of the breath alcohol testing form), in person or by telephone or electronic means, but the BAT shall ensure immediate transmission to the employer of results that require the employer to prevent the employee from performing a safety-sensitive function.

(3) If the initial transmission is not in writing (e.g., by telephone), the employer shall establish a mechanism to verify the identity of the BAT providing the information.

(4) If the initial transmission is not in writing, the BAT shall follow the initial transmission by providing to the employer the employer's copy of the breath alcohol testing form. The employer shall store the information so as to ensure that confidentiality is maintained as required by §40.81.

§40.67 Refusals to test and uncompleted tests.

(a) Refusal by an employee to complete and sign the breath alcohol testing form (Step 2), to provide breath, to provide an adequate amount of breath, or otherwise to cooperate with the testing process in a way that prevents the completion of the test, shall be noted by the BAT in the remarks section of the form. The testing process shall be terminated and the BAT shall immediately notify the employer.

(b) If a screening or confirmation test cannot be completed, or if an event occurs that would invalidate the test, the BAT shall, if practicable, begin a new screening or confirmation test, as applicable, using a new breath alcohol testing form with a new sequential test number (in the case of a screening test conducted on an EBT that meets the requirements of §40.53(b) or in the case of a confirmation test).

§40.69 Inability to provide an adequate amount of breath.

(a) This section sets forth procedures to be followed in any case in which an employee is unable, or alleges that he or she is unable, to provide an amount of breath sufficient to permit a valid breath test because of a medical condition.

(b) The BAT shall again instruct the employee to attempt to provide an adequate amount of breath. If the employee refuses to make the attempt, the BAT shall immediately inform the employer.

(c) If the employee attempts and fails to provide an adequate amount of breath, the BAT shall so note in the "Remarks" section of the breath alcohol testing form and immediately inform the employer.

(d) If the employee attempts and fails to provide an adequate amount of breath, the employer shall proceed as follows:

(1) [Reserved]

(2) The employer shall direct the employee to obtain, as soon as practical after the attempted provision of breath, an evaluation from a licensed physician who is acceptable to the employer concerning the employee's medical ability to provide an adequate amount of breath.

(i) If the physician determines, in his or her reasonable medical judgment, that a medical condition has, or with a high degree of probability, could have, precluded the employee from providing an adequate amount of breath, the employee's failure to provide an adequate amount of breath shall not be deemed a refusal to take a test. The physician shall provide to the employer a written statement of the basis for his or her conclusion.

(ii) If the licensed physician, in his or her reasonable medical judgment, is unable to make the determination set forth in paragraph (d)(2)(i) of this section the employee's failure to provide an adequate amount of breath shall be regarded as a refusal to take a test. The licensed physician shall provide a written statement of the basis for his or her conclusion to the employer.

§§40.71 to 40.77 [Reserved]

§40.79 Invalid tests.

(a) A breath alcohol test shall be invalid under the following circumstances:

(1) The next external calibration check of an EBT produces a result that differs by more than the tolerance stated in the QAP from the known value of the test standard. In this event, every test result of 0.02 or above obtained on the device since the last valid external calibration check shall be invalid;

(2) The BAT does not observe the minimum 15-minute waiting period prior to the confirmation test, as provided in §40.65(b);

(3) The BAT does not perform an air blank of the EBT before a confirmation test, or an air blank does not result in a reading of 0.00 prior to the administration of the test, as provided in §40.65;

(4) The BAT does not sign the form as required by ¤§40.63 and 40.65;

(5) The BAT has failed to note on the remarks section of the form that the employee has failed or refused to sign the form following the recording or printing on or attachment to the form of the test result;

(6) An EBT fails to print a confirmation test result; or

(7) On a confirmation test and, where applicable, on a screening test, the sequential test number or alcohol concentration displayed on the EBT is not the same as the sequential test number or alcohol concentration on the printed result.

(b) [Reserved]

§40.81 Availability and disclosure of alcohol testing information about individual employees.

(a) Employers shall maintain records in a secure manner, so that disclosure of information to unauthorized persons does not occur.

(b) Except as required by law or expressly authorized or required in this section, no employer shall release covered employee information that is contained in the records required to be maintained by this part or by DOT agency alcohol misuse rules.

(c) An employee subject to testing is entitled, upon written request, to obtain copies of any records pertaining to the employee's use of alcohol, including any records pertaining to his or her alcohol tests. The employer shall promptly provide the records requested by the employee. Access to an employee's records shall not be contingent upon payment for records other than those specifically requested.

(d) Each employer shall permit access to all facilities utilized in complying with the requirements of this part and DOT agency alcohol misuse rules to the Secretary of Transportation, any DOT agency with regulatory authority over the employer, or a state agency with regulatory authority over the employer (as authorized by DOT agency regulations).

(e) When requested by the Secretary of Transportation, any DOT agency with regulatory authority over the employer, or a state agency with regulatory authority over the employer (as authorized by DOT agency regulations), each employer shall make available copies of all results for employer alcohol testing conducted under the requirements of this part and any other information pertaining to the employer's alcohol misuse prevention program. The information shall include name-specific alcohol test results, records and reports.

(f) When requested by the National Transportation Safety Board as part of an accident investigation, an employer shall disclose information related to the employer's administration of any post-accident alcohol tests administered following the accident under investigation.

(g) An employer shall make records available to a subsequent employer upon receipt of a written request from a covered employee. Disclosure by the subsequent employer is permitted only as expressly authorized by the terms of the employee's written request.

(h) An employer may disclose information required to be maintained under this part pertaining to a covered employee to that employee or to the decisionmaker in a lawsuit, grievance, or other proceeding initiated by or on behalf of the individual, and arising from the results of an alcohol test administered under the requirements of this part, or from the employer's determination that the employee engaged in conduct prohibited by a DOT agency alcohol misuse regulation (including, but not limited to, a worker's compensation, unemployment compensation, or other proceeding relating to a benefit sought by the employee).

(i) An employer shall release information regarding a covered employee's records as directed by the specific, written consent of the employee authorizing release of the information to an identified person. Release of such information is permitted only in accordance with the terms of the employee's consent.

§40.83 Maintenance and disclosure of records concerning EBTs and BATs.

(a) Each employer or its agent shall maintain the following records for two years:

(1) Records of the inspection and maintenance of each EBT used in employee testing;

(2) Documentation of the employer's compliance with the QAP for each EBT it uses for alcohol testing under this part;

(3) Records of the training and proficiency testing of each BAT used in employee testing;

(4) The log books required by §40.59(c).

(b) Each employer or its agent shall maintain for five years records pertaining to the calibration of each EBT used in alcohol testing under this part, including records of the results of external calibration checks.

(c) Records required to be maintained by this section shall be disclosed on the same basis as provided in §40.81.

SUBPART D—NON-EVIDENTIAL ALCOHOL SCREENING DEVICES

§40.91 Authorization for use of non-evidential alcohol screening devices.

Non-evidential alcohol screening tests, performed using screening devices included by the National Highway Traffic Safety Administration on its conforming products list for non-evidential screening devices, may be used in lieu of EBTs to perform screening tests required by operating administrations' alcohol testing regulations. Non-evidential screening devices may not be used for confirmation alcohol tests, which must be conducted using EBTs as provided in Subpart C of this Part.

§40.93 The screening test technician.

(a) Anyone meeting the requirements of this Part to be a BAT may act as a screening test technician (STT), provided that the individual has demonstrated proficiency in the operation of the non-evidential screening device he or she is using.

(b) Any other individual may act as an STT if he or she successfully completes a course of instruction concerning the procedures required by this Part for conducting alcohol screening tests. Only the Department of Transportation model course, or a course of instruction determined by the Department of Transportation's Office of Drug Enforcement and Program Compliance to be equivalent to it, may be used for this purpose.

(c) With respect to any non-evidential screening device involving changes, contrasts, or other readings that are indicated on the device in terms of color, STTs shall, in order to be regarded as proficient, be able to discern correctly these changes, contrasts or readings.

(d) The STT shall receive additional training, as needed, to ensure proficiency, concerning new or additional devices or changes in technology that he or she will use.

(e) The employer or its agent shall document the training and proficiency of each STT it uses to test employees and maintain the documentation as provided in §40.83.

(f) The provisions of §40.51(b) and (c); §40.57; §40.59; §40.61; §40.63(e)(1)-(2), (f), (g), and (h); §40.69; and §40.81; and other provisions, as applicable, of this Part apply to STTs as well as to BATs.

§40.95 Quality assurance plans for non-evidential screening devices.

(a) In order to be used for alcohol screening tests subject to this part, a non-evidential screening device shall have an approved quality assurance plan (QAP) developed by the manufacturer and approved by the National Highway Traffic Safety Administration (NHTSA).

(1) The plan shall designate the method or methods to be used to perform quality control checks; the temperatures at which the non-evidential screening device shall be stored and used, as well as other environmental conditions (e.g., altitude, humidity) that may affect the performance of the device; and, where relevant, the shelf life of the device.

(2) The QAP shall prohibit the use of any device that does not pass the specified quality control checks or that has passed its expiration date.

(b) The manufacturers' instructions on or included in the package for each saliva testing device shall include directions on the proper use of the device, the time frame within which the device must be read and the manner in which the reading is made.

(c) The employer and its agents shall comply with the QAP and manufacturer's instructions for each non-evidential screening device it uses for alcohol screening tests subject to this Part.

§40.97 Locations for non-evidential alcohol screening tests.

(a) Locations for non-evidential alcohol screening tests shall meet the same requirements set forth for breath alcohol testing in §40.57 of this Part.

(b) The STT shall supervise only one employee's use of a non-evidential screening device at a time. The STT shall not leave the alcohol testing location while the screening test procedure for a given employee is in progress.

§40.99 Testing forms.

STTs conducting tests using a non-evidential screening device shall use the alcohol testing form as provided in §40.59 and Appendix B of this Part for the screening test.

§40.101 Screening test procedure.

(a) The steps for preparation for testing shall be the same as provided for breath alcohol testing in §40.61 of this Part.

(b) The STT shall complete Step 1 on the form required by §40.99. The employee shall then complete Step 2 on the form, signing the certification. Refusal by the employee to sign this certification shall be regarded as a refusal to take the test.

(c) If the employer is using a non-evidential breath testing device, the STT shall follow the same steps outlined for screening tests using EBTs in §40.63.

(d) If the employer is using a saliva testing device, the STT shall take the following steps:

(1) The STT shall explain the testing procedure to the employee.

(2) The STT shall check the expiration date of the saliva testing device, show the date to the employee, and shall not use a device at any time subsequent to the expiration date.

(3) The STT shall open an individually sealed package containing the device in the presence of the employee.

(4) The STT shall offer the employee the opportunity to use the swab. If the employee chooses to use the swab, the STT shall instruct the employee to insert the absorbent end of the swab into the employee's mouth, moving it actively throughout the mouth for a sufficient time to ensure that it is completely saturated, as provided in the manufacturer's instructions for the device.

(5) If the employee chooses not to use the swab, or in all cases in which a new test is nec-

essary because the device did not activate (see paragraph (d)(8) of this section), the STT shall insert the absorbent end of the swab into the employee's mouth, moving it actively throughout the mouth for a sufficient time to ensure that it is completely saturated, as provided in the manufacturer's instructions for the device. The STT shall wear a surgical grade glove while doing so.

(6) The STT shall place the device on a flat surface or otherwise in a position in which the swab can be firmly placed into the opening provided in the device for this purpose. The STT shall insert the swab into this opening and maintain firm pressure on the device until the device indicates that it is activated.

(7) If the procedures of paragraph (d)(3)-(d)(5) of this section are not followed successfully (e.g., the swab breaks, the STT drops the swab on the floor or another surface, the swab is removed or falls from the device before the device is activated), the STT shall discard the device and swab and conduct a new test using a new device. The new device shall be one that has been under the control of the employer or STT prior to the test. The STT shall note in the remarks section of the form the reason for the new test. In this case, the STT shall offer the employee the choice of using the swab himself or herself or having the STT use the swab. If the procedures of paragraph (d)(3)-(d)(5) of this section are not followed successfully on the new test, the collection shall be terminated and an explanation provided in the remarks section of the form. A new test shall then be conducted, using an EBT for both the screening and confirmation tests.

(8) If the procedures of paragraph (d)(3)-(d)(5) of this section are followed successfully, but the device is not activated, the STT shall discard the device and swab and conduct a new test, in the same manner as provided in paragraph (d)(7) of this section. In this case, the STT shall place the swab into the employee's mouth to collect saliva for the new test.

(9) The STT shall read the result displayed on the device two minutes after inserting the swab into the device. The STT shall show the device and its reading to the employee and enter the result on the form.

(10) Devices, swabs, gloves and other materials used in saliva testing shall not be reused, and shall be disposed of in a sanitary manner following their use, consistent with applicable requirements.

(e) In the case of any screening test performed under this section, the STT, after determining the alcohol concentration result, shall follow the applicable provisions of §40.63(e)(1)-(2), (f), (g), and (h). The STT shall also enter, in the "Remarks" section of the form, a notation that the screening test was performed using a non-evidential breath testing device or a saliva device, as applicable. Following completion of the screening test, the STT shall date the form and sign the certification in Step 3 of the form.

§40.103 Refusals to test and uncompleted tests.

(a) Refusal by an employee to complete and sign the alcohol testing form required by §40.99 (Step 2), to provide a breath or saliva sample, to provide an adequate amount of breath, or otherwise to cooperate in a way that prevents the completion of the testing process, shall be noted by the STT in the remarks section of the form. This constitutes a refusal to test. The testing process shall be terminated and the STT shall immediately notify the employer.

(b) If the screening test cannot be completed, for reasons other than a refusal by the employee, or if an event occurs that would invalidate the test, the STT shall, if practicable, immediately begin a new screening test, using a new testing form and, in the case of a test using a saliva screening device, a new device.

§40.105 Inability to provide an adequate amount of breath or saliva.

(a) If an employee is unable to provide sufficient breath to complete a test on a non-evidential breath testing device, the procedures of §40.69 apply.

(b) If an employee is unable to provide sufficient saliva to complete a test on a saliva screening device (e.g., the employee does not provide sufficient saliva to activate the device), the STT, as provided in §40.101 of this Part, shall conduct a new test using a new device. If the employee refuses to complete the new test, the STT shall terminate testing and immediately inform the employer. This constitutes a refusal to test.

(c) If the new test is completed, but there is an insufficient amount of saliva to activate the device, STT shall immediately inform the employer, which shall immediately cause an alcohol test to be administered to the employee using an EBT.

§40.107 Invalid tests.

An alcohol test using a non-evidential screening device shall be invalid under the following circumstances:

(a) With respect to a test conducted on a saliva device—

(1) The result is read before two minutes or after 15 minutes from the time the swab is inserted into the device;

(2) The device does not activate;

(3) The device is used for a test after the expiration date printed on its package; or

(4) The STT fails to note in the remarks section of the form that the screening test was conducted using a saliva device;

(b) With respect to a test conducted on any non-evidential alcohol testing device, the STT has failed to note on the remarks section of the form that the employee has failed or refused to sign the form following the recording on the form of the test result.

§40.109 Availability and disclosure of alcohol testing information about individual employees.

The provisions of §40.81 apply to records of non-evidential alcohol screening tests.

§40.111 Maintenance and disclosure of records concerning non-evidential testing devices and STTs.

Records concerning STTs and non-evidential testing devices shall be maintained and disclosed following the same requirements applicable to BATs and EBTs under §40.81 of this Part.

APPENDIX A TO PART 40—FEDERAL DRUG TESTING CUSTODY AND CONTROL FORM

FEDERAL DRUG TESTING CUSTODY AND CONTROL FORM

|||||||| *F211254*

SPECIMEN ID NO. **F211254**   A   LABORATORY ACCESSION NO.

SPECIMEN BOTTLE SEALS

▶ **STEP 1: TO BE COMPLETED BY COLLECTOR OR EMPLOYER REPRESENTATIVE**

A. Employer Name, Address and I.D. No.   B. MRO Name and Address

C. Donor SSN or Employee I.D. No. _____

D. Reason for Test: ☐ Pre-employment ☐ Random ☐ Reasonable Suspicion/Cause ☐ Post Accident
☐ Return to Duty ☐ Follow-up ☐ Other (specify) _____

E. Tests to be Performed: ☐ THC, Cocaine, PCP, Opiates and Amphetamines
☐ Only THC and Cocaine ☐ OTHER (specify) _____

▶ **STEP 2: TO BE COMPLETED BY COLLECTOR** - Specimen temperature must be read within 4 minutes of collection.

Specimen temperature within range: ☐ Yes, 90° - 100°F/32° - 38°C   ☐ No, Record specimen temperature here _____

▶ **STEP 3: TO BE COMPLETED BY COLLECTOR AND DONOR** - Collector affixes bottle seal(s) to bottle(s). Collector dates seal(s). Donor initials seal(s).
▶ **STEP 4: TO BE COMPLETED BY DONOR** - Go to copy 4 (pink page); STEP 4
▶ **STEP 5: TO BE COMPLETED BY COLLECTOR**

COLLECTION SITE LOCATION:

_____   ( )_____   SPLIT SPECIMEN COLLECTION
Collection Facility   Collector's Business Phone No.   ☐ YES ☐ NO

_____   _____   _____ _____
Address   City   State   Zip

REMARKS: _____

I certify that the specimen identified on this form is the specimen presented to me by the donor providing the certification on Copy 4 of this form, that it bears the same specimen identification number as that set forth above, and that it has been collected, labeled and sealed as in accordance with applicable Federal requirements.

X _____   _____   _____   AM/PM
(PRINT) Collector's Name (First, MI, Last)   Signature of Collector   Date (Mo./Day/Yr.)   Time

▶ **STEP 6: TO BE INITIATED BY THE COLLECTOR AND COMPLETED AS NECESSARY THEREAFTER**

DATE MO. DAY YR.	SPECIMEN RELEASED BY	SPECIMEN RECEIVED BY	PURPOSE OF CHANGE
/ /	DONOR - NO SIGNATURE	Signature ____ Name	PROVIDE SPECIMEN FOR TESTING
/ /	Signature ____ Name	Signature ____ Name	
/ /	Signature ____ Name	Signature ____ Name	
/ /	Signature ____ Name	Signature ____ Name	

STEP 7: TO BE COMPLETED BY THE LABORATORY - Specimen Bottle Seal(s) Intact: ☐ YES ☐ NO, Explain in Remarks Below.

THE RESULTS FOR THE ABOVE IDENTIFIED SPECIMEN ARE IN ACCORDANCE WITH THE APPLICABLE INITIAL TEST AND CONFIRMATORY TEST CUTOFF LEVELS ESTABLISHED BY THE HHS *MANDATORY GUIDELINES FOR FEDERAL WORKPLACE DRUG TESTING PROGRAMS*

☐ NEGATIVE ☐ POSITIVE, for the following: ☐ CANNABINOIDS as Carboxy—THC ☐ COCAINE METABOLITES as Benzoylecgonine ☐ PHENCYCLIDINE
☐ TEST NOT PERFORMED   ☐ OPIATES: ☐ AMPHETAMINES:
☐ codeine   ☐ amphetamine   ☐ OTHER _____
☐ morphine   ☐ methamphetamine

REMARKS _____

TEST LAB (if different from above) _____   _____   ( )_____
NAME   ADDRESS   PHONE NO.

I certify that the specimen identified by the laboratory accession number on this form is the same specimen that bears the specimen identification number set forth above, that the specimen has been examined upon receipt, handled and analyzed in accordance with applicable Federal requirements, and that the results set forth are for that specimen.

_____   _____   _____
(PRINT) Certifying Scientist's Name (First, MI, Last)   Signature of Certifying Scientist   Date (Mo. / Day / Yr.)

STEP 8: TO BE COMPLETED BY THE MEDICAL REVIEW OFFICER

I have reviewed the laboratory results for the specimen identified by this form in accordance with applicable Federal requirements. My determination/verification is:
☐ Negative ☐ Positive ☐ Test Not Performed ☐ Test Cancelled   REMARKS _____

_____   _____   _____
(PRINT) Medical Review Officer's Name (First, MI, Last)   Signature of Medical Review Officer   Date (Mo. / Day / Yr.)

OMB No. 9999-0023
Expiration Date 6/30/97

COPY 1 - ORIGINAL - MUST ACCOMPANY SPECIMEN TO LABORATORY

F211254 SPECIMEN ID NO   F211254 SPECIMEN ID NO
B (SPLIT)   A

PLACE OVER CAP   PLACE OVER CAP   PLACE OVER CAP   PLACE OVER CAP

Date (Mo. Day Yr.)   Date (Mo. Day Yr.)
Donor's Initials   Donor's Initials

SHIPPING CONTAINER SEAL

/ /
Date (Mo. / Day / Yr.)

Collector's Initials

Paperwork Reduction Act Notice (as required by 5 CFR 1320.21)

Public reporting burden for this collection of information, including the time for reviewing instructions, gathering and maintaining the data needed, and completing and reviewing the collection of information is estimated for each respondent to average: 5 minutes/donor; 4 minutes/collector; 3 minutes/laboratory; and 3 minutes/Medical Review Officer. Federal employees may send comments regarding these burden estimates, or any other aspect of this collection of information, including suggestions for reducing the burden, to Public Health Service Reports Clearance Officer, Attn: PRA, Hubert H. Humphrey Building, Rm 721-B, 200 Independence Ave. S.W., Washington, D.C. 20201. Individuals from the private sector may send comments/suggestions to: Department of Transportation, Drug Enforcement and Program Compliance, Rm 9404, 400 Seventh St. S.W., Washington, D.C. 20590. In addition, copies of all comments/suggestions may be sent to: Office of Management and Budget, Paperwork Reduction Project, Rm 3001, 725 Seventeenth St. N.W., Washington, D.C. 20503.

FEDERAL DRUG TESTING CUSTODY AND CONTROL FORM

SPECIMEN ID NO. **F211254** **A** LABORATORY ACCESSION NO.

STEP 1: TO BE COMPLETED BY COLLECTOR OR EMPLOYER REPRESENTATIVE

A. Employer Name, Address and I.D. No.   B. MRO Name and Address

C. Donor SSN or Employee I.D. No. _____

D. Reason for Test: ☐ Pre-employment ☐ Random ☐ Reasonable Suspicion/Cause ☐ Post Accident
     ☐ Return to Duty ☐ Follow-up ☐ Other (specify) _____

E. Tests to be Performed: ☐ THC, Cocaine, PCP, Opiates and Amphetamines
     ☐ Only THC and Cocaine ☐ OTHER (specify) _____

STEP 2: TO BE COMPLETED BY COLLECTOR - Specimen temperature must be read within 4 minutes of collection.

Specimen temperature within range: ☐ Yes, 90° - 100°F/32° - 38°C ☐ No, Record specimen temperature here _____

STEP 3: TO BE COMPLETED BY COLLECTOR AND DONOR - Collector affixes bottle seal(s) to bottle(s). Collector dates seal(s). Donor initials seal(s).

STEP 4: TO BE COMPLETED BY DONOR - Go to copy 4 (pink page); STEP 4

STEP 5: TO BE COMPLETED BY COLLECTOR

COLLECTION SITE LOCATION: SPLIT SPECIMEN COLLECTION

_____   (   )
Collection Facility   Collector's Business Phone No.   ☐ YES ☐ NO

_____
Address   City   State   Zip

REMARKS: _____

I certify that the specimen identified on this form is the specimen presented to me by the donor providing the certification on Copy 4 of this form, that it bears the same specimen identification number as that set forth above, and that it has been collected, labeled and sealed as in accordance with applicable Federal requirements.

_____ / / _____
(PRINT) Collector's Name (First, MI, Last)   Signature of Collector   Date (Mo./Day/Yr.)   Time   AM PM

STEP 6: TO BE INITIATED BY THE COLLECTOR AND COMPLETED AS NECESSARY THEREAFTER

DATE MO. DAY YR.	SPECIMEN RELEASED BY	SPECIMEN RECEIVED BY	PURPOSE OF CHANGE
/ /	DONOR - NO SIGNATURE	Signature / Name	PROVIDE SPECIMEN FOR TESTING
/ /	Signature / Name	Signature / Name	
/ /	Signature / Name	Signature / Name	
	Signature / Name	Signature / Name	

STEP 7: TO BE COMPLETED BY THE LABORATORY - Specimen Bottle Seal(s) Intact: ☐ YES ☐ NO, Explain in Remarks Below.

THE RESULTS FOR THE ABOVE IDENTIFIED SPECIMEN ARE IN ACCORDANCE WITH THE APPLICABLE INITIAL TEST AND CONFIRMATORY TEST CUTOFF LEVELS ESTABLISHED BY THE HHS *MANDATORY GUIDELINES FOR FEDERAL WORKPLACE DRUG TESTING PROGRAMS*

☐ NEGATIVE ☐ POSITIVE, for the following: ☐ CANNABINOIDS as Carboxy—THC ☐ COCAINE METABOLITES as Benzoylecgonine ☐ PHENCYCLIDINE
☐ TEST NOT PERFORMED   ☐ OPIATES: ☐ codeine ☐ morphine   ☐ AMPHETAMINES: ☐ amphetamine ☐ methamphetamine   ☐ OTHER _____

REMARKS _____

TEST LAB (if different from above) _____ (   )
     NAME   ADDRESS   PHONE NO.

I certify that the specimen identified by the laboratory accession number on this form is the same specimen that bears the specimen identification number set forth above, that the specimen has been examined upon receipt, handled and analyzed in accordance with applicable Federal requirements, and that the results set forth are for that specimen.

_____ / /
(PRINT) Certifying Scientist's Name (First, MI, Last)   Signature of Certifying Scientist   Date (Mo. / Day / Yr.)

STEP 8: TO BE COMPLETED BY THE MEDICAL REVIEW OFFICER

I have reviewed the laboratory results for the specimen identified by this form in accordance with applicable Federal requirements. My determination/verification is:

☐ Negative ☐ Positive ☐ Test Not Performed ☐ Test Cancelled   REMARKS _____

_____ / /
(PRINT) Medical Review Officer's Name (First, MI, Last)   Signature of Medical Review Officer   Date (Mo. / Day / Yr.)

COPY 2 - 2nd ORIGINAL - MUST ACCOMPANY SPECIMEN TO LABORATORY

OMB No. 9999-0023 Expiration Date: 6/30/97

FEDERAL DRUG TESTING CUSTODY AND CONTROL FORM

SPECIMEN ID NO. **F211254**   **B (SPLIT)**   LABORATORY ACCESSION NO.

STEP 1: TO BE COMPLETED BY COLLECTOR OR EMPLOYER REPRESENTATIVE

A. Employer Name, Address and I.D. No.   B. MRO Name and Address

C. Donor SSN or Employee I.D. No. _____

D. Reason for Test: ☐ Pre-employment   ☐ Random   ☐ Reasonable Suspicion/Cause   ☐ Post Accident
                     ☐ Return to Duty   ☐ Follow-up   ☐ Other (specify) _____

E. Tests to be Performed: ☐ THC, Cocaine, PCP, Opiates and Amphetamines
                           ☐ Only THC and Cocaine   ☐ OTHER (specify) _____

STEP 2: TO BE COMPLETED BY COLLECTOR - Specimen temperature must be read within 4 minutes of collection.

Specimen temperature within range: ☐ Yes, 90° - 100°F/32° - 38°C   ☐ No, Record specimen temperature here _____

STEP 3: TO BE COMPLETED BY COLLECTOR AND DONOR - Collector affixes bottle seal(s) to bottle(s). Collector dates seal(s). Donor initials seal(s).

STEP 4: TO BE COMPLETED BY DONOR - Go to copy 4 (pink page); STEP 4

STEP 5: TO BE COMPLETED BY COLLECTOR

COLLECTION SITE LOCATION:			SPLIT SPECIMEN COLLECTION
_____ Collection Facility	( ) _____ Collector's Business Phone No.		☐ YES ☐ NO
_____ Address	_____ _____ _____ City State Zip		

REMARKS: _____

I certify that the specimen identified on this form is the specimen presented to me by the donor providing the certification on Copy 4 of this form, that it bears the same specimen identification number as that set forth above, and that it has been collected, labeled and sealed as in accordance with applicable Federal requirements.

_____   _____   / /   ___ AM / PM
(PRINT) Collector's Name (First, MI, Last)   Signature of Collector   Date (Mo./Day/Yr.)   Time

STEP 6: TO BE INITIATED BY THE COLLECTOR AND COMPLETED AS NECESSARY THEREAFTER

DATE MO. DAY YR.	SPECIMEN RELEASED BY	SPECIMEN RECEIVED BY	PURPOSE OF CHANGE
/ /	DONOR - NO SIGNATURE	Signature Name	PROVIDE SPECIMEN FOR TESTING
/ /	Signature Name	Signature Name	
/ /	Signature Name	Signature Name	
/ /	Signature Name	Signature Name	

STEP 7: TO BE COMPLETED BY THE LABORATORY - Specimen Bottle Seal(s) Intact: ☐ YES ☐ NO, Explain in Remarks Below.

THE RESULTS FOR THE ABOVE IDENTIFIED SPECIMEN ARE IN ACCORDANCE WITH THE APPLICABLE PROCEDURES ESTABLISHED BY THE HHS MANDATORY GUIDELINES FOR FEDERAL WORKPLACE DRUG TESTING PROGRAMS

☐ RECONFIRMED for the following: ☐ CANNABINOIDS as Carboxy—THC   ☐ COCAINE METABOLITES as Benzoylecgonine   ☐ PHENCYCLIDINE
☐ FAILED TO RECONFIRM   ☐ OPIATES: ☐ AMPHETAMINES:
☐ TEST NOT PERFORMED   ☐ codeine   ☐ amphetamine   ☐ OTHER _____
                                      ☐ morphine   ☐ methamphetamine

REMARKS _____

TEST LAB (if different from above) _____   ( )
                                   NAME   ADDRESS   PHONE NO.

I certify that the specimen identified by the laboratory accession number on this form is the same specimen that bears the specimen identification number set forth above, that the specimen has been examined upon receipt, handled and analyzed in accordance with applicable Federal requirements, and that the results set forth are for that specimen.

_____   _____   / /
(PRINT) Certifying Scientist's Name (First, MI, Last)   Signature of Certifying Scientist   Date (Mo. / Day / Yr.)

STEP 8: TO BE COMPLETED BY THE MEDICAL REVIEW OFFICER

I have reviewed the laboratory results for the specimen identified by this form in accordance with applicable Federal requirements. My determination/verification is:

☐ Reconfirmed   ☐ Failed to reconfirm-   ☐ Test not performed   REMARKS _____
                    Both tests cancelled   Both tests cancelled

_____   _____   / /
(PRINT) Medical Review Officer's Name (First, MI, Last)   Signature of Medical Review Officer   Date (Mo. / Day / Yr.)

COPY 3 - SPLIT SPECIMEN - MUST ACCOMPANY SPLIT SPECIMEN TO LABORATORY

OMB No. 9999-0023
Expiration Date: 6/30/97

FEDERAL DRUG TESTING CUSTODY AND CONTROL FORM

SPECIMEN ID NO. **F211254**   **A**   LABORATORY ACCESSION NO.

STEP 1: TO BE COMPLETED BY COLLECTOR OR EMPLOYER REPRESENTATIVE

A. Employer Name, Address and I.D. No.   B. MRO Name and Address

C. Donor SSN or Employee I.D. No. _____

D. Reason for Test: ☐ Pre-employment   ☐ Random   ☐ Reasonable Suspicion/Cause   ☐ Post Accident
                     ☐ Return to Duty   ☐ Follow-up   ☐ Other (specify) _____

E. Tests to be Performed: ☐ THC, Cocaine, PCP, Opiates and Amphetamines
                            ☐ Only THC and Cocaine   ☐ OTHER (specify) _____

STEP 2: TO BE COMPLETED BY COLLECTOR - Specimen temperature must be read within 4 minutes of collection.

Specimen temperature within range: ☐ Yes, 90° - 100°F/32° - 38°C   ☐ No, Record specimen temperature here _____

STEP 3: TO BE COMPLETED BY COLLECTOR AND DONOR - Collector affixes bottle seal(s) to bottle(s). Collector dates seal(s). Donor initials seal(s).

▶ **STEP 4: SEE BELOW**

STEP 5: TO BE COMPLETED BY COLLECTOR - RETURN TO COPY 1

COLLECTION SITE LOCATION: SPLIT SPECIMEN COLLECTION

_____   ( )
         Collection Facility   Collector's Business Phone No.   ☐ YES   ☐ NO

_____   _____ _____ _____
         Address   City   State   Zip

REMARKS: _____

I certify that the specimen identified on this form is the specimen presented to me by the donor providing the certification on Copy 4 of this form, that it bears the same specimen
identification number as that set forth above, and that it has been collected, labeled and sealed as in accordance with applicable Federal requirements.
                                                                                                    AM
_____   _____   _____/_____/_____   _____ PM
(PRINT) Collector's Name (First, MI, Last)   Signature of Collector   Date (Mo./Day/Yr.)   Time

STEP 6: TO BE INITIATED BY THE COLLECTOR AND COMPLETED AS NECESSARY THEREAFTER

DATE MO. DAY YR.	SPECIMEN RELEASED BY	SPECIMEN RECEIVED BY	PURPOSE OF CHANGE
/ /	DONOR - NO SIGNATURE	Signature _____ Name	PROVIDE SPECIMEN FOR TESTING
/ /	Signature _____ Name	Signature _____ Name	
/ /	Signature _____ Name	Signature _____ Name	
/ /	Signature _____ Name	Signature _____ Name	

▶ **STEP 4: TO BE COMPLETED BY DONOR**

Daytime Phone No. ( )   Evening Phone No. ( )   Date of Birth ____/____/____
                                                                           Mo. Day Yr.

I certify that I provided my urine specimen to the collector; that I have not adulterated it in any manner; that each specimen bottle used was sealed with a tamper-evident
seal in my presence; and, that the information provided on this form and on the label affixed to each specimen bottle is correct.

                                          X
_____   _____   ____/____/____
(PRINT) Donor's Name (First, MI, Last)   Signature of Donor   Date (Mo. / Day / Yr.)

Should the results of the laboratory tests for the specimen identified by this form be confirmed positive, the Medical Review Officer will contact you to
ask about prescriptions and over-the-counter medications you may have taken. Therefore, you may want to make a list of those medications as a
"memory jogger." THIS LIST IS NOT NECESSARY. If you choose to make a list, do so either on a separate piece of paper or on the back of your copy
(Copy 5).—DO NOT LIST ON THE BACK OF ANY OTHER COPY OF THE FORM. TAKE COPY 5 WITH YOU.

STEP 8: TO BE COMPLETED BY THE MEDICAL REVIEW OFFICER

I have reviewed the laboratory results for the specimen identified by this form in accordance with applicable Federal requirements. My determination/verification is:

☐ Negative   ☐ Positive   ☐ Test Not Performed   ☐ Test Cancelled   REMARKS _____

_____   _____   ____/____/____
(PRINT) Medical Review Officer's Name (First, MI, Last)   Signature of Medical Review Officer   Date (Mo. / Day / Yr.)

COPY 4 - SEND DIRECTLY TO MEDICAL REVIEW OFFICER - DO NOT SEND TO LABORATORY

OMB No. 9999-0023
Expiration Date: 6/30/97

FEDERAL DRUG TESTING CUSTODY AND CONTROL FORM

SPECIMEN ID NO. **F211254** **A** LABORATORY ACCESSION NO.

STEP 1: TO BE COMPLETED BY COLLECTOR OR EMPLOYER REPRESENTATIVE

A. Employer Name, Address and I.D. No.   B. MRO Name and Address

C. Donor SSN or Employee I.D. No. _____

D. Reason for Test: ☐ Pre-employment ☐ Random ☐ Reasonable Suspicion/Cause ☐ Post Accident
                     ☐ Return to Duty   ☐ Follow-up ☐ Other (specify) _____

E. Tests to be Performed: ☐ THC, Cocaine, PCP, Opiates and Amphetamines
                           ☐ Only THC and Cocaine   ☐ OTHER (specify) _____

STEP 2: TO BE COMPLETED BY COLLECTOR - Specimen temperature must be read within 4 minutes of collection.

Specimen temperature within range: ☐ Yes, 90° - 100°F/32° - 38°C   ☐ No, Record specimen temperature here _____

STEP 3: TO BE COMPLETED BY COLLECTOR AND DONOR - Collector affixes bottle seal(s) to bottle(s). Collector dates seal(s). Donor initials seal(s)

STEP 4: SEE BELOW

STEP 5: TO BE COMPLETED BY COLLECTOR - RETURN TO COPY 1

COLLECTION SITE LOCATION:				SPLIT SPECIMEN COLLECTION
_____ Collection Facility	( ) _____ Collector's Business Phone No.			☐ YES ☐ NO
_____ Address	_____ City	_____ State	___ Zip	

REMARKS: _____

I certify that the specimen identified on this form is the specimen presented to me by the donor providing the certification on Copy 4 of this form, that it bears the same specimen identification number as that set forth above, and that it has been collected, labeled and sealed as in accordance with applicable Federal requirements.

_____ _____ ___/___/___ A P
(PRINT) Collector's Name (First, MI, Last) Signature of Collector Date (Mo./Day/Yr.) Time

STEP 6: TO BE INITIATED BY THE COLLECTOR AND COMPLETED AS NECESSARY THEREAFTER

DATE MO. DAY YR.	SPECIMEN RELEASED BY	SPECIMEN RECEIVED BY	PURPOSE OF CHANGE
___/___/___	DONOR - NO SIGNATURE	Signature _____ Name	PROVIDE SPECIMEN FOR TESTING
___/___/___	Signature _____ Name	Signature _____ Name	
___/___/___	Signature _____ Name	Signature _____ Name	
___/___/___	Signature _____ Name	Signature _____ Name	

STEP 4: TO BE COMPLETED BY DONOR

Daytime Phone No. ( ) _____   Evening Phone No. ( ) _____   Date of Birth ___/___/___ Mo. Day Yr.

I certify that I provided my urine specimen to the collector; that I have not adulterated it in any manner; that each specimen bottle used was sealed with a tamper-evident seal in my presence; and, that the information provided on this form and on the label affixed to each specimen bottle is correct.

X
_____ _____ ___/___/___
(PRINT) Donor's Name (First, MI, Last) Signature of Donor Date (Mo. / Day / Yr.)

Should the results of the laboratory tests for the specimen identified by this form be confirmed positive, the Medical Review Officer will contact you to ask about prescriptions and over-the-counter medications you may have taken. Therefore, you may want to make a list of those medications as a "memory jogger." THIS LIST IS NOT NECESSARY. If you choose to make a list, do so either on a separate piece of paper or on the back of your copy (Copy 5).—DO NOT LIST ON THE BACK OF ANY OTHER COPY OF THE FORM. TAKE COPY 5 WITH YOU.

STEP 8: TO BE COMPLETED BY THE MEDICAL REVIEW OFFICER

I have reviewed the laboratory results for the specimen identified by this form in accordance with applicable Federal requirements. My determination/verification is:

☐ Negative ☐ Positive ☐ Test Not Performed ☐ Test Cancelled   REMARKS _____

_____ _____ ___/___/___
(PRINT) Medical Review Officer's Name (First, MI, Last) Signature of Medical Review Officer Date (Mo. / Day / Yr.)

COPY 5 - GIVE TO DONOR - DO NOT SEND TO LABORATORY

OMB No. 9999-0023
Expiration Date 6/30/97

Privacy Act Statement: (For Federal Employees Only)

Submission of the information on the attached form is voluntary. However, incomplete submission of the information, refusal to provide a urine specimen, or substitution or adulteration of a specimen may result in delay or denial of your application for employment/appointment or may result in removal from the Federal service or other disciplinary action.

The authority for obtaining the urine specimen and identifying information contained herein is Executive Order 12564 ("Drug-Free Federal Workplace"), 5 U.S.C. § 3301 (2), 5 U.S.C. § 7301 and Section 503 of Public Law 100-71, 5 U.S.C. § 7301 note. Under provisions of Executive Order 12564 and 5 U.S.C. 7301, test results may only be disclosed to agency officials on a need-to-know basis. This may include the agency Medical Review Officer, the administrator of the Employee Assistance Program, and a supervisor with authority to take adverse personnel action. This information may also be disclosed to a court where necessary to defend against a challenge to an adverse personnel action.

Submission of your SSN is not required by law and is voluntary. Your refusal to furnish your number will not result in the denial of any right, benefit, or privilege provided by law. Your SSN is solicited, pursuant to Executive Order 9397, for purposes of associating information in agency files relating to you and for purposes of identifying the specimen provided for urinalysis testing for illegal drugs. If you refuse to indicate your SSN, a substitute number or other identifier will be assigned, as required, to process the specimen.

In the event laboratory analysis determines the presence of one or more illegal drugs in the specimen you provide, you will be contacted by an agency Medical Review Officer (MRO). The MRO will determine whether there is a legitimate medical explanation for the drug(s) identified by urinalysis.

Paperwork Reduction Act Notice (as required by 5 CFR 1320.21)

Public reporting burden for this collection of information, including the time for reviewing instructions, gathering and maintaining the data needed, and completing and reviewing the collection of information is estimated for each respondent to average: 5 minutes/donor; 4 minutes/collector; 3 minutes/laboratory; and 3 minutes/Medical Review Officer. Federal employees may send comments regarding these burden estimates, or any other aspect of this collection of information, including suggestions for reducing the burden, to Public Health Service Reports Clearance Officer, Attn: PRA, Hubert H. Humphrey Building, Rm 721-B, 200 Independence Ave. S.W., Washington, D.C. 20201. Individuals from the private sector may send comments/suggestions to: Department of Transportation, Drug Enforcement and Program Compliance, Rm 9404, 400 Seventh St. S.W., Washington, D.C. 20590. In addition, copies of all comments/suggestions may be sent to: Office of Management and Budget, Paperwork Reduction Project, Rm 3001, 725 Seventeenth St. N.W., Washington, D.C. 20503.

Back of Copy 5.

FEDERAL DRUG TESTING CUSTODY AND CONTROL FORM

SPECIMEN ID NO. **F211254**   **A**   LABORATORY ACCESSION NO.

STEP 1: TO BE COMPLETED BY COLLECTOR OR EMPLOYER REPRESENTATIVE

A. Employer Name, Address and I.D. No.	B. MRO Name and Address

C. Donor SSN or Employee I.D. No. _____

D. Reason for Test: ☐ Pre-employment ☐ Random ☐ Reasonable Suspicion/Cause ☐ Post Accident
☐ Return to Duty ☐ Follow-up ☐ Other (specify) _____

E. Tests to be Performed: ☐ THC, Cocaine, PCP, Opiates and Amphetamines
☐ Only THC and Cocaine ☐ OTHER (specify) _____

STEP 2: TO BE COMPLETED BY COLLECTOR - Specimen temperature must be read within 4 minutes of collection.

Specimen temperature within range: ☐ Yes, 90° - 100°F/32° - 38°C   ☐ No, Record specimen temperature here _____

STEP 3: TO BE COMPLETED BY COLLECTOR AND DONOR - Collector affixes bottle seal(s) to bottle(s). Collector dates seal(s). Donor initials seal(s)

STEP 4: SEE BELOW

STEP 5: TO BE COMPLETED BY COLLECTOR - RETURN TO COPY 1

COLLECTION SITE LOCATION:

	SPLIT SPECIMEN COLLECTION

_____   ( ) _____
Collection Facility   Collector's Business Phone No.   ☐ YES ☐ NO

_____
Address   City   State   Zip

REMARKS: _____
I certify that the specimen identified on this form is the specimen presented to me by the donor providing the certification on Copy 4 of this form, that it bears the same specimen identification number as that set forth above, and that it has been collected, labeled and sealed as in accordance with applicable Federal requirements.

_____   _____   / /   A
(PRINT) Collector's Name (First, MI, Last)   Signature of Collector   Date (Mo./Day/Yr.)   P   Time

STEP 6: TO BE INITIATED BY THE COLLECTOR AND COMPLETED AS NECESSARY THEREAFTER

DATE MO. DAY YR.	SPECIMEN RELEASED BY	SPECIMEN RECEIVED BY	PURPOSE OF CHANGE
/ /	DONOR - NO SIGNATURE	Signature ____ Name	PROVIDE SPECIMEN FOR TESTING
/ /	Signature ____ Name	Signature ____ Name	
/ /	Signature ____ Name	Signature ____ Name	
/ /	Signature ____ Name	Signature ____ Name	

STEP 4: TO BE COMPLETED BY DONOR

Daytime Phone No. ▨▨▨▨▨▨   Evening Phone No. ▨▨▨▨▨▨   Date of Birth / /
Mo.   Day   Yr.

I certify that I provided my urine specimen to the collector; that I have not adulterated it in any manner; that each specimen bottle used was sealed with a tamper-evident seal in my presence; and, that the information provided on this form and on the label affixed to each specimen bottle is correct.

X _____   _____   / /
(PRINT) Donor's Name (First, MI, Last)   Signature of Donor   Date (Mo. / Day /Yr.)

Should the results of the laboratory tests for the specimen identified by this form be confirmed positive, the Medical Review Officer will contact you to ask about prescriptions and over-the-counter medications you may have taken. Therefore, you may want to make a list of those medications as a "memory jogger." THIS LIST IS NOT NECESSARY. If you choose to make a list, do so either on a separate piece of paper or on the back of your copy (Copy 5).—DO NOT LIST ON THE BACK OF ANY OTHER COPY OF THE FORM. TAKE COPY 5 WITH YOU.

STEP 8: TO BE COMPLETED BY THE MEDICAL REVIEW OFFICER

I have reviewed the laboratory results for the specimen identified by this form in accordance with applicable Federal requirements. My determination/verification is:

☐ Negative ☐ Positive ☐ Test Not Performed ☐ Test Cancelled   REMARKS _____

_____   _____   / /
(PRINT) Medical Review Officer's Name (First, MI, Last)   Signature of Medical Review Officer   Date (Mo. / Day / Yr.)

COPY 6 - COLLECTOR RETAINS - DO NOT SEND TO LABORATORY

OMB No. 9999-0023 Expiration Date 6/30/97

FEDERAL DRUG TESTING CUSTODY AND CONTROL FORM

SPECIMEN ID NO. **F211254**   **A**   LABORATORY ACCESSION NO.

STEP 1: TO BE COMPLETED BY COLLECTOR OR EMPLOYER REPRESENTATIVE

A. Employer Name, Address and I.D. No.   B. MRO Name and Address

C. Donor SSN or Employee I.D. No. _____

D. Reason for Test: ☐ Pre-employment   ☐ Random   ☐ Reasonable Suspicion/Cause   ☐ Post Accident
                     ☐ Return to Duty   ☐ Follow-up   ☐ Other (specify) _____

E. Tests to be Performed: ☐ THC, Cocaine, PCP, Opiates and Amphetamines
                             ☐ Only THC and Cocaine   ☐ OTHER (specify) _____

STEP 2: TO BE COMPLETED BY COLLECTOR - Specimen temperature must be read within 4 minutes of collection.

Specimen temperature within range: ☐ Yes, 90° - 100°F/32° - 38°C   ☐ No, Record specimen temperature here _____

STEP 3: TO BE COMPLETED BY COLLECTOR AND DONOR - Collector affixes bottle seal(s) to bottle(s). Collector dates seal(s). Donor initials seal(s).

STEP 4: SEE BELOW

STEP 5: TO BE COMPLETED BY COLLECTOR - RETURN TO COPY 1

COLLECTION SITE LOCATION: SPLIT SPECIMEN
                                                                                   COLLECTION
_____   (_____) _____
   Collection Facility   Collector's Business Phone No.   ☐ YES   ☐ NO

_____   _____ _____ _____
       Address   City   State   Zip

REMARKS: _____

I certify that the specimen identified on this form is the specimen presented to me by the donor providing the certification on Copy 4 of this form, that it bears the same specimen identification number as that set forth above, and that it has been collected, labeled and sealed as in accordance with applicable Federal requirements.

_____   _____/____/____   A
(PRINT) Collector's Name (First, MI, Last)   Signature of Collector   Date (Mo./Day/Yr.)   PM
                                                                                              Time

STEP 6: TO BE INITIATED BY THE COLLECTOR AND COMPLETED AS NECESSARY THEREAFTER

DATE MO. DAY YR.	SPECIMEN RELEASED BY	SPECIMEN RECEIVED BY	PURPOSE OF CHANGE
__/__/__	DONOR - NO SIGNATURE	Signature _____ Name _____	PROVIDE SPECIMEN FOR TESTING
__/__/__	Signature _____ Name _____	Signature _____ Name _____	
__/__/__	Signature _____ Name _____	Signature _____ Name _____	
__/__/__	Signature _____ Name _____	Signature _____ Name _____	

STEP 4: TO BE COMPLETED BY DONOR

Daytime Phone No. ▓▓▓▓▓▓▓▓▓▓   Evening Phone No. ▓▓▓▓▓▓▓▓▓▓   Date of Birth __/__/__
                                                                                  Mo. Day Yr.

I certify that I provided my urine specimen to the collector; that I have not adulterated it in any manner; that each specimen bottle used was sealed with a tamper-evident seal in my presence; and, that the information provided on this form and on the label affixed to each specimen bottle is correct.

                          X
_____   _____   ____/____/____
(PRINT) Donor's Name (First, MI, Last)   Signature of Donor   Date (Mo. / Day / Yr.)

Should the results of the laboratory tests for the specimen identified by this form be confirmed positive, the Medical Review Officer will contact you to ask about prescriptions and over-the-counter medications you may have taken. Therefore, you may want to make a list of those medications as a "memory jogger." THIS LIST IS NOT NECESSARY. If you choose to make a list, do so either on a separate piece of paper or on the back of your copy (Copy 5).—DO NOT LIST ON THE BACK OF ANY OTHER COPY OF THE FORM. TAKE COPY 5 WITH YOU.

STEP 8: TO BE COMPLETED BY THE MEDICAL REVIEW OFFICER

I have reviewed the laboratory results for the specimen identified by this form in accordance with applicable Federal requirements. My determination/verification is:
☐ Negative   ☐ Positive   ☐ Test Not Performed   ☐ Test Cancelled
                                                      REMARKS _____

_____   _____   ____/____/____
(PRINT) Medical Review Officer's Name (First, MI, Last)   Signature of Medical Review Officer   Date (Mo. / Yr.)

COPY 7 - FORWARD TO EMPLOYER - DO NOT SEND TO LABORATORY

OMB No. 9999-0023
Expiration Date: 6/30/97

INSTRUCTION FOR COMPLETING DRUG TESTING CUSTODY AND CONTROL FORM

The following instructions are in accordance with procedures established by the Department of Health and Human Services and the Department of Transportation mandatory guidelines for federal and transportation workplace drug testing programs.

NOTE: Use ballpoint pen, press hard, and check all copies for legibility.

STEP 1

If the information in STEP 1 has not been completed, collector (not donor) completes STEP 1 (A-E).

NOTE: Donor refusal to provide SSN or Employee I.D. number must be annotated in STEP 5 collector's REMARKS section.

STEP 2.

Upon receiving specimen from donor, check specimen temperature. This must be accomplished within 4 minutes.

Check block marked "Yes" if temperature is within range.

If specimen temperature is not within range, check block marked "No" and record specimen temperature.

STEP 3. FOR SPLIT SPECIMEN COLLECTIONS ONLY

Secure caps on both specimen bottles and affix specimen bottle seal labeled A over the cap and down the sides of the primary specimen (bottle containing at least 30ml of urine).

Affix specimen bottle seal labeled B (split) on the split specimen (bottle containing at least 15ml of urine) in the same manner.

Record date on both specimen bottle seals.

FOR SINGLE SPECIMEN COLLECTION ONLY

Secure cap on specimen bottle (containing at least 30ml of urine) and affix specimen bottle seal labeled A over the cap and down the sides of the specimen bottle.

Record date on specimen bottle seal.

Instruct donor to initial the specimen bottle seal.

STEP 4.

Turn to Copy 4 (pink page). STEP 4.

Instruct donor to complete STEP 4.

Ensure donor provides his/her daytime and evening phone number and date of birth.

Instruct donor to read certification statement. Ensure donor prints his/her name and signs and dates the certification statement.

NOTE: Donor refusal to sign must be annotated in STEP 5, collector's remarks section.

Upon completion, check donor entries, return to Copy 1.

STEP 5.

After returning to Copy 1, go to STEP 5.

Complete the name and address of the facility at which the collection is taking place.

List a business telephone number where collector can be reached.

Place a check in the box indicating whether or not a split specimen was collected.

Record any unusual occurrences concerning the collection (e.g. donor refusal to provide information sign certification statement, specimen collected under direct observation, suspected adulteration) in the remarks section.

Collector completes collection certification section by printing and signing his/her name, recording the date and time of collection. Be sure to circle A.M. or P.M.

STEP 6. CHAIN OF CUSTODY SECTION

NOTE: Each time the specimen is handled, transferred, or placed into storage prior to being packaged for shipment, every individual must be identified (including a direct observer, if required) and the date and purpose of change recorded. The following instructions pertain to a collection in which the donor provides a specimen directly to the collector who seals, packages, and ships the specimen to the laboratory.

Record date of collection.

In the "Specimen Received By" column, sign and print your name indicating that you have received the specimen from the donor.

The "Purpose of Change" entry in the next column is pre-printed (Provide Specimen for Testing) and explains the transfer of the specimen from the donor to the collector.

On the next line, record the date the specimen was released by you.

Complete the "Specimen Released By" block by signing and printing your name.

If you are preparing the specimen for shipment to the laboratory complete the "Specimen Received By" block by printing the carrier or shipment provider name only. (See Example)

Complete the "Purpose of Change" block explaining the transfer of the specimen from the collector to the carrier or shipment provider (e.g. Ship Specimen to Lab).

NO.	DATE DAY YR	SPECIMEN RELEASED BY	SPECIMEN RECEIVED BY	PURPOSE OF CHANGE
	8 / 15 / 94	DONOR - NO SIGNATURE	Signature *Connie Collector* / Name *Connie Collector*	PROVIDE SPECIMEN FOR TESTING
	8 / 15 / 94	Signature *Connie Collector* / Name *Connie Collector*	Signature / Name *ABC Courier Service*	SHIP SPECIMEN TO LAB
	/ /	Signature / Name	Signature / Name	
	/ /	Signature / Name	Signature / Name	

COMPLETING THE COLLECTION PROCESS

Upon completing Step 6, give donor his/her copy. Copy 5 (green page) of the Drug Testing Custody and Control Form.

Donor may leave the collection site at this point.

If a split specimen collection was performed, place both specimen bottles and Copies 1, 2, and 3 of the Drug Testing Custody and Control Form in the shipping container.

If a single collection was performed, place the specimen bottle and Copies 1 and 2 of the Drug Testing Custody and Control Form in the shipping container. Discard Copy 3.

Secure the shipping container. On the shipping container seal, record your initials and the date.

Send Copy 4 (pink page) directly to the Medical Review Officer. Do not send to laboratory.

Retain Copy 6 (yellow page) for your records.

Forward Copy 7 (blue page) to the employer. Do not send to laboratory.

U.S. Department of Transportation (DOT)
Breath Alcohol Testing Form

[THE INSTRUCTIONS FOR COMPLETING THIS FORM ARE ON THE BACK OF COPY 3]

▶ **STEP 1: TO BE COMPLETED BY BREATH ALCOHOL TECHNICIAN**

A. Employee Name _____
   (PRINT) (First, M.I., Last)

B. SSN or Employee ID No. _____

C. Employer Name, _____
   Address, &
   Telephone No. _____

   _____

   _____ ( )
   Telephone Number

D. Reason for Test: ❏ Pre-employment ❏ Random ❏ Post-accident

   ❏ Reasonable Suspicion/Cause ❏ Return to Duty ❏ Follow-up

▶ **STEP 2: TO BE COMPLETED BY EMPLOYEE**

I certify that I am about to submit to breath alcohol testing required by U.S. Department of Transportation regulations and that the identifying information provided on this form is true and correct.

_____   ___/___/___
Signature of Employee   Date Month Day Year

▶ **STEP 3: TO BE COMPLETED BY BREATH ALCOHOL TECHNICIAN**

I certify that I have conducted breath alcohol testing on the above named individual in accordance with the procedures established in the U.S. Department of Transportation regulation, 49 CFR Part 40, that I am qualified to operate the testing devices identified, and that the results are as recorded.

Screening test: Complete **only if** the testing device is not designed to **print** the following.

AM
PM
_____ _____ _____ _____ _____
Test No. Testing Device Name Testing Device Serial Number Time Result

Confirmation test: Confirmation test results **MUST** be affixed to the back of each copy of this form or printed on the space to the right of each front copy.

Remarks: _____

_____

_____

_____
(PRINT) Breath Alcohol Technician's Name (First, M.I., Last)

_____   ___/___/___
Signature of Breath Alcohol Technician Date Month Day Year

▶ **STEP 4: TO BE COMPLETED BY EMPLOYEE**

I certify that I have submitted to the breath alcohol test the results of which are accurately recorded on this form. I understand that I must not drive, perform safety-sensitive duties, or operate heavy equipment if the results are 0.02 or greater.

_____   ___/___/___
Signature of Employee   Date Month Day Year

OMB No. 2105-0529
371-FS-C3
COPY 1 - ORIGINAL - FORWARD TO THE EMPLOYER   (Rev. 9/97)

```
┌─────────────────────────────────────┐   ┌─────────────────────────────────────┐
│   AFFIX SCREENING TEST RESULTS HERE  │   │  AFFIX CONFIRMATION TEST RESULTS HERE │
│           (IF APPLICABLE)            │   │                                       │
│                                      │   │                                       │
│                                      │   │                                       │
│      USE TAMPER-EVIDENT TAPE         │   │       USE TAMPER-EVIDENT TAPE         │
│                                      │   │                                       │
│                                      │   │                                       │
└─────────────────────────────────────┘   └─────────────────────────────────────┘
```

COPY 1 - ORIGINAL - FORWARD TO THE EMPLOYER   OMB No. 2105-0529

U.S. Department of Transportation (DOT)
Breath Alcohol Testing Form

[THE INSTRUCTIONS FOR COMPLETING THIS FORM ARE ON THE BACK OF COPY 3]

▶ **STEP 1: TO BE COMPLETED BY BREATH ALCOHOL TECHNICIAN**

A. Employee Name _____
   (PRINT) (First, M.I., Last)

B. SSN or Employee ID No. _____

C. Employer Name, _____
   Address, &
   Telephone No. _____

   _____

   ( ) _____
   Telephone Number

D. Reason for Test: ❑ Pre-employment ❑ Random ❑ Post-accident
   ❑ Reasonable Suspicion/Cause ❑ Return to Duty ❑ Follow-up

▶ **STEP 2: TO BE COMPLETED BY EMPLOYEE**

I certify that I am about to submit to breath alcohol testing required by U.S. Department of Transportation regulations and that the identifying information provided on this form is true and correct.

_____   ___/___/___
Signature of Employee   Date Month Day Year

▶ **STEP 3: TO BE COMPLETED BY BREATH ALCOHOL TECHNICIAN**

I certify that I have conducted breath alcohol testing on the above named individual in accordance with the procedures established in the U.S. Department of Transportation regulation, 49 CFR Part 40, that I am qualified to operate the testing devices identified, and that the results are as recorded.

Screening test: Complete **only if** the testing device is not designed to **print** the following.

                                                    AM
                                                    PM _____
_____ _____ _____ _____ _____
Test No. Testing Device Name Testing Device Serial Number Time Result

Confirmation test: Confirmation test results **MUST** be affixed to the back of each copy of this form or printed on the space to the right of each front copy.

Remarks: _____

_____

_____

_____
(PRINT) Breath Alcohol Technician's Name (First, M.I., Last)

_____   ___/___/___
Signature of Breath Alcohol Technician   Date Month Day Year

▶ **STEP 4: TO BE COMPLETED BY EMPLOYEE**

I certify that I have submitted to the breath alcohol test the results of which are accurately recorded on this form. I understand that I must not drive, perform safety-sensitive duties, or operate heavy equipment if the results are 0.02 or greater.

_____   ___/___/___
Signature of Employee   Date Month Day Year

OMB No. 2105-0529
371-FS-C3
(Rev. 9/97)

COPY 2 - EMPLOYEE RETAINS

Privacy Act Statement

(applicable in those cases where completed Breath Alcohol Testing Forms are retained in a Federal Privacy Act system of records)

Except for your Social Security Number (SSN), submission of the information on the front side of this form is mandatory. Incomplete submission of the information, failure to provide an adequate breath specimen for testing without a valid medical explanation, engaging in conduct that clearly obstructs the testing process, or failure to sign the certification statements on the front side of this form may result in delay or denial of your application for employment/appointment, your inability to resume performing safety-sensitive duties, removal from a safety-sensitive position, or other disciplinary action.

The authority for obtaining the breath specimen required by the U.S. Department of Transportation is the Omnibus Transportation Employee Testing Act of 1991, Pub. L. 102-143, Title V. The principal purpose for which the information sought is to be used is to ensure that you have submitted to breath alcohol testing and to ensure that you are promptly notified in the event of noncompliance with the U.S. Department of Transportation breath alcohol testing requirements.

Submission of your SSN is not required by law and is voluntary. If you object to the use of your SSN in this form, you will not be denied any right, benefit, or privilege provided by law; a substitute number or other identifier will be assigned.

The information provided in this form may be disclosed, as a routine use, to a Federal, State, or local agency for authorized investigative or enforcement purposes or to a court or an administrative tribunal when the Government or one of its agencies is a party to a judicial proceeding before the court or involved in administrative proceedings before the tribunal.

PAPERWORK REDUCTION ACT NOTICE (as required by 5 CFR 1320.21)

Public reporting burden for this collection of information is estimated for each respondent to average: 1 minute/employee, 4 minutes/Breath Alcohol Technician. Individuals may send comments regarding these burden estimates, or any other aspect of this collection of information, including suggestions for reducing the burden, to U.S. Department of Transportation, Drug Enforcement and Program Compliance, Room 9404, 400 Seventh St., SW, Washington, D.C. 20590 or Office of Management and Budget, Paperwork Reduction Project, Room 3001, 725 Seventeenth St., NW, Washington, D.C. 20503.

U.S. Department of Transportation (DOT)
Breath Alcohol Testing Form

[THE INSTRUCTIONS FOR COMPLETING THIS FORM ARE ON THE BACK OF COPY 3]

▶ **STEP 1: TO BE COMPLETED BY BREATH ALCOHOL TECHNICIAN**

A. Employee Name _____
    (PRINT) (First, M.I., Last)

B. SSN or Employee ID No. _____

C. Employer Name, _____
    Address, &
    Telephone No. _____

    _____

    _____ (___) _____
                                        Telephone Number

D. Reason for Test: ☐ Pre-employment ☐ Random ☐ Post-accident
    ☐ Reasonable Suspicion/Cause ☐ Return to Duty ☐ Follow-up

▶ **STEP 2: TO BE COMPLETED BY EMPLOYEE**

I certify that I am about to submit to breath alcohol testing required by U.S. Department of Transportation regulations and that the identifying information provided on this form is true and correct.

_____   _____ / _____ / _____
        Signature of Employee   Date   Month   Day   Year

▶ **STEP 3: TO BE COMPLETED BY BREATH ALCOHOL TECHNICIAN**

I certify that I have conducted breath alcohol testing on the above named individual in accordance with the procedures established in the U.S. Department of Transportation regulation, 49 CFR Part 40, that I am qualified to operate the testing devices identified, and that the results are as recorded.

Screening test: Complete **only if** the testing device is not designed to **print** the following.

                                                                    AM
_____ _____ _____ _____ PM _____
Test No. Testing Device Name Testing Device Serial Number Time Result

Confirmation test: Confirmation test results **MUST** be affixed to the back of each copy of this form or printed on the space to the right of each front copy.

Remarks: _____

_____

_____

_____

_____
(PRINT) Breath Alcohol Technician's Name (First, M.I., Last)

_____   _____ / _____ / _____
  Signature of Breath Alcohol Technician Date Month   Day   Year

▶ **STEP 4: TO BE COMPLETED BY EMPLOYEE**

I certify that I have submitted to the breath alcohol test the results of which are accurately recorded on this form. I understand that I must not drive, perform safety-sensitive duties, or operate heavy equipment if the results are 0.02 or greater.

_____   _____ / _____ / _____
        Signature of Employee   Date   Month   Day   Year

OMB No. 2105-0529
371-FS-C3
COPY 3 - BREATH ALCOHOL TECHNICIAN RETAINS   (Rev. 9/97)

<table>
<tr><td>

AFFIX SCREENING TEST RESULTS HERE
(IF APPLICABLE)

USE TAMPER-EVIDENT TAPE

</td><td>

AFFIX CONFIRMATION TEST RESULTS HERE

USE TAMPER-EVIDENT TAPE

</td></tr>
</table>

INSTRUCTIONS FOR COMPLETING THE U.S. DEPARTMENT OF TRANSPORTATION BREATH ALCOHOL TESTING FORM

NOTE: Use a ballpoint pen, press hard, and check <u>all</u> copies for legibility.

STEP 1   The Breath Alcohol Technician (BAT) completes the information required in this step. Be sure to <u>print</u> the employee's name and check the box identifying the reason for the test.

        NOTE: If the employee refuses to provide SSN or I.D. number, be sure to indicate this in the remarks section in STEP 3. Proceed with STEP 2.

STEP 2   Instruct the employee to read, sign, and date the employee certification statement in STEP 2.

        NOTE: If the employee refuses to sign the certification statement, <u>do not proceed</u> with the alcohol test. Contact the designated employer representative.

STEP 3   The Breath Alcohol Technician (BAT) completes the information required in this step. After conducting the alcohol screening test, do the following (as appropriate):

        If the breath testing device used in conducting the screening test <u>is not capable</u> of printing the screening test information located on the front of this form (test number, testing device name, testing device serial number, time of test and results), complete this information in the space provided on the front of this form,

        NOTE: Be sure to enter the result of the test exactly as it is indicated on the breath testing device, i.e., 0.00, 0.02, 0.04, etc.

        OR, If the breath testing device used in conducting the screening test <u>is capable</u> of printing the screening test information located on the front of this form, affix the printed information in the <u>space provided above. Be sure to use tamper-evident tape.</u>

        If the results of the screening test are less than 0.02, print, sign your name, and enter today's date in the space provided. Go to STEP 4.

        If the results of the screening test are 0.02 or greater, a confirmation test must be administered in accordance with DOT regulations. An EVIDENTIAL BREATH TESTING device that is capable of printing confirmation test information <u>must</u> be used in conducting this test.

        After conducting the alcohol confirmation test, affix the printed information in the space provided above. <u>Be sure to use tamper-evident tape.</u>

        Print, sign your name, and enter the date in the space provided. Go to STEP 4.

STEP 4   Instruct the employee to read, sign, and date the employee certification statement in STEP 4.

        NOTE: If the employee refuses to sign the certification statement in STEP 4, be sure to indicate this in the remarks section in STEP 3.

        Forward **Copy 1** (white page) to the employer.
        Give **Copy 2** (green page) to the employee.
        Retain **Copy 3** (blue page) for BAT records.

COPY 3 - BREATH ALCOHOL TECHNICIAN RETAINS   **OMB No. 2105-0529**

FHWA Regulations, 49 CFR PART 382 ■

Code of Federal Regulations
Title 49—Transportation
Subtitle B—Other Regulations Relating to Transportation
Chapter III—Federal Highway Administration, Department of Transportation
Subchapter—Federal Motor Carrier Safety Regulations
PART 382—Controlled Substances and Alcohol Use and Testing
Current through January 1, 1999; 63 FR 72352

SUBPART A—GENERAL

§382.101 Purpose.

The purpose of this part is to establish programs designed to help prevent accidents and injuries resulting from the misuse of alcohol or use of controlled substances by drivers of commercial motor vehicles.

§382.103 Applicability.

(a) This part applies to every person and to all employers of such persons who operate a commercial motor vehicle in commerce in any State, and is subject to:

(1) The commercial driver's license requirements of part 383 of this subchapter;

(2) The Licencia Federal de Conductor (Mexico) requirements; or

(3) The commercial driver's license requirements of the Canadian National Safety Code.

(b) An employer who employs himself/herself as a driver must comply with both the requirements in this part that apply to employers and the requirements in this part that apply to drivers. An employer who employs only himself/herself as a driver shall implement a random alcohol and controlled substances testing program of two or more covered employees in the random testing selection pool.

(c) The exceptions contained in §390.3(f) of this subchapter do not apply to this part. The employers and drivers identified in §390.3(f) must comply with the requirements of this part, unless otherwise specifically provided in paragraph (d) of this section.

(d) Exceptions. This part shall not apply to employers and their drivers:

(1) Required to comply with the alcohol and/or controlled substances testing requirements of parts 653 and 654 of this title (Federal Transit Administration alcohol and controlled substances testing regulations); or

(2) Who a State must waive from the requirements of part 383 of this subchapter. These individuals include active duty military personnel; members of the reserves; and members of the national guard on active duty, including personnel on full-time national guard duty, personnel on part-time national guard training and national guard military technicians (civilians who are required to wear military uniforms), and active duty U.S. Coast Guard personnel;

(3) Who a State has, at its discretion, exempted from the requirements of part 383 of this subchapter. These individuals may be:

(i) Operators of a farm vehicle which is:

(A) Controlled and operated by a farmer;

(B) Used to transport either agricultural products, farm machinery, farm supplies, or both to or from a farm;

(C) Not used in the operations of a common or contract motor carrier; and

(D) Used within 241 kilometers (150 miles) of the farmer's farm.

(ii) Firefighters or other persons who operate commercial motor vehicles which are necessary for the preservation of life or property or the execution of emergency governmental functions, are equipped with audible and visual signals, and are not subject to normal traffic regulation.

§382.105 Testing procedures.

Each employer shall ensure that all alcohol or controlled substances testing conducted under this part complies with the procedures set forth in part 40 of this title. The provisions of part 40 of this title that address alcohol or controlled substances testing are made applicable to employers by this part.

§382.107 Definitions.

Words or phrases used in this part are defined in ¤§386.2 and 390.5 of this subchapter, and §40.3 of this title, except as provided herein—

Alcohol means the intoxicating agent in beverage alcohol, ethyl alcohol, or other low molecular weight alcohols including methyl and isopropyl alcohol.

Alcohol concentration (or content) means the alcohol in a volume of breath expressed in terms of grams of alcohol per 210 liters of breath as indicated by an evidential breath test under this part.

Alcohol use means the consumption of any beverage, mixture, or preparation, including any medication, containing alcohol.

Commerce means:

(1) Any trade, traffic or transportation within the jurisdiction of the United States between a place in a State and a place outside of such State, including a place outside of the United States and

(2) Trade, traffic, and transportation in the United States which affects any trade, traffic, and transportation described in paragraph (1) of this definition.

Commercial motor vehicle means a motor vehicle or combination of motor vehicles used in commerce to transport passengers or property if the motor vehicle—

(1) Has a gross combination weight rating of 11,794 or more kilograms (26,001 or more pounds) inclusive of a towed unit with a gross vehicle weight rating of more than 4,536 kilograms (10,000 pounds); or

(2) Has a gross vehicle weight rating of 11,794 or more kilograms (26,001 or more pounds); or

(3) Is designed to transport 16 or more passengers, including the driver; or

(4) Is of any size and is used in the transportation of materials found to be hazardous for the purposes of the Hazardous Materials Transportation Act and which require the motor vehicle to be placarded under the Haz-ardous Materials Regulations (49 CFR part 172, subpart F).

Confirmation test for alcohol testing means a second test, following a screening test with a result of 0.02 or greater, that provides quantitative data of alcohol concentration. For controlled substances testing means a second analytical procedure to identify the presence of a specific drug or metabolite which is independent of the screen test and which uses a different technique and chemical principle from that of the screen test in order to ensure reliability and accuracy. (Gas chromatography/mass spectrometry (GC/MS) is the only authorized confirmation method for cocaine, marijuana, opiates, amphetamines, and phencyclidine.)

Consortium means an entity, including a group or association of employers or contractors, that provides alcohol or controlled substances testing as required by this part, or other DOT alcohol or controlled substances testing rules, and that acts on behalf of the employers.

Controlled substances mean those substances identified in §40.21(a) of this title.

Disabling damage means damage which precludes departure of a motor vehicle from the scene of the accident in its usual manner in daylight after simple repairs.

(1) Inclusions. Damage to motor vehicles that could have been driven, but would have been further damaged if so driven.

(2) Exclusions.

(i) Damage which can be remedied temporarily at the scene of the accident without special tools or parts.

(ii) Tire disablement without other damage even if no spare tire is available.

(iii) Headlight or taillight damage.

(iv) Damage to turn signals, horn, or windshield wipers which make them inoperative.

DOT Agency means an agency (or "operating administration") of the United States Department of Transportation administering regulations requiring alcohol and/or drug testing (14 CFR parts 61, 63, 65, 121, and 135; 49 CFR parts 199, 219, 382, 653 and 654), in accordance with part 40 of this title.

Driver means any person who operates a commercial motor vehicle. This includes, but is not limited to: Full time, regularly employed drivers; casual, intermittent or occasional drivers; leased drivers and independent, owner-operator contractors who are either directly employed by or under lease to an employer or who operate a commercial motor vehicle at the direction of or with the consent of an employer.

Employer means any person (including the United States, a State, District of Columbia, tribal government, or a political subdivision of a State) who owns or leases a commercial motor vehicle or assigns persons to operate such a vehicle. The term employer includes an employer's agents, officers and representatives.

Licensed medical practitioner means a person who is licensed, certified, and/or registered, in accordance with applicable Federal, State, local, or foreign laws and regulations, to prescribe controlled substances and other drugs.

Performing (a safety-sensitive function) means a driver is considered to be performing a safety-sensitive function during any period in which he or she is actually performing, ready to perform, or immediately available to perform any safety-sensitive functions.

Positive rate means the number of positive results for random controlled substances tests conducted under this part plus the number of refusals of random controlled substances tests required by this part, divided by the total of random controlled substances tests conducted under this part plus the number of refusals of random tests required by this part.

Refuse to submit (to an alcohol or controlled substances test) means that a driver:

(1) Fails to provide adequate breath for alcohol testing as required by part 40 of this title, without a valid medical explanation, after he or she has received notice of the requirement for breath testing in accordance with the provisions of this part,

(2) Fails to provide an adequate urine sample for controlled substances testing as required by part 40 of this title, without a genuine inability to provide a specimen (as determined by a medical evaluation), after he or she has received notice of the requirement for urine testing in accordance with the provisions of this part, or

(3) Engages in conduct that clearly obstructs the testing process.

Safety-sensitive function means all time from the time a driver begins to work or is required to be in readiness to work until the time he/she is relieved from work and all responsibility for performing work. Safety-sensitive functions shall include:

(1) All time at an employer or shipper plant, terminal, facility, or other property, or on any public property, waiting to be dispatched, unless the driver has been relieved from duty by the employer;

(2) All time inspecting equipment as required by ¤§392.7 and 392.8 of this subchapter or otherwise inspecting, servicing, or conditioning any commercial motor vehicle at any time;

(3) All time spent at the driving controls of a commercial motor vehicle in operation;

(4) All time, other than driving time, in or upon any commercial motor vehicle except time spent resting in a sleeper berth (a berth conforming to the requirements of §393.76 of this subchapter);

(5) All time loading or unloading a vehicle, supervising, or assisting in the loading or unloading, attending a vehicle being loaded or unloaded, remaining in readiness to operate the vehicle, or in giving or receiving receipts for shipments loaded or unloaded; and

(6) All time repairing, obtaining assistance, or remaining in attendance upon a disabled vehicle.

Screening test (also known as initial test) In alcohol testing, it means an analytical procedure to determine whether a driver may have a prohibited concentration of alcohol in his or her system. In controlled substance testing, it means an immunoassay screen to eliminate "negative" urine specimens from further consideration.

Violation rate means the number of drivers (as reported under §382.305 of this part) found during random tests given under this part to have an alcohol concentration of 0.04 or greater, plus the number of drivers who refuse a random test required by this part, divided by the total reported number of drivers in the industry given random alcohol tests under this part plus the total reported number of drivers in the industry who refuse a random test required by this part.

§382.109 Preemption of State and local laws.

(a) Except as provided in paragraph (b) of this section, this part preempts any State or local law, rule, regulation, or order to the extent that:

(1) Compliance with both the State or local requirement and this part is not possible; or

(2) Compliance with the State or local requirement is an obstacle to the accomplishment and execution of any requirement in this part.

(b) This part shall not be construed to preempt provisions of State criminal law that impose sanctions for reckless conduct leading to actual loss of life, injury, or damage to property, whether the provisions apply specifically to transportation employees, employers, or the general public.

§382.111 Other requirements imposed by employers.

Except as expressly provided in this part, nothing in this part shall be construed to affect the authority of employers, or the rights of drivers, with respect to the use of alcohol, or the use of controlled substances, including authority and rights with respect to testing and rehabilitation.

§382.113 Requirement for notice.

Before performing an alcohol or controlled substances test under this part, each employer shall notify a driver that the alcohol or controlled substances test is required by this part. No employer shall falsely represent that a test is administered under this part.

§382.115 Starting date for testing programs.

(a) All domestic employers. Each domestic-domiciled employer that begins commercial motor vehicle operations will implement the requirements of this part on the date the employer begins such operations.

(b) Large foreign employers. Each foreign-domiciled employer with fifty or more drivers assigned to operate commercial motor vehicles in North America on December 17, 1995, must implement the requirements of this part beginning on July 1, 1996.

(c) Small foreign employers. Each foreign-domiciled employer with less than fifty drivers assigned to operate commercial motor vehicles in North America on December 17, 1995, must implement the requirements of this part beginning on July 1, 1997.

(d) All foreign employers. Each foreign-domiciled employer that begins commercial motor vehicle operations in the United States after December 17, 1995, but before July 1, 1997, must implement the requirements of this part beginning on July 1, 1997. A foreign employer that begins commercial motor vehicle operations in the United States on or after July 1, 1997, must implement the requirements of this part on the date the foreign employer begins such operations.

SUBPART B—PROHIBITIONS

§382.201 Alcohol concentration.

No driver shall report for duty or remain on duty requiring the performance of safety-sensitive functions while having an alcohol concentration of 0.04 or greater. No employer having actual knowledge that a driver has an alcohol concentration of 0.04 or greater shall permit the driver to perform or continue to perform safety-sensitive functions.

§382.205 On-duty use.

No driver shall use alcohol while performing safety-sensitive functions. No employer having actual knowledge that a driver is using alcohol while performing safety-sensitive functions shall permit the driver to perform or continue to perform safety-sensitive functions.

§382.207 Pre-duty use.

No driver shall perform safety-sensitive functions within four hours after using alcohol. No employer having actual knowledge that a driver has used alcohol within four hours shall permit a driver to perform or continue to perform safety-sensitive functions.

§382.209 Use following an accident.

No driver required to take a post-accident alcohol test under §382.303 of this part shall use alcohol for eight hours following the accident, or until he/she undergoes a post-accident alcohol test, whichever occurs first.

§382.211 Refusal to submit to a required alcohol or controlled substances test.

No driver shall refuse to submit to a post-accident alcohol or controlled substances test required under §382.303, a random alcohol or controlled substances test required under §382.305, a reasonable suspicion alcohol or controlled substances test required under §382.307, or a follow-up alcohol or controlled substances test required under §382.311. No employer shall permit a driver who refuses to submit to such tests to perform or continue to perform safety-sensitive functions.

§382.213 Controlled substances use.

(a) No driver shall report for duty or remain on duty requiring the performance of safety-sensitive functions when the driver uses any controlled substance, except when the use is pursuant to the instructions of a licensed medical practitioner, as defined in §382.107 of this part, who has advised the driver that the substance will not adversely affect the driver's ability to safely operate a commercial motor vehicle.

(b) No employer having actual knowledge that a driver has used a controlled substance shall permit the driver to perform or continue to perform a safety- sensitive function.

(c) An employer may require a driver to inform the employer of any therapeutic drug use.

§382.215 Controlled substances testing.

No driver shall report for duty, remain on duty or perform a safety-sensitive function, if the driver tests positive for controlled substances. No employer having actual knowledge that a driver has tested positive for controlled substances shall permit the driver to perform or continue to perform safety- sensitive functions.

SUBPART C—TESTS REQUIRED

§382.301 Pre-employment testing.

(a) Prior to the first time a driver performs safety-sensitive functions for an employer, the driver shall undergo testing for alcohol and controlled substances as a condition prior to being used, unless the employer uses the exception in paragraphs (c) and (d) of this section. No employer shall allow a driver, who the employer intends to hire or use, to perform safety-sensitive functions unless the driver has been administered an alcohol test with a result indicating an alcohol concentration less than 0.04, and has received a controlled substances test result from the MRO indicating a verified negative test result. If a pre-employment alcohol test result under this section indicates an alcohol content of 0.02 or greater but less than 0.04, the provision of §382.505 shall apply.

(b) Exception for pre-employment alcohol testing. An employer is not required to administer an alcohol test required by paragraph (a) of this section if:

(1) The driver has undergone an alcohol test required by this section or the alcohol misuse rule of another DOT agency under part 40 of

this title within the previous six months, with a result indicating an alcohol concentration less than 0.04; and

(2) The employer ensures that no prior employer of the driver of whom the employer has knowledge has records of a violation of this part or the alcohol misuse rule of another DOT agency within the previous six months.

(c) Exception for pre-employment controlled substances testing. An employer is not required to administer a controlled substances test required by paragraph (a) of this section if:

(1) The driver has participated in a controlled substances testing program that meets the requirements of this part within the previous 30 days; and

(2) While participating in that program, either

(i) Was tested for controlled substances within the past 6 months (from the date of application with the employer) or

(ii) Participated in the random controlled substances testing program for the previous 12 months (from the date of application with the employer); and

(3) The employer ensures that no prior employer of the driver of whom the employer has knowledge has records of a violation of this part or the controlled substances use rule of another DOT agency within the previous six months.

(d)(1) An employer who exercises the exception in either paragraph (b) or (c) of this section shall contact the alcohol and/or controlled substances testing program(s) in which the driver participates or participated and shall obtain and retain from the testing program(s) the following information:

(i) Name(s) and address(es) of the program(s).

(ii) Verification that the driver participates or participated in the program(s).

(iii) Verification that the program(s) conforms to part 40 of this title.

(iv) Verification that the driver is qualified under the rules of this part, including that the driver has not refused to be tested for controlled substances.

(v) The date the driver was last tested for alcohol or controlled substances.

(vi) The results of any tests taken within the previous six months and any other violations of subpart B of this part.

(2) An employer who uses, but does not employ, a driver more than once a year to

operate commercial motor vehicles must obtain the information in paragraph (d)(1) of this section at least once every six months. The records prepared under this paragraph shall be maintained in accordance with §382.401. If the employer cannot verify that the driver is participating in a controlled substances testing program in accordance with this part and part 40, the employer shall conduct a pre-employment alcohol and/or controlled substances test.

(e) Notwithstanding any other provisions of this subpart, all provisions and requirements in this section pertaining to pre-employment testing for alcohol are vacated as of May 1, 1995.

§382.303 Post-accident testing.

(a) As soon as practicable following an occurrence involving a commercial motor vehicle operating on a public road in commerce, each employer shall test for alcohol and controlled substances each surviving driver:

(1) Who was performing safety-sensitive functions with respect to the vehicle, if the accident involved the loss of human life; or

(2) Who receives a citation under State or local law for a moving traffic violation arising from the accident, if the accident involved:

(i) Bodily injury to any person who, as a result of the injury, immediately receives medical treatment away from the scene of the accident; or

(ii) One or more motor vehicles incurring disabling damage as a result of the accident, requiring the motor vehicle to be transported away from the scene by a tow truck or other motor vehicle.

(3) This table notes when a post-accident test is required to be conducted by paragraphs (a)(1) and (a)(2) of this section.

Table for §382.303(a)(3)

Type of accident involved	Citation issued to the CMV driver	Test must be performed by employer
Human fatality	YES NO	YES. YES.
Bodily injury with immediate medical treatment away from the scene	YES NO	YES. NO.
Disabling damage to any motor vehicle requiring tow away	YES NO	YES. NO.

(b)(1) Alcohol tests. If a test required by this section is not administered within two hours following the accident, the employer shall prepare and maintain on file a record stating the reasons the test was not promptly administered. If a test required by this section is not administered within eight hours following the accident, the employer shall cease attempts to administer an alcohol test and shall prepare and maintain the same record. Records shall be submitted to the FHWA upon request of the Associate Administrator.

(2) For the years stated in this paragraph, employers who submit MIS reports shall submit to the FHWA each record of a test required by this section that is not completed within eight hours. The employer's records of tests that are not completed within eight hours shall be submitted to the FHWA by March 15, 1996; March 15, 1997, and March 15, 1998, for calendar years 1995, 1996, and 1997, respectively. Employers shall append these records to their MIS submissions. Each record shall include the following information:

(i) Type of test (reasonable suspicion/post-accident);

(ii) Triggering event (including date, time, and location);

(iii) Reason(s) test could not be completed within eight hours;

(iv) If blood alcohol testing could have been completed within eight hours, the name, address, and telephone number of the testing site where blood testing could have occurred; and

(3) Records of alcohol tests that could not be completed in eight hours shall be submitted to the FHWA at the following address: Attn: Alcohol Testing Program, Office of Motor Carrier Research and Standards (HCS-1), Federal Highway Administration, 400 Seventh Street, SW., Washington, DC 20590.

(4) Controlled substance tests. If a test required by this section is not administered within 32 hours following the accident, the employer shall cease attempts to administer a controlled substances test, and prepare and maintain on file a record stating the reasons the test was not promptly administered. Records shall be submitted to the FHWA upon request of the Associate Administrator.

(c) A driver who is subject to post-accident testing shall remain readily available for such testing or may be deemed by the employer to have refused to submit to testing. Nothing in this section shall be construed to require the delay of necessary medical attention for injured people following an accident or to prohibit a driver from leaving the scene of an accident for the period necessary to obtain assistance in responding to the accident, or to obtain necessary emergency medical care.

(d) An employer shall provide drivers with necessary post-accident information, procedures and instructions, prior to the driver operating a commercial motor vehicle, so that drivers will be able to comply with the requirements of this section.

(e)(1) The results of a breath or blood test for the use of alcohol, conducted by Federal, State, or local officials having independent authority for the test, shall be considered to meet the requirements of this section, provided such tests conform to the applicable Federal, State or local alcohol testing requirements, and that the results of the tests are obtained by the employer.

(2) The results of a urine test for the use of controlled substances, conducted by Federal, State, or local officials having independent authority for the test, shall be considered to meet the requirements of this section, provided such tests conform to the applicable Federal, State or local controlled substances testing requirements, and that the results of the tests are obtained by the employer.

(f) Exception. This section does not apply to:

(1) An occurrence involving only boarding or alighting from a stationary motor vehicle; or

(2) An occurrence involving only the loading or unloading of cargo; or

(3) An occurrence in the course of the operation of a passenger car or a multipurpose passenger vehicle (as defined in §571.3 of this title) by an employer unless the motor vehicle is transporting passengers for hire or hazardous materials of a type and quantity that require the motor vehicle to be marked or placarded in accordance with §177.823 of this title.

§382.305 Random testing.

(a) Every employer shall comply with the requirements of this section. Every driver shall submit to random alcohol and controlled substance testing as required in this section.

(b)(1) Except as provided in paragraphs (c) through (e) of this section, the minimum annual percentage rate for random alcohol testing shall be 25 percent of the average number of driver positions.

(2) Except as provided in paragraphs (f) through (h) of this section, the minimum annual percentage rate for random controlled substances testing shall be 50 percent of the average number of driver positions.

(c) The FHWA Administrator's decision to increase or decrease the minimum annual percentage rate for alcohol testing is based on the reported violation rate for the entire industry. All information used for this determination is drawn from the alcohol management information system reports required by §382.403 of this part. In order to ensure reliability of the data, the FHWA Administrator considers the quality and completeness of the reported data, may obtain additional information or reports from employers, and may make appropriate modifications in calculating the industry violation rate. Each year, the FHWA Administrator will publish in the Federal Register the minimum annual percentage rate for random alcohol testing of drivers. The new minimum annual percentage rate for random alcohol testing will be applicable starting January 1 of the calendar year following publication.

(d)(1) When the minimum annual percentage rate for random alcohol testing is 25 percent or more, the FHWA Administrator may lower this rate to 10 percent of all driver positions if the FHWA Administrator determines that the data received under the reporting requirements of §382.403 for two consecutive calendar years indicate that the violation rate is less than 0.5 percent.

(2) When the minimum annual percentage rate for random alcohol testing is 50 percent, the FHWA Administrator may lower this rate to 25 percent of all driver positions if the FHWA Administrator determines that the data received under the reporting requirements of §382.403 for two consecutive calendar years indicate that the violation rate is less than 1.0 percent but equal to or greater than 0.5 percent.

(e)(1) When the minimum annual percentage rate for random alcohol testing is 10 percent, and the data received under the reporting requirements of §382.403 for that calendar year indicate that the violation rate is equal to or greater than 0.5 percent, but less than 1.0 percent, the FHWA Administrator will increase the minimum annual percentage rate for random alcohol testing to 25 percent for all driver positions.

(2) When the minimum annual percentage rate for random alcohol testing is 25 percent or less, and the data received under the report-

ing requirements of §382.403 for that calendar year indicate that the violation rate is equal to or greater than 1.0 percent, the FHWA Administrator will increase the minimum annual percentage rate for random alcohol testing to 50 percent for all driver positions.

(f) The FHWA Administrator's decision to increase or decrease the minimum annual percentage rate for controlled substances testing is based on the reported positive rate for the entire industry. All information used for this determination is drawn from the controlled substances management information system reports required by §382.403 of this part. In order to ensure reliability of the data, the FHWA Administrator considers the quality and completeness of the reported data, may obtain additional information or reports from employers, and may make appropriate modifications in calculating the industry positive rate. Each year, the FHWA Administrator will publish in the Federal Register the minimum annual percentage rate for random controlled substances testing of drivers. The new minimum annual percentage rate for random controlled substances testing will be applicable starting January 1 of the calendar year following publication.

(g) When the minimum annual percentage rate for random controlled substances testing is 50 percent, the FHWA Administrator may lower this rate to 25 percent of all driver positions if the FHWA Administrator determines that the data received under the reporting requirements of §382.403 for two consecutive calendar years indicate that the positive rate is less than 1.0 percent. However, after the initial two years of random testing by large employers and the initial first year of testing by small employers under this section, the FHWA Administrator may lower the rate the following calendar year, if the combined positive testing rate is less than 1.0 percent, and if it would be in the interest of safety.

(h) When the minimum annual percentage rate for random controlled substances testing is 25 percent, and the data received under the reporting requirements of §382.403 for any calendar year indicate that the reported positive rate is equal to or greater than 1.0 percent, the FHWA Administrator will increase the minimum annual percentage rate for random controlled substances testing to 50 percent of all driver positions.

(i) The selection of drivers for random alcohol and controlled substances testing shall be made by a scientifically valid method, such as a random number table or a computer-based random number generator that is matched with drivers' Social Security numbers, payroll identification numbers, or other comparable identifying numbers. Under the selection process used, each driver shall have an equal chance of being tested each time selections are made.

(j) The employer shall randomly select a sufficient number of drivers for testing during each calendar year to equal an annual rate not less than the minimum annual percentage rate for random alcohol and controlled substances testing determined by the FHWA Administrator. If the employer conducts random testing for alcohol and/or controlled substances through a consortium, the number of drivers to be tested may be calculated for each individual employer or may be based on the total number of drivers covered by the consortium who are subject to random alcohol and/or controlled substances testing at the same minimum annual percentage rate under this part or any DOT alcohol or controlled substances random testing rule.

(k) Each employer shall ensure that random alcohol and controlled substances tests conducted under this part are unannounced and that the dates for administering random alcohol and controlled substances tests are spread reasonably throughout the calendar year.

(l) Each employer shall require that each driver who is notified of selection for random alcohol and/or controlled substances testing proceeds to the test site immediately; provided, however, that if the driver is performing a safety-sensitive function, other than driving a commercial motor vehicle, at the time of notification, the employer shall instead ensure that the driver ceases to perform the safety-sensitive function and proceeds to the testing site as soon as possible.

(m) A driver shall only be tested for alcohol while the driver is performing safety-sensitive functions, just before the driver is to perform safety- sensitive functions, or just after the driver has ceased performing such functions.

(n) If a given driver is subject to random alcohol or controlled substances testing under the random alcohol or controlled substances testing rules of more than one DOT agency for the same employer, the driver shall be subject to random alcohol and/or controlled substances testing at the annual percentage rate established for the calendar year by the DOT agency regulating more than 50 percent of the driver's function.

(o) If an employer is required to conduct random alcohol or controlled substances testing under the alcohol or controlled substances testing rules of more than one DOT agency, the employer may—

(1) Establish separate pools for random selection, with each pool containing the DOT-covered employees who are subject to testing at the same required minimum annual percentage rate; or

(2) Randomly select such employees for testing at the highest minimum annual percentage rate established for the calendar year by any DOT agency to which the employer is subject.

§382.307 Reasonable suspicion testing.

(a) An employer shall require a driver to submit to an alcohol test when the employer has reasonable suspicion to believe that the driver has violated the prohibitions of subpart B of this part concerning alcohol. The employer's determination that reasonable suspicion exists to require the driver to undergo an alcohol test must be based on specific, contemporaneous, articulable observations concerning the appearance, behavior, speech or body odors of the driver.

(b) An employer shall require a driver to submit to a controlled substances test when the employer has reasonable suspicion to believe that the driver has violated the prohibitions of subpart B of this part concerning controlled substances. The employer's determination that reasonable suspicion exists to require the driver to undergo a controlled substances test must be based on specific, contemporaneous, articulable observations concerning the appearance, behavior, speech or body odors of the driver. The observations may include indications of the chronic and withdrawal effects of controlled substances.

(c) The required observations for alcohol and/or controlled substances reasonable suspicion testing shall be made by a supervisor or company official who is trained in accordance with §382.603 of this part. The person who makes the determination that reasonable suspicion exists to conduct an alcohol test shall not conduct the alcohol test of the driver.

(d) Alcohol testing is authorized by this section only if the observations required by paragraph (a) of this section are made during, just preceding, or just after the period of the work day that the driver is required to be in compliance with this part. A driver may be directed by the employer to only undergo reasonable suspicion testing while the driver is performing safety- sensitive functions, just before the driver is to perform safety-sensitive functions, or just after the driver has ceased performing such functions.

(e)(1) If an alcohol test required by this section is not administered within two hours following the determination under paragraph (a) of this section, the employer shall prepare and maintain on file a record stating the reasons the alcohol test was not promptly administered. If an alcohol test required by this section is not administered within eight hours following the determination under paragraph (a) of this section, the employer shall cease attempts to administer an alcohol test and shall state in the record the reasons for not administering the test.

(2) For the years stated in this paragraph, employers who submit MIS reports shall submit to the FHWA each record of a test required by this section that is not completed within 8 hours. The employer's records of tests that could not be completed within 8 hours shall be submitted to the FHWA by March 15, 1996; March 15, 1997; and March 15, 1998; for calendar years 1995, 1996, and 1997, respectively. Employers shall append these records to their MIS submissions. Each record shall include the following information:

(i) Type of test (reasonable suspicion/post-accident);

(ii) Triggering event (including date, time, and location);

(iii) Reason(s) test could not be completed within 8 hours; and

(iv) If blood alcohol testing could have been completed within eight hours, the name, address, and telephone number of the testing site where blood testing could have occurred.

(3) Records of tests that could not be completed in eight hours shall be submitted to the FHWA at the following address: Attn.: Alcohol Testing program, Office of Motor Carrier Research and Standards (HCS-1), Federal Highway Administration, 400 Seventh Street, SW., Washington, DC 20590.

(4) Notwithstanding the absence of a reasonable suspicion alcohol test under this section, no driver shall report for duty or remain on duty requiring the performance of safety-sensitive functions while the driver is under the influence of or impaired by alcohol, as shown by the behavioral, speech, and performance indicators of alcohol misuse, nor shall an employer permit the driver to perform or

continue to perform safety-sensitive functions, until:

(i) An alcohol test is administered and the driver's alcohol concentration measures less than 0.02; or

(ii) Twenty four hours have elapsed following the determination under paragraph (a) of this section that there is reasonable suspicion to believe that the driver has violated the prohibitions in this part concerning the use of alcohol.

(5) Except as provided in paragraph (e)(2) of this section, no employer shall take any action under this part against a driver based solely on the driver's behavior and appearance, with respect to alcohol use, in the absence of an alcohol test. This does not prohibit an employer with independent authority of this part from taking any action otherwise consistent with law.

(f) A written record shall be made of the observations leading to a controlled substance reasonable suspicion test, and signed by the supervisor or company official who made the observations, within 24 hours of the observed behavior or before the results of the controlled substances test are released, whichever is earlier.

§382.309 Return-to-duty testing.

(a) Each employer shall ensure that before a driver returns to duty requiring the performance of a safety-sensitive function after engaging in conduct prohibited by subpart B of this part concerning alcohol, the driver shall undergo a return-to-duty alcohol test with a result indicating an alcohol concentration of less than 0.02.

(b) Each employer shall ensure that before a driver returns to duty requiring the performance of a safety-sensitive function after engaging in conduct prohibited by subpart B of this part concerning controlled substances, the driver shall undergo a return-to-duty controlled substances test with a result indicating a verified negative result for controlled substances use.

§382.311 Follow-up testing.

(a) Following a determination under §382.605(b) that a driver is in need of assistance in resolving problems associated with alcohol misuse and/or use of controlled substances, each employer shall ensure that the driver is subject to unannounced follow-up alcohol and/or controlled substances testing as directed by a substance abuse professional

in accordance with the provisions of §382.605(c)(2)(ii).

(b) Follow-up alcohol testing shall be conducted only when the driver is performing safety-sensitive functions, just before the driver is to perform safety-sensitive functions, or just after the driver has ceased performing safety-sensitive functions.

SUBPART D—HANDLING OF TEST RESULTS, RECORD RETENTION, AND CONFIDENTIALITY

§382.401 Retention of records.

(a) General requirement. Each employer shall maintain records of its alcohol misuse and controlled substances use prevention programs as provided in this section. The records shall be maintained in a secure location with controlled access.

(b) Period of retention. Each employer shall maintain the records in accordance with the following schedule:

(1) Five years. The following records shall be maintained for a minimum of five years:

(i) Records of driver alcohol test results indicating an alcohol concentration of 0.02 or greater,

(ii) Records of driver verified positive controlled substances test results,

(iii) Documentation of refusals to take required alcohol and/or controlled substances tests,

(iv) Driver evaluation and referrals,

(v) Calibration documentation,

(vi) Records related to the administration of the alcohol and controlled substances testing programs, and

(vii) A copy of each annual calendar year summary required by §382.403.

(2) Two years. Records related to the alcohol and controlled substances collection process (except calibration of evidential breath testing devices).

(3) One year. Records of negative and canceled controlled substances test results (as defined in part 40 of this title) and alcohol test results with a concentration of less than 0.02 shall be maintained for a minimum of one year.

(4) Indefinite period. Records related to the education and training of breath alcohol technicians, screening test technicians, supervisors,

THE MEDICAL REVIEW OFFICER'S MANUAL

and drivers shall be maintained by the employer while the individual performs the functions which require the training and for two years after ceasing to perform those functions.

(c) Types of records. The following specific types of records shall be maintained. "Documents generated" are documents that may have to be prepared under a requirement of this part. If the record is required to be prepared, it must be maintained.

(1) Records related to the collection process:

(i) Collection logbooks, if used;

(ii) Documents relating to the random selection process;

(iii) Calibration documentation for evidential breath testing devices;

(iv) Documentation of breath alcohol technician training;

(v) Documents generated in connection with decisions to administer reasonable suspicion alcohol or controlled substances tests;

(vi) Documents generated in connection with decisions on post-accident tests;

(vii) Documents verifying existence of a medical explanation of the inability of a driver to provide adequate breath or to provide a urine specimen for testing; and

(viii) Consolidated annual calendar year summaries as required by §382.403.

(2) Records related to a driver's test results:

(i) The employer's copy of the alcohol test form, including the results of the test;

(ii) The employer's copy of the controlled substances test chain of custody and control form;

(iii) Documents sent by the MRO to the employer, including those required by §382.407(a).

(iv) Documents related to the refusal of any driver to submit to an alcohol or controlled substances test required by this part; and

(v) Documents presented by a driver to dispute the result of an alcohol or controlled substances test administered under this part.

(vi) Documents generated in connection with verifications of prior employers' alcohol or controlled substances test results that the employer:

(A) Must obtain in connection with the exception contained in §382.301 of this part, and

(B) Must obtain as required by §382.413 of this subpart.

(3) Records related to other violations of this part.

(4) Records related to evaluations:

(i) Records pertaining to a determination by a substance abuse professional concerning a driver's need for assistance; and

(ii) Records concerning a driver's compliance with recommendations of the substance abuse professional.

(5) Records related to education and training:

(i) Materials on alcohol misuse and controlled substance use awareness, including a copy of the employer's policy on alcohol misuse and controlled substance use;

(ii) Documentation of compliance with the requirements of §382.601, including the driver's signed receipt of education materials;

(iii) Documentation of training provided to supervisors for the purpose of qualifying the supervisors to make a determination concerning the need for alcohol and/or controlled substances testing based on reasonable suspicion;

(iv) Documentation of training for breath alcohol technicians as required by §40.51(a) of this title, and

(v) Certification that any training conducted under this part complies with the requirements for such training.

(6) Administrative records related to alcohol and controlled substances testing:

(i) Agreements with collection site facilities, laboratories, breath alcohol technicians, screening test technicians, medical review officers, consortia, and third party service providers;

(ii) Names and positions of officials and their role in the employer's alcohol and controlled substances testing program(s);

(iii) Quarterly laboratory statistical summaries of urinalysis required by §40.29(g)(6) of this title; and

(iv) The employer's alcohol and controlled substances testing policy and procedures.

(d) Location of records. All records required by this part shall be maintained as required by §390.31 of this subchapter and shall be made available for inspection at the employer's principal place of business within two business days after a request has been made by an authorized representative of the Federal Highway Administration.

(e)(1) OMB control number. The information collection requirements of this part have been reviewed by the Office of Management and Budget pursuant to the Paperwork Reduction Act of 1995 (44 U.S.C. 3501 et seq.) and have been assigned OMB control number 2125-0543.

(2) The information collection requirements of this part are found in the following sections: Section 382.105, 382.113, 382.301, 382.303, 382.305, 382.307, 382.309, 382.311, 382.401, 382.403, 382.405, 382.407, 382.409, 382.411, 382.413, 382.601, 382.603, 382.605.

§382.403 Reporting of results in a management information system.

(a) An employer shall prepare and maintain a summary of the results of its alcohol and controlled substances testing programs performed under this part during the previous calendar year, when requested by the Secretary of Transportation, any DOT agency, or any State or local officials with regulatory authority over the employer or any of its drivers.

(b) If an employer is notified, during the month of January, of a request by the Federal Highway Administration to report the employer's annual calendar year summary information, the employer shall prepare and submit the report to the Federal Highway Administration by March 15 of that year. The employer shall ensure that the annual summary report is accurate and received by March 15 at the location that the Federal Highway Administration specifies in its request. The report shall be in the form and manner prescribed by the Federal Highway Administration in its request. When the report is submitted to the Federal Highway Administration by mail or electronic transmission, the information requested shall be typed, except for the signature of the certifying official. Each employer shall ensure the accuracy and timeliness of each report submitted by the employer or a consortium.

(c) Detailed summary. Each annual calendar year summary that contains information on a verified positive controlled substances test result, an alcohol screening test result of 0.02 or greater, or any other violation of the alcohol misuse provisions of subpart B of this part shall include the following informational elements:

(1) Number of drivers subject to Part 382;

(2) Number of drivers subject to testing under the alcohol misuse or controlled substances use rules of more than one DOT agency, identified by each agency;

(3) Number of urine specimens collected by type of test (e.g., pre-employment, random, reasonable suspicion, post-accident);

(4) Number of positives verified by a MRO by type of test, and type of controlled substance;

(5) Number of negative controlled substance tests verified by a MRO by type of test;

(6) Number of persons denied a position as a driver following a pre-employment verified positive controlled substances test and/or a pre-employment alcohol test that indicates an alcohol concentration of 0.04 or greater;

(7) Number of drivers with tests verified positive by a medical review officer for multiple controlled substances;

(8) Number of drivers who refused to submit to an alcohol or controlled substances test required under this subpart;

(9)(i) Number of supervisors who have received required alcohol training during the reporting period; and

(ii) Number of supervisors who have received required controlled substances training during the reporting period;

(10)(i) Number of screening alcohol tests by type of test; and

(ii) Number of confirmation alcohol tests, by type of test;

(11) Number of confirmation alcohol tests indicating an alcohol concentration of 0.02 or greater but less than 0.04, by type of test;

(12) Number of confirmation alcohol tests indicating an alcohol concentration of 0.04 or greater, by type of test;

(13) Number of drivers who were returned to duty (having complied with the recommendations of a substance abuse professional as described in ¤§382.503 and 382.605), in this reporting period, who previously:

(i) Had a verified positive controlled substance test result, or

(ii) Engaged in prohibited alcohol misuse under the provisions of this part;

(14) Number of drivers who were administered alcohol and drug tests at the same time, with both a verified positive drug test result and an alcohol test result indicating an alcohol concentration of 0.04 or greater; and

(15) Number of drivers who were found to have violated any non-testing prohibitions of subpart B of this part, and any action taken in response to the violation.

(d) Short summary. Each employer's annual calendar year summary that contains only negative controlled substance test results, alcohol screening test results of less than 0.02, and does not contain any other violations of subpart B of this part, may prepare and submit, as required by paragraph (b) of this section, either a standard report form containing all the information elements specified in paragraph (c) of this section, or an "EZ" report form. The "EZ" report shall include the following information elements:

(1) Number of drivers subject to this Part 382;

(2) Number of drivers subject to testing under the alcohol misuse or controlled substance use rules of more than one DOT agency, identified by each agency;

(3) Number of urine specimens collected by type of test (e.g., pre-employment, random, reasonable suspicion, post-accident);

(4) Number of negatives verified by a medical review officer by type of test;

(5) Number of drivers who refused to submit to an alcohol or controlled substances test required under this subpart;

(6)(i) Number of supervisors who have received required alcohol training during the reporting period; and

(ii) Number of supervisors who have received required controlled substances training during the reporting period;

(7) Number of screen alcohol tests by type of test; and

(8) Number of drivers who were returned to duty (having complied with the recommendations of a substance abuse professional as described in ¤§382.503 and 382.605), in this reporting period, who previously:

(i) Had a verified positive controlled substance test result, or

(ii) Engaged in prohibited alcohol misuse under the provisions of this part.

(e) Each employer that is subject to more than one DOT agency alcohol or controlled substances rule shall identify each driver covered by the regulations of more than one DOT agency. The identification will be by the total number of covered functions. Prior to conducting any alcohol or controlled substances test on a driver subject to the rules of more than one DOT agency, the employer shall determine which DOT agency rule or rules authorizes or requires the test. The test result information shall be directed to the appropriate DOT agency or agencies.

(f) A consortium may prepare annual calendar year summaries and reports on behalf of individual employers for purposes of compliance with this section. However, each employer shall sign and submit such a report and shall remain responsible for ensuring the accuracy and timeliness of each report prepared on its behalf by a consortium.

§382.405 Access to facilities and records.

(a) Except as required by law or expressly authorized or required in this section, no employer shall release driver information that is contained in records required to be maintained under §382.401.

(b) A driver is entitled, upon written request, to obtain copies of any records pertaining to the driver's use of alcohol or controlled substances, including any records pertaining to his or her alcohol or controlled substances tests. The employer shall promptly provide the records requested by the driver. Access to a driver's records shall not be contingent upon payment for records other than those specifically requested.

(c) Each employer shall permit access to all facilities utilized in complying with the requirements of this part to the Secretary of Transportation, any DOT agency, or any State or local officials with regulatory authority over the employer or any of its drivers.

(d) Each employer shall make available copies of all results for employer alcohol and/or controlled substances testing conducted under this part and any other information pertaining to the employer's alcohol misuse and/or controlled substances use prevention program, when requested by the Secretary of Transportation, any DOT agency, or any State or local officials with regulatory authority over the employer or any of its drivers.

(e) When requested by the National Transportation Safety Board as part of an accident investigation, employers shall disclose information related to the employer's administration of a post-accident alcohol and/or controlled substance test administered following the accident under investigation.

(f) Records shall be made available to a subsequent employer upon receipt of a written request from a driver. Disclosure by the subsequent employer is permitted only as expressly authorized by the terms of the driver's request.

(g) An employer may disclose information required to be maintained under this part pertaining to a driver, the decisionmaker in a lawsuit, grievance, or other proceeding initiated by or on behalf of the individual, and arising from the results of an alcohol and/or controlled substance test administered under this part, or from the employer's determination that the driver engaged in conduct prohibited by subpart B of this part (including, but not limited to, a worker's compensation, unemployment compensation, or other proceeding relating to a benefit sought by the driver.)

(h) An employer shall release information regarding a driver's records as directed by the specific, written consent of the driver authorizing release of the information to an identified person. Release of such information by the person receiving the information is permitted only in accordance with the terms of the employee's consent.

§382.407 Medical review officer notifications to the employer.

(a) The medical review officer may report to the employer using any communications device, but in all instances a signed, written notification must be forwarded within three business days of completion of the medical review officer's review, pursuant to part 40 of this title. A legible photocopy of the fourth copy of Part 40 Appendix A subtitled COPY 4—SEND DIRECTLY TO MEDICAL REVIEW OFFICER—DO NOT SEND TO LABORATORY of the Federal Custody and Control Form OMB Number 9999-0023 may be used to make the signed, written notification to the employer for all test results (positive, negative, canceled, etc.), provided that the controlled substance(s) verified as positive, and the MRO's signature, shall be legibly noted in the remarks section of step 8 of the form completed by the medical review officer. The MRO must sign all verified positive test results. An MRO may sign or rubber stamp negative test results. An MRO's staff may rubber stamp negative test results under written authorization of the MRO. In no event shall an MRO, or his/her staff, use electronic signature technology to comply with this section. All reports, both oral and in writing, from the medical review officer to an employer shall clearly include:

(1) A statement that the controlled substances test being reported was in accordance with part 40 of this title and this part, except for legible photocopies of Copy 4 of the Federal Custody and Control Form;

(2) The full name of the driver for whom the test results are being reported;

(3) The type of test indicated on the custody and control form (i.e. random, post-accident, follow-up);

(4) The date and location of the test collection;

(5) The identities of the persons or entities performing the collection, analyzing the specimens, and serving as the medical review officer for the specific test;

(6) The results of the controlled substances test, positive, negative, test canceled, or test not performed, and if positive, the identity of the controlled substance(s) for which the test was verified positive.

(b) A medical review officer shall report to the employer that the medical review officer has made all reasonable efforts to contact the driver as provided in §40.33(c) of this title. The employer shall, as soon as practicable, request that the driver contact the medical review officer prior to dispatching the driver or within 24 hours, whichever is earlier.

§382.409 Medical review officer record retention for controlled substances.

(a) A medical review officer shall maintain all dated records and notifications, identified by individual, for a minimum of five years for verified positive controlled substances test results.

(b) A medical review officer shall maintain all dated records and notifications, identified by individual, for a minimum of one year for negative and canceled controlled substances test results.

(c) No person may obtain the individual controlled substances test results retained by a medical review officer, and no medical review officer shall release the individual controlled substances test results of any driver to any person, without first obtaining a specific, written authorization from the tested driver. Nothing in this paragraph shall prohibit a medical review officer from releasing, to the employer or to officials of the Secretary of Transportation, any DOT agency, or any State or local officials with regulatory authority over the controlled substances testing program under this part, the information delineated in §382.407(a) of this subpart.

§382.411 Employer notifications.

(a) An employer shall notify a driver of the results of a pre-employment controlled substance test conducted under this part, if the driver requests such results within 60 calendar days of being notified of the disposition of the employment application. An employer shall notify a driver of the results of random, reasonable suspicion and post-accident tests for controlled substances conducted under this part if the test results are verified positive. The employer shall also inform the driver which controlled substance or substances were verified as positive.

(b) The designated management official shall make reasonable efforts to contact and request each driver who submitted a specimen under the employer's program, regardless of the driver's employment status, to contact and discuss the results of the controlled substances test with a medical review officer who has been unable to contact the driver.

(c) The designated management official shall immediately notify the medical review officer that the driver has been notified to contact the medical review officer within 24 hours.

§382.413 Inquiries for alcohol and controlled substances information from previous employers.

(a)(1) An employer shall, pursuant to the driver's written authorization, inquire about the following information on a driver from the driver's previous employers, during the preceding two years from the date of application, which are maintained by the driver's previous employers under §382.401(b)(1)(i) through (iii) of this subpart:

(i) Alcohol tests with a result of 0.04 alcohol concentration or greater;

(ii) Verified positive controlled substances test results; and

(iii) Refusals to be tested.

(2) The information obtained from a previous employer may contain any alcohol and drug information the previous employer obtained from other previous employers under paragraph (a)(1) of this section.

(b) If feasible, the information in paragraph (a) of this section must be obtained and reviewed by the employer prior to the first time a driver performs safety-sensitive functions for the employer. If not feasible, the information must be obtained and reviewed as soon as possible, but no later than 14- calendar days after the first time a driver performs safety-sensitive functions for the employer. An employer may not permit a driver to perform safety- sensitive functions after 14 days without having made a good faith effort to obtain the information as soon as possible. If a driver hired or used by the employer ceases performing safety-sensitive functions for the employer before expiration of the 14-day period or before the employer has obtained the information in paragraph (a) of this section, the employer must still make a good faith effort to obtain the information.

(c) An employer must maintain a written, confidential record of the information obtained under paragraph (a) or (f) of this section. If, after making a good faith effort, an employer is unable to obtain the information from a previous employer, a record must be made of the efforts to obtain the information and retained in the driver's qualification file.

(d) The prospective employer must provide to each of the driver's previous employers the driver's specific, written authorization for release of the information in paragraph (a) of this section.

(e) The release of any information under this section may take the form of personal interviews, telephone interviews, letters, or any other method of transmitting information that ensures confidentiality.

(f) The information in paragraph (a) of this section may be provided directly to the prospective employer by the driver, provided the employer assures itself that the information is true and accurate.

(g) An employer may not use a driver to perform safety-sensitive functions if the employer obtains information on a violation of the prohibitions in subpart B of this part by the driver, without obtaining information on subsequent compliance with the referral and rehabilitation requirements of §382.605 of this part.

(h) Employers need not obtain information under paragraph (a) of this section generated by previous employers prior to the starting dates in §382.115 of this part.

SUBPART E—CONSEQUENCES FOR DRIVERS ENGAGING IN SUBSTANCE USE-RELATED CONDUCT

§382.501 Removal from safety-sensitive function.

(a) Except as provided in subpart F of this part, no driver shall perform safety-sensitive functions, including driving a commercial motor vehicle, if the driver has engaged in conduct prohibited by subpart B of this part or an alcohol or controlled substances rule of another DOT agency.

(b) No employer shall permit any driver to perform safety-sensitive functions, including driving a commercial motor vehicle, if the employer has determined that the driver has violated this section.

(c) For purposes of this subpart, commercial motor vehicle means a commercial motor vehicle in commerce as defined in §382.107, and a commercial motor vehicle in interstate commerce as defined in Part 390 of this subchapter.

§382.503 Required evaluation and testing.

No driver who has engaged in conduct prohibited by subpart B of this part shall perform safety-sensitive functions, including driving a commercial motor vehicle, unless the driver has met the requirements of §382.605. No employer shall permit a driver who has engaged in conduct prohibited by subpart B of this part to perform safety-sensitive functions, including driving a commercial motor vehicle, unless the driver has met the requirements of §382.605.

§382.505 Other alcohol-related conduct.

(a) No driver tested under the provisions of subpart C of this part who is found to have an alcohol concentration of 0.02 or greater but less than 0.04 shall perform or continue to perform safety-sensitive functions for an employer, including driving a commercial motor vehicle, nor shall an employer permit the driver to perform or continue to perform safety-sensitive functions, until the start of the driver's next regularly scheduled duty period, but not less than 24 hours following administration of the test.

(b) Except as provided in paragraph (a) of this section, no employer shall take any action under this part against a driver based solely on test results showing an alcohol concentration less than 0.04. This does not prohibit an employer with authority independent of this part from taking any action otherwise consistent with law.

§382.507 Penalties.

Any employer or driver who violates the requirements of this part shall be subject to the penalty provisions of 49 U.S.C. section 521(b).

SUBPART F—ALCOHOL MISUSE AND CONTROLLED SUBSTANCES USE INFORMATION, TRAINING, AND REFERRAL

§382.601 Employer obligation to promulgate a policy on the misuse of alcohol and use of controlled substances.

(a) General requirements. Each employer shall provide educational materials that explain the requirements of this part and the employer's policies and procedures with respect to meeting these requirements.

(1) The employer shall ensure that a copy of these materials is distributed to each driver prior to the start of alcohol and controlled substances testing under this part and to each driver subsequently hired or transferred into a position requiring driving a commercial motor vehicle.

(2) Each employer shall provide written notice to representatives of employee organizations of the availability of this information.

(b) Required content. The materials to be made available to drivers shall include detailed discussion of at least the following:

(1) The identity of the person designated by the employer to answer driver questions about the materials;

(2) The categories of drivers who are subject to the provisions of this part;

(3) Sufficient information about the safety-sensitive functions performed by those drivers to make clear what period of the work day the driver is required to be in compliance with this part;

(4) Specific information concerning driver conduct that is prohibited by this part;

(5) The circumstances under which a driver will be tested for alcohol and/or controlled substances under this part, including post-accident testing under §382.303(d);

(6) The procedures that will be used to test for the presence of alcohol and controlled substances, protect the driver and the integrity of the testing processes, safeguard the validity of the test results, and ensure that those results are attributed to the correct driver, including post-accident information, procedures and instructions required by §382.303(d) of this part;

(7) The requirement that a driver submit to alcohol and controlled substances tests administered in accordance with this part;

(8) An explanation of what constitutes a refusal to submit to an alcohol or controlled substances test and the attendant consequences;

(9) The consequences for drivers found to have violated subpart B of this part, including the requirement that the driver be removed immediately from safety-sensitive functions, and the procedures under §382.605;

(10) The consequences for drivers found to have an alcohol concentration of 0.02 or greater but less than 0.04;

(11) Information concerning the effects of alcohol and controlled substances use on an individual's health, work, and personal life; signs and symptoms of an alcohol or a controlled substances problem (the driver's or a coworker's); and available methods of intervening when an alcohol or a controlled substances problem is suspected, including confrontation, referral to any employee assistance program and or referral to management.

(c) Optional provision. The materials supplied to drivers may also include information on additional employer policies with respect to the use of alcohol or controlled substances, including any consequences for a driver found to have a specified alcohol or controlled substances level, that are based on the employer's authority independent of this part. Any such additional policies or consequences must be clearly and obviously described as being based on independent authority.

(d) Certificate of receipt. Each employer shall ensure that each driver is required to sign a statement certifying that he or she has received a copy of these materials described in this section. Each employer shall maintain the original of the signed certificate and may provide a copy of the certificate to the driver.

§382.603 Training for supervisors.

Each employer shall ensure that all persons designated to supervise drivers receive at least 60 minutes of training on alcohol misuse and receive at least an additional 60 minutes of training on controlled substances use. The training will be used by the supervisors to determine whether reasonable suspicion exists to require a driver to undergo testing under §382.307. The training shall include the physical, behavioral, speech, and performance indicators of probable alcohol misuse and use of controlled substances.

§382.605 Referral, evaluation, and treatment.

(a) Each driver who has engaged in conduct prohibited by subpart B of this part shall be advised by the employer of the resources available to the driver in evaluating and resolving problems associated with the misuse of alcohol and use of controlled substances, including the names, addresses, and telephone numbers of substance abuse professionals and counseling and treatment programs.

(b) Each driver who engages in conduct prohibited by subpart B of this part shall be evaluated by a substance abuse professional who shall determine what assistance, if any, the employee needs in resolving problems associated with alcohol misuse and controlled substances use.

(c)(1) Before a driver returns to duty requiring the performance of a safety-sensitive function after engaging in conduct prohibited by subpart B of this part, the driver shall undergo a return-to-duty alcohol test with a result indicating an alcohol concentration of less than 0.02 if the conduct involved alcohol, or a controlled substances test with a verified negative result if the conduct involved a controlled substance.

(2) In addition, each driver identified as needing assistance in resolving problems associated with alcohol misuse or controlled substances use,

(i) Shall be evaluated by a substance abuse professional to determine that the driver has properly followed any rehabilitation program prescribed under paragraph (b) of this section, and

(ii) Shall be subject to unannounced follow-up alcohol and controlled substances tests administered by the employer following the driver's return to duty. The number and frequency of such follow-up testing shall be as directed by the substance abuse professional, and consist of at least six tests in the first 12 months following the driver's return to duty. The employer may direct the driver to undergo return-to-duty and follow-up testing for both alcohol and controlled substances, if the substance abuse professional determines that return-to-duty and follow-up testing for both alcohol and controlled substances is necessary for that particular driver. Any such testing shall be performed in accordance with the requirements of 49 CFR part 40. Follow-up testing shall not exceed 60 months from the date of the driver's return to duty. The substance abuse professional may terminate the requirement for follow-up testing at any time after the first six tests have been administered, if the substance abuse professional determines that such testing is no longer necessary.

(d) Evaluation and rehabilitation may be provided by the employer, by a substance abuse professional under contract with the employer, or by a substance abuse professional not affiliated with the employer. The choice of substance abuse professional and assignment of costs shall be made in accordance with employer/driver agreements and employer policies.

(e) The employer shall ensure that a substance abuse professional who determines that a driver requires assistance in resolving problems with alcohol misuse or controlled substances use does not refer the driver to the substance abuse professional's private practice or to a person or organization from which the substance abuse professional receives remuneration or in which the substance abuse professional has a financial interest. This paragraph does not prohibit a substance abuse professional from referring a driver for assistance provided through—

(1) A public agency, such as a State, county, or municipality;

(2) The employer or a person under contract to provide treatment for alcohol or controlled substance problems on behalf of the employer;

(3) The sole source of therapeutically appropriate treatment under the driver's health insurance program; or

(4) The sole source of therapeutically appropriate treatment reasonably accessible to the driver.

(f) The requirements of this section with respect to referral, evaluation and rehabilitation do not apply to applicants who refuse to submit to a pre- employment alcohol or controlled substances test or who have a pre-employment alcohol test with a result indicating an alcohol concentration of 0.04 or greater or a controlled substances test with a verified positive test result.

Index ■

Hair tests, 113, 114t–115t, 116
Health Inca Tea, 69
Hemp products, food use of, 69
Heroin, 82
  effects of, 74t
  illicit uses of, 74t, 83
  See also Opiates

Immunoassays, 33
  types of, 33t
Impairment, defined, 67
Isomer testing, 34

Klear, See Nitrites

Laboratories, 5–6
  accuracy level of, 29
  certification of, 20–30
  reports of, 40–41
  specimen storage, 41
  types of tests performed by, 31–34
Limit of detection, 96
Litigation package, 41

Marijuana
  cutoff concentration for, 31t
  effects of, 74t
  food use of, 69
  half-life of, 46
  illicit uses of, 74t, 81
  laboratory issues regarding, 81–82
  medical uses of, 58t, 74t, 80–81
  passive inhalation of, 68
  pharmacology of, 81–82
  prescription use of, 58t
  results interpretation for, 82
Mass spectrometry, 34
Medical Examiner's Certificate, 66–67
Medical Review Officer
  administrative review of tests by, 47
  ancillary roles of, 6–7
  contacting the donor, 52–54, 61
  continuing education for, 3
  and drug testing marketplace, 7–8
  Federal requirements for, 1
  functions of, 1
  identifying the donor, 55–56
  in-house vs. off-site, 4–5, 5t
  and laboratories, 5–6
  liability insurance for, 10–11
  licensure of, 2–3
  punchlist, 53, 54f
  receipt of forms and results by, 45
  reporting requirements for, 105, 107
  responsibilities of, 4
  risk management for, 9–11
  role after positive test, 52–53, 55–56, 60–61
  state requirements for, 1–2

as substance abuse professional, 128
and third-party administrators, 6, 7
training of, 3
Medical Review Officer Certification Council (MROCC), 3
  certification by, 139–140
  examinations, 140–142
  philosophy and raison d'etre of, 139–140
  research funding by, 142
Medications lists, 21
Memorandum for Record (MFR), 48–49, 49f
Methadone, 83
  effects of, 75t
  illicit uses of, 75t
  laboratory issues regarding, 92
  medical uses of, 75t, 92
  pharmacology of, 91–92
  results interpretation for, 92
Methamphetamine
  cutoff concentration for, 31t
  effects of, 74t
  illicit uses of, 74t, 76
  medical uses of, 73, 74t, 76
  passive inhalation of, 68
  pharmacology of, 76
  testing for, 34
Methaqualone
  effects of, 75t
  illicit uses of, 75t, 92
  medical uses of, 59t, 75t
  pharmacology of, 92
  results interpretation for, 92
Metronidazole, interfering with testing, 51
Miranda rights, 56
6-Monoacetylmorphine, *See* 6-Acetylmorphine
Morphine, *See* Opiates
Multiple positive results, 65

National Laboratory Certification Program (NLCP), 29
NIDA certification, 29
Nitrite, as adulterant, 35, 36t, 37, 39
Noncontact positives, 53, 55
Nuclear Regulatory Commission, drug testing rules of, 14
Nurse practitioner, 2

Omnibus Transportation Employee Testing Act, 13–14
On-site urine tests, 111–112, 114t–115t
Opiates, 82
  clinical evidence of abuse, 86
  concentration, reports of, 45
  cutoff concentration for, 31t
  illicit uses of, 74t, , 83
  in foreign medications, 70–71

Test not performed
    action after, 62t
    conditions for, 35t
    procedure in case of, 50–52, 101–102
THC (tetrahydrocannabinol). *See* Marijuana
Third-party administrators, 6, 7
Tolmetin, interfering with testing, 51

Uncorrected flaw
    action after, 62t
    meaning of, 35t
    procedure in case of, 50, 101

United States Coast Guard, drug testing
    rules of, 13
Unsuitable specimens, 35t, 39–40, 51–52,
    62t, 101–102

Vicks inhaler, positive results caused by,
    57t, 73, 76, 78

Water loading, 38
Weight loss, 73, 81
Witnessed collections, *See* Collection of
    specimens, direct observation
Workers' compensation, 15